Yale Studies in Political Science, 23

POLITICAL ROLES IN A NEW STATE

TANZANIA'S FIRST DECADE

by Raymond F. Hopkins

New Haven and London, Yale University Press, 1971

Published with assistance from the foundation
established in memory of Calvin Chapin
of the class of 1788, Yale College.

Library of Congress catalog card number: 70–140532
International standard book number: 0–300–01410–4

Designed by John O. C. McCrillis
and set in Granjon type.
Printed in the United States of America by
Colonial Press, Inc., Clinton, Massachusetts.

Distributed in Great Britain, Europe, and Africa by
Yale University Press, Ltd., London; in Canada by
McGill-Queen's University Press, Montreal; in Mexico
by Centro Interamericano de Libros Académicos,
Mexico City; in Central and South America by Kaiman
& Polon, Inc., New York City; in Australasia by
Australia and New Zealand Book Co., Pty., Ltd.,
Artarmon, New South Wales; in India by UBS Publishers'
Distributors Pvt., Ltd., Delhi; in Japan by John
Weatherhill, Inc., Tokyo.

TO CAROL

Contents

Preface

This study attempts two tasks. The first is to explore the character of national politics in Tanzania from the perspective of members of the political elite; the second is to apply theories developed in the analysis of roles to empirical data collected from a sample of the Tanzanian elite.

This research was first conceived as a study of political change viewed in the context of role conflict. The conservative effects of recruitment and socialization into roles have been widely discussed as explaining the maintenance of similar behavior in political systems. I reasoned that since these forces secure continuity in the behavior of successive role occupants, then political change would demand changes in role norms. Clashes between old and new political forms in a recently independent state such as Tanzania seemed a likely focus for studying the role conflict that accompanied political change.

After completing my field work in Tanzania in 1966, however, it seemed clear that the most important phenomenon which I had studied was not role conflict, probably more acute at an earlier period, but the institutionalization of role norms that spelled out emerging rules of the game for the new political system. As a result, this study focuses more on order than conflict in Tanzania, more on institutionalization than change.

Since the field data for the book was gathered, Tanzania has taken a number of new steps toward implementing its ideology of socialism. These include nationalizing major firms and industries and creating leadership codes designed to prevent economic aggrandizement by politicians. Nevertheless, most of the features of politics that I observed in 1966 seem true four years later. Differences between bourgeois-oriented and militant political leaders remain, while TANU continues in its paramount if structurally weak position. The elections in November 1970 paralleled those in 1965, with local personalities and issues providing the major focus of campaigning. Over three and a half million Tanzanians voted, 72 percent of those registered, reelecting President Julius Nyerere with nearly 97 percent of the vote and indicating confidence in the government and party.

This study began with field research in Tanzania in 1965 and 1966, was first completed at Yale University in 1966-68, and was revised at Swarthmore College in 1969-70. All data based on my interviews are from 1966.

Events in Tanzania since then are described because they enrich the context for interpreting these interviews. Portions of chapter 5 appeared as an article in the *American Political Science Review* 64 (September 1970). In the text, few Swahili terms are employed, with the exception of those of special importance. In the case of tribal names, the nonprefixed root is given, such as Haya rather than Bahaya, or Chagga rather than Wachagga.

Several statistical methods were used to analyze the data and test them for significance. The results of statistical tests are presented when appropriate. I have not, however, always limited my discussion and interpretation of the data to statistically significant findings, because the sample size (109 elite) is so small that noticeable differences among subgroups seemed significant, although not in a statistical sense. The sample size compared with the chosen universe of Tanzanian elite is relatively large (approximately 30 percent).

This book was completed only with the assistance and advice of a number of people. Above all I am indebted to the many Tanzanians who patiently answered my several questions. Without the generous donation of their time and thoughts none of what follows would have been possible. I cannot express too warmly my appreciation for their invaluable contribution; in many respects this book is their collective story.

I wish to acknowledge with gratitude the Foreign Area Fellowship Program, which supported my field research and subsequent period of analysis, and the Yale University International Relations Council, which provided funds for computer and technical expenses.

I also want to thank the University of Dar es Salaam, where I was a Research Associate, and my political science colleagues at the then University College, for facilitating my research. I further want to express thanks to E. Kapinga and Thomas Mkude, second-year law students, who enthusiastically devoted their long vacation to carrying out varied tasks as research assistants; to Dr. Gordon Wilson and his associates at Marco Surveys, who were continually accommodating; and to all the helpful and kind Tanzanians I encountered at University College, at Kivukoni College, and in several government ministries. The insights and suggestions of these many thoughtful people were invaluable.

I am indebted to Professors William J. Foltz and Leonard W. Doob, whose comments and encouragement have made my task much easier, and to Professors Hayward R. Alker, Jr., Barnett Baron, Ronald D. Brunner, Karl W. Deutsch, Robert E. Lane, and J. Roland Pennock, each of whom contributed valuable suggestions and criticisms at various stages of this book. Deeply appreciated typing assistance was performed by Miss Norma Ostertag and by Mrs. Janice De Ancona, supported in part by Yale University's Office of Advanced Political Studies from a grant from the Advanced Research Projects Agency. The book has been made much more readable by the editorial guidance of Mrs. Ruth Kaufman and Mrs. Marian Ash and the assistance of Yale University Press.

Above all I owe an enormous debt to my wife, Carol, who not only performed the common wifely functions of typist, critic, and supporter, but also did extraordinary work as a programmer. Among the several programs she wrote were those for the content analysis and the calculation of role consensus.

R.F.H.

Swarthmore, Pa.
December 1970

1. The Tanzanian Political System

Since the end of World War II, with the dissolution of the major nine-teenth-century empires, over sixty new states have come into existence. Most of these new countries differ sharply from the more established industrialized nations. Commonly they have peasant economies, low rates of literacy, little urbanization, and a number of subnational ethnic and language groups that promote internal hostilities and vitiate nascent national sentiments. Fascinated by the affairs of the newly established governments in these states, American political scientists have increasingly turned their attention to the subject of political development,[1] focusing on two major questions: how democratic is the new state; and how stable will it become? Tanzania, a young African state, has displayed novelty and flexibility in its attempts to resolve the classic problems of order and freedom.[2]

Like dozens of other newly independent nations, Tanzania is charac-

1. Political scientists do not agree on exactly what this term refers to. A number of alternative definitions have been suggested, emphasizing one or another aspect of social change or modernization as the central organizing concept of political development. For a discussion of alternative approaches see Robert A. Pakenham, "Approaches to the Study of Political Development," *World Politics, 17* (October 1964), 108–20; Samuel P. Huntington, "Political Development and Political Decay," *World Politics, 17* (April 1965), 386–430; Lucian W. Pye, *Aspects of Political Development* (Boston: Little, Brown, 1965), pp. 31–48; and Samuel P. Huntington, "The Change to Change: Modernization, Development, and Politics," (unpublished manuscript, Harvard University, Spring 1970).

2. Tanzania, formally the United Republic of Tanzania, consists of the former countries of Tanganyika (which became independent on December 9, 1961) and Zanzibar (whose independence was granted on December 10, 1963). On April 25, 1964, following a revolution in Zanzibar, a union between these two countries was declared by their presidents. Because Zanzibar still has a separate government and special constitutional status in the Republic, much of the discussion in the book refers only to mainland Tanzania (the former Tanganyika). Zanzibar will be considered a part of Tanzania only after 1964, when it became incorporated in some degree into the national political system of Tanganyika. Developments in Tanzania prior to 1964 will relate only to events in the former Tanganyika. For a summary of politics in pre-union Zanzibar, see Michael Lofchie, *Zanzibar: Background to Revolution* (Princeton: Princeton University Press, 1965), and John Middleton and Jane Campbell, *Zanzibar: Its Society and Its Politics* (London: Oxford University Press, 1965). The political history of Tanganyika prior to independence is discussed in J. Claggett Taylor, *The Political Development of Tanganyika* (Stanford: Stanford University Press, 1963) and Margaret L. Bates, "Tanganyika," in Gwendolyn M. Carter, ed., *African One-Party States* (Ithaca: Cornell University Press, 1962).

terized by transitional, ambiguous, and new situations in which political leaders lack an established body of precedents, rules, and norms to guide their behavior. Africans of varied backgrounds, abilities, and ideas have assumed roles reserved until recently for the European colonial community. Not until the period of independence were hundreds of expatriates replaced in the upper levels of the bureaucracy, nor till then did the Legislative Council embrace any but a token number of Africans. When Tanzanians were elevated to formal political roles as M.P.'s and administrators, they officially inherited a set of rules and practices hastily transferred from the British. These norms, partially codified in the 1961 constitution and the General Orders of the civil service, were considered inappropriate by many of the new officeholders. In fact, the British had left two sets of norms: one based on their behavior as colonial masters of the African territory, and another based on the political culture of Great Britain.[3] While it was the latter which they consciously handed over to the Tanzanians at independence, the former has proved to be much more potent in providing guidelines and styles of action. Tanzanians, newly inducted to positions of political responsibility, have had the task of reconciling this mixed colonial heritage with their past experiences in family, tribal, and educational institutions, with increasing demands for rapid modernization, and with their own conceptions of desirable political organization.

After a decade of self-government, many changes have occurred. The outline of a fairly stable pattern of politics has emerged. It represents a nascent political system, embedded in the expectations, demands, and identities of the major political actors and shaped by their interactions. By interviewing a sample of those individuals who through legislative or high administrative office play one or more important roles in the system, this study approaches the basic questions of democracy and stability through an analysis of the institutionalization of political roles. Three crucial roles are examined: the civil servant, the M.P., and the president. Some rules that seem to govern role behavior and set the style for politics are extrapolated

3. For a discussion of this culture see Richard Rose, "England: The Traditionally Modern Political Culture," in Lucian W. Pye and Sidney Verba, eds., *Political Culture and Political Development* (Princeton: Princeton University Press, 1965). Fred G. Burke concludes that "the British legacy, then, is less English 'democracy' and welfare socialism than it is the mores of colonial government, administration and economy, which are essentially oligarchic," in "Research Design for Intensive Study of National Planning in Tanganyika" (Program of East African Studies, Syracuse University, Occasional Paper No. 5, July 1964), p. 37.

from the expectations of those interviewed. Propositions about the relationship between background, role expectations, and behavior are considered in light of the statistical evidence from the interviews. Finally, by examining role consensus and the differences among attitudes, national stability and the strength of democratic practices are assessed.

THE CONTEMPORARY SITUATION

Tanzania is located just south of the equator along 550 miles of the coast of East Africa. Its 342,170 square miles contain a population of over twelve million.[4] One finds several images of the land, the climate, the people, and their politics. The dry savannah and scrub forest of the tsetse-infested central plateau differ sharply from the tropical lowlands along the coast. Dissimilar to both these areas are the highlands, mountains, and regions near Lakes Victoria and Nyasa, where adequate rainfall, pleasant climate, and fertile soil have combined to support the bulk of Tanzania's cash-crop agriculture.

The population of Tanzania is concentrated around the edges of the country; many areas in the dry central plateau are virtually uninhabited. This highly uneven distribution of population is illustrated by the fact that Zanzibar, the coastal areas, and the regions around Lake Victoria and Mount Kilimanjaro are from five to one hundred times more densely settled than central or southern districts. Nevertheless, in a country the size of Germany and France combined, with a population about one tenth of theirs, overpopulation is not a problem except in a few densely settled rural areas.

Urbanization in towns over 10,000 is about 5.5 percent.[5] Even with a continuing rapid growth in urban centers, Tanzania is and will remain a predominantly rural country. The population of Dar es Salaam, the capital

4. Tanzania's population in 1967 was 12,231,342. If the 1957 census figure of 9,084,000 in Tanzania is accurate, the average annual population increase was not the 1.8 to 2.0 percent expected in 1966 but slightly over 3.0 percent. See *Recorded Population Changes, 1948–1967, Tanzania* (Dar es Salaam: Central Statistical Bureau, 1968), p. 6, and *Economic and Statistical Review*, no. 18 (East African Statistical Department, March 1966), pp. 4–5. Not included in the estimate of area are 20,650 square miles of inland water in mainland Tanzania.

5. The urbanization in towns of 10,000 or more in 1948 was 1.7% and in 1957, 3.3%. The 5.5% figure for 1967 urbanization is calculated from figures in Allison Butler Herrick et al., *Area Handbook for Tanzania* (Washington: U.S. Government Printing Office, 1968), p. 78, and *Recorded Population Changes*, pp. 11, 13–14.

and largest city, is 272,515.[6] The problems that large numbers of urban poor and unemployed generally create for political stability are not likely to be faced in Tanzania for some time. To further insure against unstable urban populations, the government instituted in March 1967 a work card system in Dar es Salaam and other towns throughout the country and the police rounded up unemployed persons and returned them to their home areas.[7]

There are over 120 different African tribes in Tanzania along with Arabs, Asians, and Europeans.[8] No single ethnic, religious, or economic group dominates the society. Tribal conflict, for example, is mitigated by a the large number of tribal identities and the absence of tribal structures capable of organizing sustained military or political activity.[9] These major tribes are located in areas that serve as traditional homes; hence the common usage of terms like "Chaggaland" or "Sukumaland." The 1957 census suggested that 29 of 52 districts had a dominant majority tribe, 9 had a dominant tribe which comprised 40 percent or more of the population, and 14 districts were tribally heterogeneous. Five of these heterogeneous districts were coastal.[10] Table 1.1 presents the major tribal and ethnic groups with their relative numerical strengths.

Religious affiliations often coincide with tribal and ethnic identities, but only imperfectly. Christianity, through missionary schools, has been a mobilizing force, and the three most economically active tribes—the Chagga, Haya, and Nyakusa—are also among the most Christianized groups.[11]

---

6. This 1967 figure is reported in *The Standard* (Dar es Salaam), December 29, 1967, p. 1. In 1948, the Dar es Salaam population was 69,227 and in 1957 it was 128,742. The average annual growth, therefore, has been 7.5 percent (compared to a total population growth of 2.4 percent) in 1948–67.

7. *The Nationalist,* April 1–4, 1967.

8. In the 1948 census "over 201 tribes" were classified, but 110 had less than 10,000 population. The 1957 census classified 126 distinct tribes. Zanzibar has numerous inhabitants belonging to mainland tribes and three indigenous African tribes: the Hadimu, Tumbatu, and Pemba. See J. P. Moffett, *Tanganyika: A Review of Its Resources and Their Development* (Dar es Salaam: Government Printer, 1955), pp. 29–41; *African Census Report 1957* (Dar es Salaam: Government Printer, 1963), pp. 40 ff., and Middleton and Campbell, pp. 12–23. A summary description of the people can also be found in Taylor, pp. 26–37, and Bates, pp. 432–35.

9. The important "groups" (including tribal) in politics will be discussed later in this chapter.

10. *African Census Report 1957,* pp. 47–51.

11. The percentages in 1957 were for the Chagga, 75%, for the Haya, 58%, and for the Nyakusa, 27%. The average for the country was 24.9% Christian.

TABLE 1.1. Major Ethnic Groups in Mainland Tanzania, 1957

Tribe or Race	Number	Percent of Total
Sukuma	1,093,430	12.5
Nyamwezi	362,841	4.1
Makonde	333,897	3.8
Haya	325,429	3.7
Chagga	318,167	3.6
Gogo	299,417	3.4
Ha	289,792	3.3
Hehe	251,624	2.9
Nyakusa	219,678	2.5
Luguru	202,297	2.3
Bena	195,802	2.2
Turu	195,709	2.2
Sambaa	193,802	2.2
Zaramo	183,260	2.1
Other tribes	4,197,539	47.9
Asian	76,417	0.9
Arab	19,088	0.2
European	20,534	0.2

Sources: *Statistical Abstract 1964* (Dar es Salaam: Government Printer, 1965), pp. 22–23. In Zanzibar, which had a population estimated at 354,360 in 1967, the racial breakdown differs. According to 1957 data, Africans form only 75.7% of the total compared to 98.7% on the mainland; 16.9% are Arabs and 5.8% are Asians. Since the 1964 revolution, a large number of Arabs and Asians have left Zanzibar, so their percentage is substantially reduced from these earlier figures. See John Middleton and Jane Campbell, *Zanzibar: Its Society and Politics* (London: Oxford University Press, 1965), pp. 10–13.

Islam, accepted by about 30 percent of the population, has somewhat more adherents. Muslims are found particularly in Zanzibar, along the coast, and in the central regions of the country. The three coast provinces in 1957 (Tanga, Eastern, and Southern) were all above 70 percent Muslim. The coast was dominated by Arabs and Swahilis for several centuries while Christians and Islams moved inland about the same time. Tabora and Ujiji were important trading areas for Arabs, which accounts in part for the acceptance of Islam in the central areas of the country.[12]

12. The percentages of population professing various religions (1957) were: mainland —Protestants 10.7%, Roman Catholic 14.2%, Muslim 30.9%, Animist 43.2%; Zanzibar— Christian 1.4% and Muslim 96.8%. These figures are my changes from faulty 1957 census estimates. While possibly 70 to 80% of the Chagga accept Christianity, about half of

Since independence, the largely expatriate European community has declined somewhat in numbers and has changed radically in its composition and functions. As colonial civil servants have departed they have been replaced by foreign emissaries and assistance personnel. Americans, Germans, Russians, Chinese, Italians, and Canadians have all arrived to teach, organize, and build. The Asian community, consisting of Indians and Pakistanis, nearly half of whom are Ismailis (Muslim followers of the Aga Khan), has increased through natural growth, but the influx of new immigrants has stopped.[13] Racial tensions among these groups clearly exist. Asians especially are objects of African hostility because of their predominance as skilled workers, small traders, and businessmen. The small size of their communities, the fact that fewer than half have become citizens, and the suspicion and distrust with which Africans regard most Europeans and Asians explain why these groups have little or no voice in policy making. Their economic and social presence, however, is an important political fact. There has been a great deal of discussion and legislation since independence directed toward changing or overthrowing the economic and social relationships between Africans and these two minority communities.

The economic picture in Tanzania is susceptible to several interpretations, but the basic outline is clear. Tanzania is a very poor country. A recent survey ranked Tanzania 108th of 122 countries in gross national product per capita.[14] In 1967 the annual per capita income was about $63.[15] Since 1964, moreover, national income has grown slowly, owing largely to the drop in prices for major exports such as coffee, sisal, and cotton. These declines largely offset gains in crop production, and coupled with unusual

---

these are Protestant. The published census estimates are 2.0% Protestant and 72.7% Catholic. Figures for the whole country are affected by this error and appropriate adjustments have been made. For Chagga religious preferences see Kathleen M. Stahl, *Tanganyika* (The Hague: Mouton and Co., 1961), p. 24; *African Census Report 1957*, pp. 61–68. These figures are for Africans only. The European population was 98% Christian; the Asian, 47% Islamic, 38% Hindu, 7% Christian, and 5.5% Sikh; the Arab population was 99% Muslim. The Muslim population is, of course, broken into several sects as is the Christian population. The few Christians in Zanzibar are found principally among the whites and mainland African immgrants. See Lofchie, p. 72.

13. See *Statistical Abstract 1964* (Dar es Salaam: Government Printer, 1965), p. 27.

14. See Bruce M. Russett et al., *World Handbook of Political and Social Indicators* (New Haven: Yale University Press, 1964), pp. 155–57.

15. See *Annual Economic Survey, 1968* (Dar es Salaam: Government Printer, 1969), p. 5. This figure is calculated from the national income figures on the mainland for 1967 and the census figures for that year.

rain damage in 1967 and 1968, resulted in a slowing in the growth of Tanzania's agricultural earnings, already advancing at only a modest pace.

Agriculture, excluding the costs of handling and processing agricultural products, accounts for over half of Tanzania's gross domestic product. Even after the subsistence economy is excluded, it is the dominant economic sector. Table 1.2 presents the contributions of major sectors to Tanzania's income. The price Tanzania receives for its agricultural products on the world market is, therefore, a basic factor in the Tanzanian economy, determining whether the economy will grow or stagnate. Since 1961 the terms of trade—that is, the cost of imports in terms of exports—have fallen. The loss in export earnings was greater than the entire inflow of foreign aid in 1965 (when the terms of trade fell from an index of 100 in 1960 to 84).

These figures, however, disguise an upsurge of economic activity since independence. For every year since independence until 1968 Tanzania has had a favorable balance of trade. These trade earnings have contributed a basic stability to the economy. Moreover, trade has become diversified among more exchange partners. Production of agricultural products has continued to expand, although the decline in world prices for Tanzania's major commodities erased potential economic gains in the period 1964–68. From 1960 to 1968 the economy grew at a reasonable rate, about 5.9 percent. The effects of the mid-60s' decline in earnings for major agricultural crops is illustrated by a slower growth rate from 1964 to 1968, of about 5.2 percent. As table 1.2 shows, the primary sectors have grown the least, although these figures may underestimate growth in small holders' cash sales (included under agriculture) and in services.[16]

Minimum wage and other regulatory legislation have improved the lot of the worker in Tanzania. Since independence, however, the number of wage-earning employees has declined, largely because of employment reductions on sisal estates. Apparent disagreements over whether future development in Tanzania should concentrate on industrialization or agricultural growth have been resolved in favor of an emphasis on agriculture, although some politicians have agitated in favor of a Marxist-prescribed reliance on heavy industry as the key to development.[17] Various economic

16. *Annual Economic Survey, 1968*, p. 7

17. The emphasis on agriculture, of course, is not to be at the expense of appropriate investment in both light and some heavy industry. See Henry Bienen, *Tanzania: Party Transformation and Economic Development* (Princeton: Princeton University Press, 1967), pp. 217–27. Bienen argues that in 1964 some highly placed officials, apparently influenced by "scientific socialism," urged industrialization as the basis for economic development,

TABLE 1.2. Gross Domestic Product at Current Factor Cost (in millions of shillings)

Industry	1960	1962	1963	1964	1965	1966	1967	1968*	Percentage Change 1967–68	Annual Growth Rate 1960–68 (%)
Agriculture	2,256	2,485	2,787	2,805	2,651	2,895	2,896	2,934	+ 1.3	+ 3.3
Mining	104	103	88	121	121	159	161	111	−31.1	+ 0.8
Primary Sector	2,360	2,588	2,875	2,926	2,772	3,054	3,057	3,045	− 0.4	+ 3.2
Manufacturing	109	154	156	194	234	283	332	377	+13.6	+16.8
Construction	91	122	124	154	151	172	208	221	+ 6.3	+11.7
Public Utilities	25	30	32	35	37	48	51	60	+17.6	+11.5
Commerce	419	484	517	600	658	767	780	853	+ 9.3	+ 9.2
Rent	160	175	187	222	246	276	293	302	+ 3.0	+ 8.2
Transport	175	188	188	197	216	247	275	298	+ 8.4	+ 6.9
Services	362	448	468	509	580	615	654	713	+ 9.0	+ 8.8
Secondary and Tertiary Sectors	1,341	1,601	1,672	1,911	2,122	2,408	2,593	2,824	+ 8.9	+ 9.7
G.D.P.	3,701	4,189	4,547	4,837	4,894	5,462	5,650	5,869	+ 3.9	+ 5.9
(Index 1960 = 100.0)	100.0	113.2	122.9	130.7	132.2	147.6	152.7	158.6		

* Provisional.

Source: *Annual Economic Survey, 1968* (Dar es Salaam: Government Printer, 1969), p. 5.

studies have indicated that Tanzania has rich untapped agricultural resources, such as the Kilombero Valley, and the ability to make rapid gains in agricultural output, as already evidenced by the rapid increase in cotton production in Sukumaland. Whether these resources can be mobilized effectively by overcoming traditional barriers to increased production in the peasant economy is not yet demonstrated.

Some analysts pessimistically forecast that government opposition to capitalist development minimizes growth potential.[18] However, a system of private property and reliance on foreign finance have been clearly rejected by the government. President Nyerere has candidly summarized the overall economic position in Tanzania:

> The truth is that our United Republic has at present a poor undeveloped and agricultural economy. We have very little capital to invest in big factories or modern machines. We are short of people with skill and experience. What we do have is land in abundance and people who are willing to work hard for their own improvement. It is the use of these latter resources which will decide whether we reach our total goals or not. If we use these resources in a spirit of self-reliance as the basis for development then we shall make progress slowly but surely and it will be real progress affecting the lives of the masses, not just having spectacular show pieces in the

exploiting agricultural and mineral resources to build heavy industry. In spite of the apparent failure of the village development schemes in which President Nyerere had placed great hope, events in Tanzania, particularly the principles contained in the Arusha Declaration of January 1967 and the new emphasis on agriculture in primary education, indicate that the government's principal development commitment is to widespread improvement of agriculture.

Nevertheless, a series of articles in *The Nationalist* by "Pressman" (regularly written by one or two important Zanzibaris in the government, A. M. Babu or A. K. Hanga, now deceased) continued to press for industrialization. In *The Nationalist*, March 31, 1967, p. 4, "Pressman" wrote: "As the Arusha Declaration emphasizes, correct and reliable leadership and reliance on the masses are two of the most fundamental conditions for a successful economic development based on self-reliance. . . . This means an economy where attention is focused on the means of production, on the problems of capital accumulation, on credit conditions, on investments in heavy and manufacturing industries— in short, focused on the progressive emergence of a diversified modern economy built around a basic industrial complex." Hanga was placed in preventive detention for over a year prior to his death in a Zanzibar prison in October 1969.

18. See Gilbert L. Rutman, "An Analysis of the Economy of Tanganyika with Special Reference to the Role of the Government" (Ph.D. dissertation, Duke University, 1965).

towns while the rest of the people in Tanzania live in their present poverty.[19]

The politics of Tanzania, like its people and economy, presents a number of contrasts. The image of democracy is contradicted by legal arrangements and informal norms designed to muffle dissension. The picture of a strident and revolutionizing one-party system contrasts with reports of organizational weakness and internal differences.[20] Finally, in spite of the sincere dedication to socialism of many leaders, there is a contrast between the principles accepted by the government and the realities of Tanzanian life. For example, the socialist principle of state ownership is limited by the fact that over 90 percent of the population secure their livelihood as small-scale peasant farmers. Certainly the principle of economic equality runs counter to the reality of sharp income differences that result when a well-paid civil servant or businessman receives twenty times the income of a semiskilled worker.[21] Thus, despite rapid transformations in the political framework of the state, major residues of the past remain. In fact, in vast areas of the country traditional norms still regulate life.

In spite of these contradictions there is a basic validity to the national government's claim to be a one-party socialist democracy. The present "interim constitution," adopted in July 1965, made de jure a single party dominance that has characterized the mainland since before independence, and Zanzibar since the time of its revolution. The Tanganyika African National Union (TANU) and the Afro-Shirazi Party (ASP) are the only legal political parties in Tanzania, each the sovereign political organization on the mainland and on Zanzibar respectively. Socialism, more

19. Julius K. Nyerere, "Education for Self-Reliance," *The Nationalist,* March 10, 1967, pp. 4–7. Other optimistic assessments as to the long-run economic possibilities for Tanzania may be found in The International Bank for Reconstruction and Development, *The Economic Development of Tanganyika* (Baltimore: Johns Hopkins Press, 1961), and Brian van Arkadie, "The Structure and Underdevelopment of the East African Economies" (unpublished manuscript, Yale University Economic Growth Center).

20. See Bienen, passim.

21. Salaries of well-paid civil servants and African businessmen—despite salary reductions announced in October 1966 of 10% across the board among top civil servants—easily average $6,000 a year, while the income for a semiskilled worker such as a house servant runs about $310 a year. See *Staff List 1965* (Dar es Salaam: Government Printer, 1966). Nevertheless, this compares favorably with the 30–50 to 1 salary ratio of these groups in most of Africa. See Andrew M. Kamarck, *The Economics of African Development* (New York: Frederick A. Praeger, 1967), p. 60.

Fabian than Marxist in character, has been the creed of Tanzania's leaders from the founding of TANU in 1954. The most recent evidence of the commitment to socialism has been the nationalization of all foreign banks, insurance companies, major trading concerns, and many of the mills and factories.[22] The September 1965 national elections for a new Assembly and president were generally free, participation was encouraged, and alternatives were offered the voters.[23] However difficult it may be to reconcile "authoritarian" practices such as prohibition of organized opposition or frequent public warnings against political dissent with the fundamental principles of democracy, Tanzania incorporates phenomena of both types in its political system. The pattern of political rhetoric and procedure in Tanzania is novel, even though various component themes within this pattern may be found in Western traditions of liberty and equality and Marxist-Leninist constructs such as democratic centralism.

The decision-making machinery in Tanzania is rather complex. The central body is the cabinet, composed of sixteen ministers, the second vice-president and president, and a secretary to the cabinet who is also head of the civil service. The broad outlines of the policies these men draw up and submit to the National Assembly, however, are first reviewed and worked out by the National Executive Committee (NEC) of TANU, a body to which a majority of the cabinet members do not belong. While it is true that the National Assembly must approve all laws, the dominance of TANU has ensured the easy passage of nearly all cabinet-sponsored legislation since independence. The day-to-day affairs of the government, particularly outside the capital and major cities, are organized under the Ministry of Regional Administration. This ministry, headed until June 1967 by Oscar Kambona, the former secretary-general of TANU, is responsible for central government administration throughout the country. Since independence, party and government have become closely interlocked, with Julius K. Nyerere, the founder of TANU, as president of both. Figure 1.1 outlines the basic structure of government and TANU. The

22. These concerns were nationalized in a series of announcements by President Nyerere the week of February 6–12, 1967. The following week Parliament passed the necessary enabling legislation. See *The Nationalist*, February 7–16, 1967. The Fabian ideas of Tanzanian leaders emerged during several important interviews.

23. See Lionel Cliffe, ed., *One-Party Democracy* (Nairobi: East African Publishing House, 1967) and Ruth Schachter Morgenthau, "Tanzanian Elections," *Africa Report, 10,* no. 10 (December 1965). The question of the degree of electoral alternatives is discussed in chapter 7.

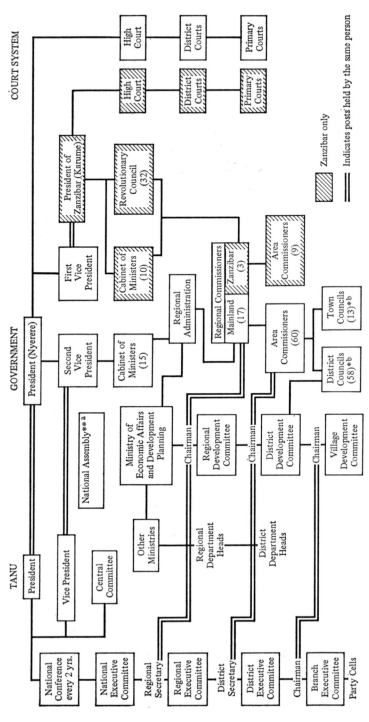

Figure 1.1. Party and Government Structure in Tanzania

a. Up to 82 appointed, including the Zanzibar Revolutionary Council; 120 elected nationally (mainland only); 15 national members elected by the Assembly.

b. Up to ten council members may be appointed by the president; the remainder are elected.

Sources: Based in part on graphic representations of these structures in Henry Bienen, *Tanzania: Party Transformation and Economic Development* (Princeton: Princeton University Press, 1967), p. 83, and in Allison Butler Herrick et al., *Area Handbook for Tanzania* (Washington: U.S. Government Printing Office, 1968), p. 208.

principal effect of the changes since independence has been to coordinate the party and government machinery. Nyerere, in his opening remarks to the newly elected National Assembly in October 1965, summarized the government's view concerning the structure of national decision making which has evolved.

> Under the new constitution the integration of TANU and Government machinery makes it possible for closer cooperation to develop without the danger of overlapping. By our new system we have demonstrated finally that the old conflicts between TANU and the Civil Service, and between TANU and the institutions of central government, are out of date. The colonialism which engendered these conflicts is dead as far as Tanzania is concerned. We can now put its attitudes behind us and concentrate on building our country in accordance with our own desires.[24]

The Historical Development of the Political System

The growth of the *national* political system in Tanzania, from the time it became a legal territorial entity under colonial rule to its present position as an independent state and evolving nation, may be divided into four periods: the initial colonization by Germany, the British trusteeship, the drive to independence, and finally the period of sovereign African rule.

German Rule

In 1885 Germany first acquired rights to mainland Tanganyika (along with what is now Rwanda and Burundi) as a result of a few treaties made by the explorer Karl Peters and subsequent agreements reached by the European powers at the Berlin Conference (1884-85). By this time, Arab influence had spread along the entire East African coast. The Sultan of Zanzibar, in fact, claimed sovereignty over the Tanganyika coastline and control of the interior region.[25] Only in 1891 was this "claim" relinquished after heavy German pressure. The German East African

---

24. Julius K. Nyerere, "President's Address at the Opening of the National Assembly after the General Election," October 12, 1965 (Dar es Salaam: Ministry of Information and Tourism), p. 4.

25. This historical tie is not only relevant to the contemporary union with Zanzibar but also reflects the long period during which Africans have been subject to claims of authority by outsiders. The resentment evidenced in the Zanzibar revolution of 1964 resulted from the many years of Arab dominance.

Company, a commercial venture, proved inadequate to the task of managing this large territory, and it was therefore entrusted to military commanders. The political organizations the Germans found in their newly acquired land were by no means static. The centralization of authority and the range of decision making were continually changing. Evidence suggests there was a fluidity among tribal units, with families or clans breaking away to form new tribal aggregates and with powerful chiefs, as among the Nyamwezi and Hehe, organizing and increasing their strength while other groups fragmented. The major problems confronting the various people inhabiting German East Africa were local and immediate. Demands for order and redress of wrongs occurred predominantly at the village level.

While there were some earlier signs of change and nation building, it was the period of German influence that marked the origin of modern Tanzania. The penetration of Arabs after the eleventh century had already resulted in some cultural innovation and change, particularly the introduction of the Muslim religion and the development of the Swahili language. However, it was the lines drawn on a map in Berlin in 1885 that were the basic determinants in organizing and setting the boundaries for Tanzania's subsequent emergence as a state. German rule, roughly from 1885 to 1916, accomplished three important tasks in the construction of a new political system: first, it laid the foundation for modern economic processes; second, it organized a nationwide network of control, imperfectly coordinated from Dar es Salaam; and third, it undermined the authority of the traditional political systems.

The Germans built railroads, roads, and telegraph systems to link the country together. And they introduced cash-crop farming, particularly the raising of sisal, of which Tanzania provides over 30 percent of the world supply.[26] Both projects demanded laborers, and through taxation and direct pressures a large number of Africans were induced into wage-labor employment. Perhaps the most significant political action of the Germans was weakening traditional political authority and undermining the will to resist. Although the Germans ruled through intermediaries and left relatively untouched areas where they had little economic interest or a low incentive to penetrate, their impact was substantial. Friedland, for instance, notes eleven major rebellions the Germans were forced

26. *Background to the Budget, 1966*, p. 14. In 1965 it supplied 37%, but this figure has declined since then.

to put down between 1888 and 1906.[27] The last of these, the Maji-Maji Rebellion (1905–06), cost an estimated 120,000 African lives. The effect of these military conquests was to set one chieftainship against another, one warring faction against another. Traditional leaders who rebelled were slain, committed suicide, or fled. Those who were unacceptable to the Germans were simply removed. By 1906, the period of rebellion and military suppression had drawn to a close.[28]

In Rwanda and Burundi, where the Germans found indigenous chieftainships firmly entrenched, they established indirect control over the two systems, which eventually were mandated to Belgium after World War I. The remainder of German East Africa (later Tanganyika) was divided into 21 administrative districts. In 1906, civilian district commissioners, responsible for maintaining order and collecting taxes, had been appointed in all but two. Each was directly accountable to the governor. In many areas where there were groups of clans without formal leaders, the Germans employed and even extended the system Zanzibar had devised for ruling the coastal region, namely appointing an Arab or Swahili as "akida," who was responsible for groups of villages. The akidas were often arbitrary and cruel rulers and generally had no local roots in the areas they administered. Beneath the akidas a system of jumbes (Islamic leaders), local headmen, and in a few areas hereditary chiefs, completed the hierarchical pyramid from the governor to the village. The use of akidas (outsiders) and the manipulation of traditional rulers, as among the Hehe and Chagga, undermined the authority of traditional political order. Local governments, managed from the center, were responsible for law and order and for labor recruitment and taxes (after 1905, a direct national poll tax was introduced). This entire governmental organization was controlled by a European administrative staff, which in 1914 numbered only 79. Obviously German administration was thinly spread, but the indigenous systems offered weak resistance to foreign domination. During World War I, from 1916 to 1918, General Von Lettow-Vorbeck led a relatively small German force (most of whom were Africans) crisscrossing the territory in guerrilla style actions. What the early German policy of repression (*Schrecklichkeit,* frightfulness)

27. See William H. Friedland, "The Evolution of Tanganyika's Political System" (Program of East African Studies, Syracuse University, Occasional Paper No. 10), p. 18.
28. See G. S. P. Freeman-Grenville, "The German Spear 1884–98," in Roland Oliver and Gervase Mathew, *History of East Africa* (Oxford: Clarendon Press, 1963), pp. 447–48.

had not accomplished in disrupting traditional systems, certainly World War I did.[29]

British Trusteeship

Following a period of British military rule from 1917 to 1920, Tanganyika Territory became a British mandate under the League of Nations. Civilian rule began in September 1920, based on the Tanganyika Order in Council which created the offices of governor and executive council. The governor was to consult the executive council, of which he was president, "except in cases where he might not deem it expedient." [30] Under British rule, the akida system and indirect rule were modified. Except along the heavily Muslim coast of the Indian Ocean where traditional systems had long been politically fragmented, traditional leaders were sought out in an effort to rule through them.

Sir Donald Cameron, who was appointed governor in 1926, officially inaugurated the system of indirect rule or "native administration," the highly refined method of ruling through traditional leaders which was becoming the keystone of British colonial policy.[31] Under Cameron, the last of the akidas was removed, the Native Authority Ordinance (1927) came into effect, and native councils were established to handle local financing, expenditures for education and public works, and adjudication of less serious offenses. British administrative officers, however, exercised strong leadership over these systems of native government. Provincial commissions, district commissioners, and district officers exercised control not only in the initial stages of colonial government but up through the pre-independence period.[32] Cameron also introduced the Legislative Council (LegCo) in 1926, which consisted of thirteen official and ten unofficial members, all appointed by the governor. Normally there were seven Europeans and three Asians holding these unofficial seats; in 1945 the composition of the Council was raised to fifteen officials and fourteen unofficials, with four seats reserved for Africans, although not until 1949 were all four seats filled.

Until 1960 the fundamental power of the governor was unimpaired

29. See Bates, pp. 400–03.

30. Instructions to the Governor, 1920 Laws of Tanganyika, quoted in B. T. G. Chidzero, *Tanganyika and International Trusteeship* (New York: Oxford University Press, 1961), p. 51.

31. See Bates, p. 405.

32. See, for example, the account in Roland Young and Henry Fosbrooke, *Land and Politics among the Luguru of Tanganyika* (London: Routledge and Kegan Paul, 1960).

by legislative or executive checks. In principle, the entire legislative and executive apparatus of the national government was subordinate to his authority, though he was of course subordinate to the Colonial Office. This was the basic pattern of formal centralized government administration which TANU inherited in 1961.

The depression and World War II drained Britain to the extent that few resources were available for investment in Tanganyika. The uncertain status of the mandate was an additional factor discouraging investment and development. As a result, the size and services of the colonial government expanded very little betwen 1929 and 1945. German farms and plantations put up for sale after World War I were purchased by Greeks, Swiss, Italians, and a few British. Along with these settlers there was a growing community of Indians, who had begun arriving even before World War I and had purchased a number of German businesses after the war. These groups, along with some Africans who, owing to taxation or more positive incentives, began serious cash farming, were primarily responsible for whatever economic growth occurred in the "modern" sector during this period.

The Nationalist Period

Two important events occurred between 1945 and 1961. First, the colonial government, in response to external pressures from both British opinion and the United Nations, as well as internal pressures from growing African nationalism, began to revamp and modernize the governmental apparatus, bringing in Africans for the first time to administrative positions, organizing elections, and debating policy issues with African leaders. Second, and even more important, was the emergence of a nationalist movement, TANU. The pattern of policy making and organization that developed in TANU during the nationalist period has come to structure to an important degree the national political decision-making process.

After World War II, Tanganyika Territory became a trust territory of Great Britain under the United Nations. The territory's special international status maintained certain pressures on the United Kingdom to prevent widespread alienation of land by colonial settlers. It also served to prevent closer integration with Kenya, which, it was feared, might place the territory under the domination of white settlers. Racial discrimination was also mitigated somewhat by the United Nations' overseership.[33] Racial harmony has been a continual theme in British policy in Tanganyika.

After World War II, the number of Africans exposed to modernity, trained beyond secondary school, and recruited to positions of responsibility rose sharply. Many men of the King's African Rifles (Tanganyika) returned home after the war, having served abroad in Ethiopia, Egypt, and Burma. Makerere College at Kampala trained an increasing number of Africans, most frequently as secondary school teachers. By 1950 there were 23 Makerere-trained African teachers in government schools and perhaps an equal number in Protestant and Catholic secondary schools. Of these 23, eight held high government posts in 1966.[34] Overseas education also became more possible, for the first time. For example, Tom Marealle, later to be elected paramount chief of the Chagga and to serve with the U.N., and Frederick Mchauru, who became a principal secretary (the chief administrator for a ministry), had two-year courses at the London School of Economics and Social Science, returning to Dar es Salaam in 1946.

In 1947 the Tanganyika African Association (TAA) began to emerge as a political interest group. Its origins can be traced back to 1924, when the Tanganyika African Civil Servants' Association was founded in Tanga. When the TAA was founded in Dar es Salaam in 1929, the rudiments of a territorial-wide organization were already in existence.[35] Until the 1940s, the TAA remained largely a mutual benefit society, a social organization catering to the interests of modernized Africans, largely government civil servants and teachers. Its lack of militancy is underscored by the fact that the colonial government provided rent-free headquarters in Dar es Salaam. In the small urban centers throughout the country tribal unions emerged during the 1930s among the Chagga, Haya, Sambaa, Sukuma, and others. Often TAA leaders were also leaders in these tribal unions, which were in fact nontraditional. In 1947, when the British government proposed a closer union between Kenya and Tanganyika in the form of an East African High Commission, the TAA interpreted this as

33. These points were made by Chidzero in *Tanganyika and International Trusteeship*.

34. These eight were included in the elite studied: six as civil servants and two as members of the National Assembly. One other Makerere teacher, Dunstan Omari, was formerly head of the civil service and then served as secretary-general of the East African Common Services Organization (EASCO).

35. See Ralph A. Austen, "Notes of the Pre-history of TANU," *Makerere Journal*, No. 9 (Kampala, 1964), pp. 1–6.

a threat to progress toward African political power and initiated its first political act by holding a large public protest at Dar es Salaam. In 1948 it told the United Nations Visiting Mission that it had 39 branches, 1,780 members, and a central committee of 30.[36] This was the growing nucleus for an African political party.

The early 1950s brought increasing articulation of African interests and nationalist sentiments. The most dramatic example was in 1952, when complaints of the Meru tribe regarding land alienation by the colonial government were taken to the United Nations by a Tanganyika African, Japhet Kirilo.[37] In the same year the Chagga elected a single paramount chief for the first time. Although the Chagga Congress, formed by the Moshi TAA branch, was soundly defeated by Marealle—the candidate of the Kilimanjaro Chagga Citizens' Union—the more stridently nationalist attitudes of the younger Africans were expressed in political organization for the first time. Among the Sukuma, African interests were furthered by the growth of producer cooperatives; under the leadership of Paul Bomani a number of small cooperatives were brought together in the Victoria Federation of Cooperative Unions. In 1954, Julius Nyerere, who had returned from Edinburgh the year before, became president of the TAA. On July 7, 1954, after several months' preparation, the TAA was formally transformed into the Tanganyika African National Union (TANU), the first African political organization. TANU quickly became the dominant force in African politics. Other parties, such as the United Tanganyika Party (UTP) and the African National Congress (ANC), were overwhelmingly defeated in elections.

The TANU constitution was modeled on that of Nkrumah's Convention People's Party. Party officials were elected by the annual delegates' conference, policy making was entrusted to the National Executive Committee (NEC) which met quarterly, while the day-to-day affairs of the party were handled by a central committee, composed of "the President and nine other members selected by him and approved by the National Executive." [38] Article 2 of the constitution contains the "aims and objects

36. George Bennett, "An Outline History of TANU," *Makerere Journal*, No. 7 (Kampala, 1963).

37. Kirilo ran for the National Assembly from Arusha Rural in the 1965 elections but lost in a close contest to Ole Mejooli, the TANU chairman. Although the election was nullified by the courts, Kirilo, the early nationalist, was defeated more decisively in a rematch.

38. See Bennett.

of TANU." In the original constitution these included: to "fight relentlessly until Tanganyika is self-governing and independent," to fight "tribalism and all isolationist tendencies against the Africans and to build a united nationalism," and to promote trade unionism, cooperatives, fair prices for producers and consumers, a minimum wage, and compulsory primary education.[39] As independence approached these aims and objects began to include broader economic goals. The 1961 constitution added the objectives of eliminating poverty, ignorance, and disease and controlling "collectively the means of producing national wealth." Then, in the revised constitution of 1965, article 2 was expanded to include the injunction "that it is the responsibility of the State to intervene actively in the economic life of the Nation . . . so as to prevent the accumulation of wealth to an extent which is inconsistent with the existence of a classless society." [40]

The immediate strategy of the party in the pre-independence period, however, was not to tackle these economic and social issues but to unite around the single goal of independence. It was Nyerere's view that:

> What was needed was unity among the people of Tanganyika in demanding their independence. In order to create that unity a clear enduring purpose was required. From the very beginning of TANU in 1954, I believed that it would be wrong for us to struggle against individual instances of discrimination. . . . Although these affected the majority of our people, they did not strike the root. There was one thing however which could combine all our people and that was the desire to achieve independence and be self-governing.[41]

As a result of this strategy, political goals were given priority over economic ones, a priority which has continued to inform Nyerere's approach to important policy decisions.

In the years between 1954 and 1958 the party expanded, opening branches throughout the country, collecting dues, and presenting its views in the press, through pamphlets, in the Legislative Council, and even before the United Nations. During this initial period, the party received little encouragement from the colonial government and was forced

---

39. Ibid.
40. *TANU Constitution* (Dar es Salaam: mimeo., 1961) and *TANU Constitution, 1965* (Dar es Salaam: Government Printer, 1965). Also see Bienen, pp. 256 ff.
41. Cited in Stahl, p. 6.

to register branch by branch at the district level. The denial of national registration, however, did not prove a detriment since the government could declare the party illegal only branch by branch. Governor Twining, in an effort to accommodate change, proposed a policy of multiracialism. This form of the separate-but-equal populations policy suggested equal political participation for very unequal populations, thus inhibiting majority rule (by Africans, therefore). Support for Twining's policies was sought from traditional leaders. The chiefs' convention of 1958, however, did not ally with the Twining regime, as many traditional leaders either vacillated or supported TANU, which vehemently opposed "multiracialism."

In 1958 a new governor, Sir Richard Turnbull, arrived on the scene. Elections had been scheduled under revised constitutional arrangements. For the first time, the "unofficial" members of LegCo were to be elected instead of appointed by the governor. One African, one Asian, and one European were to be elected from each of ten constituencies. TANU and TANU-supported candidates swept all the elections. Subsequently, five TANU legislators joined the government at the governor's invitation, while Nyerere remained outside as opposition spokesman. Nyerere's ability to command respect and friendship from many of the British in the colonial government, especially Turnbull, coupled with a persuasiveness and correct reading of events, accounts in large measure for British acquiescence to the rapid movement of Tanganyika Territory to independence. At the 1958 annual conference Nyerere had been successful in persuading a divided TANU leadership to participate in the forthcoming elections, and TANU's success in these elections was a critical event in the drive toward independence.

During the period of TANU's rise to predominance, local TANU branches gained members and support by championing local grievances, such as opposition to cattle culling, cattle dips, and other agricultural reforms disliked by African farmers. Instances of opposition to unpopular agricultural reform occurred in Iringa, Korogwe, Morogoro and Sukumaland. Other demands championed by local TANU branches were more education and the removal of agricultural training from the academic curricula. At the national and regional level, however, opposition based on these issues was discouraged, because local TANU opposition to agricultural reforms was used by the government as a justification for banning the organization in several areas—for example, in Sukumaland from 1954 to 1958. Nyerere himself made a number of trips to branches accused of undermining government and traditional authority. He announced his support for agricultural reforms, explained that opposition based on dislike for them was irresponsible, and reaffirmed TANU's *central* goal of independence.[42] In addition to a recognition of the long-range value of agricultural reforms, it was an explicit TANU strategy to avoid involvement in local grievances. Thus, a pattern of total opposition to British policies never developed.

As TANU grew into the broadly based national movement it became by the time of independence, it began to draw within its structure a variety of potential interest groups. A youth wing, which quickly became known as the TANU Youth League (TYL), was formed. Under the leadership of Rashidi Kawawa (now second vice-president), Lawi Sijaona (a minister since independence), and Joseph Nyerere (the president's brother), the TYL grew rapidly. It occasionally became involved in disorders and illegal disturbances and represented a potential element of unrest, but its principal functions were organizing and maintaining order at party rallies and spreading nationalist sentiment. By 1955 a women's group was active in Dar es Salaam and was soon spreading across the country. Organized under Bibi Titi, a self-taught and extremely colorful speaker, it emerged as an important national vehicle for TANU support.[43] The party also established an elders section, both in recognition of the traditional deference given to elders and to accommodate important African elements in Tanzanian society that might not otherwise be represented in TANU. In 1958 the Tanganyika Federation of Labour (TFL) was given permanent representation on the NEC; the union movement had long been closely linked with the party and shared leadership talent. TANU's boycott of beer sales in March 1958 in support of a brewery strike was reciprocated in 1959 when the TFL threatened a general strike if TANU's demands for internal self-government were not met. The TFL was not just formally affiliated with the party; two past presidents, Kawawa and Kamaliza, also served as members of the party's central committee.

Since 1956 the Youth League and the party had been organizing adult education classes and bush primary schools in order to further basic edu-

---

42. Judith Listowel, *The Making of Tanganyika* (London: Chatto and Windus, 1965), pp. 262–302.

43. Bibi Titi is a politician who was important in the late 1950s and early 1960s, but whose influence declined after her defeat as an M.P. in 1965. She subsequently has been "retired" from politics and jailed on charges of treason.

cation. By the time of independence this educational organization formed a separate unit, the Tanganyika African Parents' Association (TAPA), which was also formally affiliated with the party. Cooperative societies, which at various regional and local levels often had interlocking leadership with the party, were organized after independence into a broad national organization, the Cooperative Union of Tanganyika (CUT), which was soon formally affiliated with the party by representation in the NEC. Thus, during the period 1958 to 1961, as TANU moved into control of the government, formalized lines between the party and a variety of particular interests were established and the party became the prime agency responsible for articulating and representing their political interests. The Asian Association also aligned itself politically with TANU. The links were only informal, however, since Asians were not admitted to party membership until 1963, and by then the Asian Association had been dissolved.

In 1959 Governor Turnbull appointed a multiracial committee to review the election system. In 1960 new elections were held under the revisions recommended by this committee. In the 71 constituencies, 70 candidates with TANU backing were elected, 58 in uncontested elections. In the remaining 13 constituencies, only about 50 percent of the eligible voters turned out. TANU candidates received 82.8 percent of the votes cast for these contested seats, the African National Congress (ANC), a more radical party, received 0.3 percent and independent candidates, 16.9 percent (attributable largely to a successful and a near-successful candidate from Mbulu and Tukuyu). The one upset, where the TANU-supported candidate was defeated, was not, in fact, a rejection of TANU, for Sarwatt, the victor, had been the popular choice of the local TANU branches but had been rejected by the NEC. Sarwatt was soon readmitted in good standing to the party, became Deputy Speaker of the National Assembly, and in 1969 Speaker of the East African Legislative Assembly.

Following TANU's electoral victory in 1960, Britain moved to grant independence, and a year of intensive preparation preceded the formal ceremonies on December 9, 1961. During this period, TANU ran the government under the supervision of the colonial administration and Tanganyikans by the score were sent to Britain for courses in public administration, diplomacy, agriculture, police work, engineering, and health. A government modeled on the Westminster system was assembled under the aegis of the governor. Nyerere became chief minister with the estab-

lishment of responsible government in September 1960, and in May 1961
he became the prime minister. The political role structure at independence
was modeled directly on the British heritage.[44] The governor-general, as
the Queen's representative, was head of state. The prime minister was
the head of government, making policy through his cabinet and the cabinet secretariat. The Legislative Council, with its numbers increased and
its powers broadened, assumed the name and functions of Parliament.

Establishment of Sovereignty

The fourth period in the formation of Tanzania's political system began with independence, which marked not the end of change but the
beginning of even more rapid change. In 1961 there were only two important political organizations in the country, the first, TANU, centralized
policy formation on national issues through its powerful National Executive Committee and under the strong guidance of Nyerere. His intellectual abilities, coupled with his decisions in a number of strategic controversies over party strategy, gave him undisputed leadership. His
decisions, now appraised as "correct," and his ability to predict British
reactions, built up a strong feeling of trust and deference toward him
among party members. One minister remarked, "Nyerere is the greatest
living political scientist. Once he decides, he is never wrong." [45]

The party, which had been a highly unified organization in its efforts
to attain independence, began to show signs of cleavage on questions of
citizenship, the need for expatriate staff, and the implications of socialism.
Party leaders were faced with the dilemma of wanting both to maintain
the unity established during the nationalist period and to avoid undemocratic suppression of people and ideas. The effects of party competition in Kenya, Uganda, Nigeria, and the Congo could be seen as both
divisive and dangerous, with political expression of regional and economic
differences inhibiting the growth of national sentiment and steps toward

44. At the level of local government, reforms had been on the books for several years
by which the old native authority institutions could be replaced by local councils modeled
on the system of English local government. However, because of entrenched multiracial
clauses in these provisions—that is, seats reserved for Asians and Europeans—TANU opposed this "modernization" of local government. But after independence the centralized
reorganization of district and town councils moved quickly. See Stanley Dryden, "Local
Administration in Tanzania" (unpublished M.A. thesis, University of East Africa, Dar es
Salaam, 1966) and Samuel Rae, "Political Administration in Tanganyika" (unpublished
M.A. thesis, Columbia University, 1965).

45. Interview with Tanzanian cabinet minister, June 25, 1966.

greater political and economic independence. Tribalism, racial and economic differences, and competing ideologies were potential cleavages that could tear Tanzania apart. A year after independence the answer to this dilemma was suggested by Nyerere—Tanzania would have only one party and all conflicts would be resolved within the party structure.[46] In the interim constitution of 1965 the legal framework for a one-party state was adopted.[47]

The second political organization was the government. Although the structure of the government had been revised—particularly at the upper levels—in preparation for independence, many aspects of the colonial government were not susceptible to rapid change and retained much of their former character. Colonial government tended to be authoritarian and paternalistic in both its attitudes and organization, and these traits did not disappear when the veneer of British parliamentary democracy was established immediately prior to independence. Even the formal structure bristled with a colonial legacy.

Parliament, consisting of the National Assembly and the governor-general, was the supreme legislative body. The governor-general, appointed by the Queen, was only titular head of state but nevertheless exercised important powers. He was officially head of the executive, commanded the army, and had the power of both appointment and pardon. While his actions were to be "in accordance with the advice of the cabinet or Prime Minister," he had both symbolic authority and real power in ambiguous situations. The judiciary, while it was established as an independent body in the 1961 constitution, relinquished final constitutional interpretation to the Privy Council in Britain.[48] Dual systems of traditional and English law, with the implied double standard, remained. Thus, although the act of granting independence officially occurred in 1961, the process of independence in fact began several years earlier and continued at least through 1965.

46. See Nyerere's speech, "Democracy and the Party System," delivered January 14, 1963 (Dar es Salaam: Tanganyika Standard, 1963).

47. Implementation of this decision had been delayed two and a half years, first by a desire to facilitate a federation of East African states, and later by problems of the union with Zanzibar. The changes in the constitution were based largely on the conclusions of a special commission that studied a wide range of opinions. See *Report of the Presidential Commission on the Establishment of a Democratic One-Party State* (Dar es Salaam, Government Printer, 1965).

48. See *The Constitution of Tanganyika* (Dar es Salaam: Government Printer, 1961), pp. 18–19, 27.

During this fourth period of Tanzania's political growth, the two main political structures inherited at independence were remolded piece by piece. Government organization and policies experienced the greatest changes. These changes have broadened the power and scope of government and increased the authority of the executive. Local government has been modernized and placed under direct control of a central government ministry. The position of chief (often the head of former native authorities) has been abolished except as an honorary title. All land has been declared government property; freehold land tenure has been ended. Existing freehold claims have been transferred into long-term leases, with the Ministry of Lands having the power to regulate and revoke the rights to land. A unified system of laws, applicable throughout the country and administered through a single judicial hierarchical organization, has been established. Drawing heavily upon the governmental innovations introduced in Ghana, regional and district administration has incorporated politicians into key posts as commissioners throughout the country. Former administrators in the civil service, a number of whom had been promoted to district commissioner, were effectively demoted to become "administrative secretaries," responsible for the administration and financing of subnational units. Since 1964, however, a number of old politicians have been replaced as commissioners by former civil servants. A preventive detention act even stronger than Ghana's has been enacted. The republican constitution of 1962, altered only a little by the interim constitution of 1965, has introduced two new roles, those of president and second vice-president.[49]

The role of the president encompasses even more than the executive powers of the governor-general and the political responsibilities of the prime minister. One of his additional powers flows from the preventive detention act, based on the principle "that the executive, especially in the circumstances of a new nation such as ours, must have the necessary powers to carry out the functions of a modern state." [50] This act has given the president sweeping powers of preventive detention that cannot be challenged in any court; the detainee can appeal only to an advisory committee whose decisions are not binding. The president also

49. The first vice-president, Abeid Karume, is also president of Zanzibar. Creation of this special position was part of the reorganization of government necessitated by the union. Karume's scope of decision making is confined effectively to Zanzibar, and his actions on the mainland are largely ceremonial.

50. Act Number 60 of 1962.

has gained the power to "deport" citizens from one part of the country to another and to expel undesirables. Finally, under the National Union of Tanganyika Workers Establishment Act of 1964, the president may appoint the secretary-general and deputy secretary-general of the newly established National Union of Tanganyika (NUTA). With the powers of detention and pardon, military and police control, broad powers of appointment, and even the ability to summarily dismiss students,[51] the president's power seems unlimited. As Nyerere himself admitted, "I have sufficient powers under the constitution to be a dictator." [52]

One responsibility of the former prime minister, to lead government business in the National Assembly, has devolved upon the second vice-president. In fact, many of his duties resemble those of the former chief secretary to the governor. He performs a variety of ceremonial functions on behalf of the president, as well as a full range of administrative duties, with particular responsibility for justice and defense. When the second vice-president, Kawawa, was asked about the similarity of the role of governor to president and chief secretary to vice-president, he agreed there were parallels in their responsibilities but quickly noted a major difference: "We are elected." [53] Indeed, this is the very point that Nyerere himself stressed four years earlier in defending the strong presidential powers proposed in the republican constitution of 1962.

> Any government in the world is a dictator. . . . It has all the coercive means, it has the police, it has the armed forces; and it is incredible when one thinks of it. . . . And yet an individual can push these people out of power, and elect someone else to go and control the armed forces. A tyrant, Sir, is usually a person who is frightened of the people. It is incompatible with popular leadership, because popular leadership is never frightened of the people—it is a contradiction in terms.[54]

The popular leadership which Nyerere mentions has been tested in a fashion by national elections. In December 1962 Nyerere became the

51. As in October 1966, when he dismissed 393 students who protested the National Service Act.

52. Report of Nyerere's remarks on a television program in the U.K. on January 20, 1966, in *The Standard* (Tanzania), January 22, 1966.

53. Interview with Rashidi Kawawa, August 31, 1966.

54. *Tanganyika Parliamentary Debates* (Hansard), June 5 to July 3, 1962 (Dar es Salaam: Government Printer, 1962), Cols. 1105–06.

first president under the republican constitution after overwhelmingly defeating the ANC candidate, Mtemvu, by 1,127,978 to 21,276. In September 1965, under the interim constitution, Nyerere received 95.6 percent "yes" votes with 2,636,040 people voting; this was 78.1 percent of registered voters and probably represented over half the eligible population.[55] Nyerere's 1965 election, occurring simultaneously with the defeat or narrow victory of several ministers and junior ministers, reflected his popularity, which is an important element in legitimizing both the party and the government.[56]

Since independence, the *Bunge* or National Assembly has been an important forum for debating government policy and raising criticisms and objections of various sorts, and has provided a platform for broader explanation and defense of government programs and policies. In spite of the open and honest criticisms often voiced in the Assembly, in nearly all cases the Assembly has been concerned with ratifying decisions made by some other group. Not unlike the LegCo, the Assembly has been more often a sounding board and a forum for extracting approbation and applause for new government policies than a deliberative body that formulates policies or actually writes legislation. The judiciary, while remaining independent and asserting its competence, even to imprisoning political officials[57] and having its mild sentences of army mutineers upheld, still has not been tested on its independence or powers of constitutional interpretation. Moreover, with the preventive detention act and special detention powers of regional and area commissioners, the actual role of the court in politics has remained minimal.

The union with Zanzibar in April 1964 resulted more in changes of personnel than of organization in the national government. On January 12, 1964, a revolution in Zanzibar brought to power a new ruling group which included nationalist African politicians and a number of dedicated socialists with strong interests in Marxism. Zanzibaris have since been appointed members of the Bunge (they numbered 41 of 184 in March

---

55. If we estimate the population at 11 million in 1965 and assume 45% were over 21 (the voting age), that gives us a voting age population of 4,950,000, of which those voting would represent 53.3%. The portion of the population 21 or over is based on *African Census Reports 1957*, p. 29.

56. Nyerere's popularity and its implications will be discussed more thoroughly in chapter 6.

57. For example, P. Mbogo, a former M.P. and an area commissioner immediately prior to his arrest.

1966), and several have received ministerial posts or high administrative appointments. However, the two islands of the former Zanzibar Republic retain a separate government and set of ministers. The Revolutionary Council is the governing body for Zanzibar, and Sheikh Abeid Karume, a former labor leader and head of the Afro-Shirazi party, is president of Zanzibar as well as first vice-president of Tanzania.

The party has also experienced important changes. At the time of independence its finances declined, many of the most able members and party leaders acquired positions in the government, and the organization languished. Despite the fact that TANU claimed 1.25 million members (in a population of 10 million), "subscriptions had dried up, the enrollment of new members ceased, and attendance at public meetings was shrinking." [58] The inability of TANU to mobilize the population was further demonstrated, as Bienen points out, when only one quarter of the potential voters appeared at the polls at the 1962 elections.[59] Nyerere, recognizing this problem, resigned as prime minister in January 1962, leaving the government in the hands of a trusted friend, Rashidi Kawawa. In the next ten months Nyerere laid plans for changes in both the government and the party. Kivukoni College (established by TANU) had opened and began offering a year's training in social science for middle-level TANU leaders. Within a few years the TANU organization at the district and regional levels was filled with Kivukoni graduates. In 1962 the party was brought directly into the government through the reorganization of provincial administration. Politicians appointed by Nyerere to new posts of area commissioner and regional commissioner were simultaneously assigned as regional and district secretaries of the party.[60] With their dual party and government roles, their job is to bridge the gap between the party and government, explain government policies to the people, and coordinate development within their areas.

While TANU certainly has become the preeminent political organization (excluding the government), it is apparent that one reason is the relative weakness of other organizations or potential organizations in Tanzania. In absolute terms, or in relation to the ability to effect change at the

58. Bennett.
59. See Bienen, p. 57.
60. There are 69 districts or areas and 20 regions. Sixty districts and 17 regions were created in 1962–63 by dividing and realigning the former nine provinces. The union with Zanzibar added an additional three regions and nine areas. Each district has an area commissioner and each region, a regional commissioner.

local level, TANU's capacities are limited. It is handicapped by disjointed communication networks, lack of organization, inadequate education among party officers and staff, and limited finances. The army mutiny in January 1964 underlined the weakness of the party, which was unable to organize resistance to this illegal seizure of power or to restore order, tasks which required the support of British troops.

Following the army mutiny of 1964, the cell system was introduced in the party; each group of ten houses or families was clustered into a single cell. With this innovation, TANU created a pyramidal organization which stretches from the president down to the lowest member. Moreover, the cell has been given specific functions, particularly in relation to security and self-help projects. TANU leaders have exhorted cell members to report any suspicious activities or any strangers to their cell leader. The party was further strengthened by broadening its membership base. In 1963, TANU was opened to Asian and European members, a move Nyerere had been promoting since 1958. Since the army mutiny, soldiers in the newly organized army have been encouraged to join the party, though they may not hold office.[61] In July 1964, barriers to civil servants joining the party were lifted, though there are restrictions against their holding party posts.

Further changes occurred in 1965 and 1966, particularly at the national level. Salaries of key staff at the national headquarters were paid by the central government, and a new organizational arrangement at head-quarters called for expanded and upgraded positions. Ministers, regional commissioners, and other party officials in government posts were asked to establish specific office hours at party headquarters and to be available to meet the public. The president himself arranged to spend time each week at national headquarters. Finally, in January 1967, under the Arusha Declaration, party officials were brought under closer regulation and specifically prohibited from serving as members or directors of any corporation or profit-making institution, holding any property for rent, receiving multiple salaries, or engaging in capitalist activities such as owning stock or making private investments or running their own businesses.[62]

61. Another action intended to retain control over and support from the army was the appointment of Selemani Kitundu, a high party official, as a colonel and the political commissar of the army. Kitundu continued as the regional commissioner of Dar es Salaam after his appointment in 1964 until 1967, when he took over his army duties on a full-time basis.

62. *The Nationalist*, February 6, 1967, p. 1, and March 4, 1967, p. 1.

The most important phenomenon of the independence period has been the effect of all these changes—the consolidation of power by TANU. As Friedland points out, the party has become "a focal institution, an institution which pervades and dominates all other institutions and society."[63] This description is at complete variance with Bienen's view that the country is undercentralized, with the center having little power to affect decisions or behavior at the local level, and that national institutions, such as TANU, are "fragile."[64] These conflicting views are reconcilable if one considers that the first is based on TANU's strength relative to other national organizations, while the second relates TANU's strength to its ability to effect change, especially of a developmental or integrative nature, at the local level. In these terms both assessments of TANU's strength are accurate.

The relative paramountcy of TANU's position makes the group approach to understanding politics in Tanzania particularly bootless. Some groups that might be expected to be influential in politics are unorganized. Other groups that are organized are prohibited, either formally or informally, from bringing public pressure to bear on policy questions. The Chiefs' Convention dissolved itself before independence, and a year later the position of chief was abolished along with all hereditary traditional status.[65] The Asian Association and all tribal associations have been abolished. Recognition of tribalism, even in collecting simple statistics, is discouraged. All political parties except TANU have been outlawed, including the African National Congress, the People's Democratic Party (PDP), and the All Muslim National Union of Tanganyika (AMNUT).

All this does not mean that there are no chiefs or that chiefs have no influence. Nor does it mean that tribal identities are unimportant, that Asians do not have special interests which they communicate to the government, or that policy cleavages do not exist among politicians. But these groups do not organize or communicate their feelings on policy matters to each other, the public, or the government as groups. Informal

---

63. See Friedland, p. 55.

64. Bienen, pp. 12–14.

65. One of the most powerful chiefs, A. S. Fundikira, resigned from the government in 1963 in a dispute over TANU's land policy. He was brought to trial in June of that year on charges of corruption. Although the charges were eventually dropped and Fundikira was given a secure position as chairman of East African Airways and a nominated seat in the National Assembly, he has been excluded from the ruling circles of both the government and the party.

tribal associations exist in Dar es Salaam and, no doubt, other cities, and often aid members with personal affairs such as marriage, employment, or death. But they are strongly discouraged from political activity. No tribal group as such, for example, may complain openly about the conditions of roads in its area or the desirability of a textile mill.

Organizations such as churches, schools, cooperatives, labor unions, and business groups do exist. Their ability to exercise influence, however, is limited. Since the party represents, in theory, the interests of all the people, some of these groups—as we have described earlier—are associated with the party and represented on the NEC. Perhaps it is appropriate that a socialist party does not have a business group affiliate, but the fact that most businessmen are either expatriates or Asians no doubt explains in large part the absence of an organized business association within the party. There seems little doubt that businessmen, and in particular Asians, have little political influence.

Teachers are also somewhat alienated from politics. There are several reasons for this. First, they are prohibited from holding office and must therefore resign (and lose their job security) if they gain public office, even at the local level. This rule reflects in part the experience of the Bukoba Council, which in 1963 was dissolved by the central government after several teachers elected to the council balked at TANU directives. The fact that a number of teachers were arrested and detained (usually for a day or two only) following the army mutiny in 1964 left a residual fear of political involvement and a hesitancy to criticize the government openly. At present, although teachers number over 13,000 and are thus a crucial group in the country, their political interests are completely channeled through NUTA, the national labor organization, or through the Ministry of Education.

An example of how group interests are discouraged can be seen in remarks on the Hire Purchase Bill in 1966. An Asian member had suggested that the act's provisions be made more lenient in favor of the consumer. This was interpreted by one M.P. as an underhanded attempt to delay passage of the bill. "These Asians have tried all sorts of tricks and pressures to keep us from passing this. They know [such tactics are] wrong and they can't stop us." [66] The government officially stressed that this act would promote the welfare of all *wananchi* (nationals).[67]

66. Interview with M.P. No. 26, February 24, 1966

67. *Majadiliano ya Bunge* (Hansard), February 22–28, 1966 (Dar es Salaam: Government Printer, 1966), Cols. 75–110. The word citizen (*raia*) was not used.

The nomination of national members for the Assembly is another example of official pressure discouraging the expression of group interests. The NEC screens all nominees, whose names are submitted by the seven national organizations designated by the president. The NEC chose to reject all names originally submitted because many were closely associated with or even leaders of the organizations nominating them. This policy of denying the legitimacy of particular interests was established prior to independence. In October 1958, when Sheikh Sulemani Takadir, the first leader of TANU elders, questioned the absence of Muslims from TANU's list of candidates in the forthcoming elections, he was summarily expelled from the party.[68]

Thus, with many groups officially restricted and others absorbed and controlled by the party, at least with respect to their political activity, the expression of group interests is publicly muffled. Only on a few occasions have groups openly taken stands designed to influence government action.[69] One such group, which had been organized to articulate its own interests and was not yet absorbed in the party, was the university students. Though not unaware of the informal rule condemning the expression of "selfish interest," the students had been confident of their own importance. In protest against what seemed unfair treatment for them under proposed National Service legislation, 393 members of the Tanzania Students Union (from four institutions in Dar es Salaam, but largely from University College) on October 22, 1966, staged a protest on the lawn of the State House. The president expelled the students on the spot and ordered them to return to their homes. University life had obviously not conditioned them to make the sacrifices in work and to accept the pay cuts that were expected of them from political leaders. The assets of the Students Union were handed over to the TANU Youth League, the Union dissolved, and students urged to join the TYL. Six months after the expulsion, following a formal request from the Parliament, Nyerere announced that students who requested pardon might return to the university, but that "students who are opposed to socialism will not return to the college."[70]

68. See Bennett.

69. Two examples of this would be the call for implementation of socialism by NUTA at its annual conference in December 1966, a month prior to the acceptance of the Arusha Declaration by the NEC, and the regular criticisms by the Sisal Growers' Association. The latter, however, are often denounced by the government.

70. See *The Nationalist*, October 24, 1966, and April 21, 1967. Most students were re-enrolled for the term beginning in July 1967.

To the party's leaders the maintenance of unity has always been a key ingredient in their success. In a country handicapped by poor communications, local autonomy, vast contrasts between urban and rural conditions, and a myriad of ethnic and economic differences, unity has been preserved by the establishment of a one-party state, emphasis on broad issues, and continual reminders that the chief tactic of Tanzania's enemies is to divide the people. Politics as a struggle of interest and ideology is a closed game, not open to the public or the outsider.

THE MODERN POLITICAL SYSTEM: A CLOSED STYLE OF POLITICS

The political system that has emerged from colonialism in Tanzania does not operate by the rules of parliamentary democracy so quickly erected by the British prior to their exit. The pattern of rule and decision making is a mixture of the hierarchical and paternal qualities of colonial rule and the pattern of closed politics developed by TANU in its formative period. Issues often are debated not in public but in private. The private debate may be sharp; meetings of the NEC (closed to the public) are reported to be extremely lively with "no holds barred." [71] Decisions on the commitment to socialism, the establishment of a national bank, the union with Zanzibar, and the nationalization of major industries, banks, and trading firms were made privately. Consultations, of course, were held according to the president's judgment. The public and the legislature were eventually called upon to ratify such decisions, though not to debate their wisdom.

Limitations on public criticism ought not be overemphasized, however. Real efforts have been made to allow criticisms of policies and programs, as was evidenced in the debate on education in the National Assembly in February 1966, or the report on cooperatives, discussed in October 1966. Before the one-party machinery was set up, a commission gathered widespread public opinion on issues regarding implementation procedures. The commission, however, did not canvass opinion randomly, nor did it ask questions as to whether a single party was desirable or if more than one candidate should stand for the presidency.[72] The nomination of a single candidate for president is crucial to contain factional-

---

71. Interview with a member of the National Executive Committee, June 1966.

72. See *One-Party State Report*, esp. pp. 10, 22–23. The decision to become a one-party state had effectively been made at the 1963 TANU Annual Conference.

ism within the party and prevent policy disputes from erupting into public debate, thereby forcing candidates to identify with alternative positions. The public, however, seems to prefer the notion of two candidates, as indicated by a recent survey of 392 people in Dar es Salaam. To the question, "When our president retires, do you think that there should be two candidates to stand for election in that presidential election?" 226 (58%) replied "yes," 111 (28%) said "no," and 55 (14%) were in the "don't know" category.[73]

Thus, while criticisms and constructive suggestions are sought, and certainly there is no state or party apparatus to control opinion, practices that are likely to bring division or disunity to the country have been avoided. There seems to be an unwritten portion of the "National Ethic" (Nyerere's statement of principles, which has served as a surrogate for a bill of rights) that urges unity and solidarity. Unity, the policy of TANU in the independence struggle, continues not only as a description of the situation but as a goal actively sought.[74]

This unity manifests itself mostly at the national level. Locally based politicians and speakers in the National Assembly, dealing with local topics, are much more willing to discuss political problems. Bienen, in conducting interviews with political elite at the "center," found "a strong commitment to viewing both society and the political elite as cohesive

73. "Dar es Salaam Election Survey," conducted by MARCO Surveys in January 1966, for Lionel Cliffe and James S. Coleman, whom I wish to thank for allowing me to use material from the survey. The survey was part of a study of the 1965 Tanzanian election conducted under the auspices of the East African Institute of Social Research.

74. The National Ethic may be found in *One-Party State Report,* pp. 3–4. The concept of unity has been expressed frequently in the statements of Nyerere: "Once the first free government is formed, its supreme task lies ahead—the building up of the country's economy . . . calls for the maximum united effort by the whole country if it is to succeed. *There can be no room for difference or division.*" "One-Party Rule," reprinted in Paul E. Sigmund, Jr., *The Ideologies of the Developing Nations* (New York: Praeger, 1963), p. 199. "To try and import the idea of a parliamentary opposition into Africa may very likely lead to violence—because the opposition parties will tend to be regarded as traitors by the majority of our people—or at best, it will lead to the trivial manoeuverings of 'opposing' groups whose time is spent in the inflation of artificial differences into some semblance of reality 'for the sake of preserving democracy!'" "Democracy and the Party System," p. 15. "We want to maintain and expand the individual liberty which we now have, and to ensure for our nation the safeguards which are provided by freedom for criticism. . . . At present, however, we have to face the fact that in general terms the freedom for all to live a decent life must take priority. Development must be considered first, and other matters examined in relation to it." From Nyerere's speech at the opening of University College, Dar es Salaam, August 21, 1964 (Dar es Salaam: Ministry of Information and Tourism), p. 17.

and psychologically homogeneous, even if ethnically and socially heterogeneous." [75] The elite interviews that I conducted revealed a similar reluctance to identify any divisions in national leadership. But there are real and important ideological cleavages among these elite, both in elective and appointive posts, as shown in their responses to economic questions reported in chapter 3. However, these differences are only infrequently subjects for public debate, and then always in the third person. Calls for unity have declined since the general election in 1965, which seems to have restored Tanzanians' confidence in their government, badly shaken by the army mutiny the year before. This broader consolidation of support is now being translated into a new tactic to insure a minimum unity or consensus on national policy.

A new emphasis on testing the ideological conformity of TANU members was announced in the Arusha Declaration (January 1967). The steps leading up to the new attitude toward party membership may be traced by using as an example the problem of those who might support a "mixed-economy" approach to national development. In 1962 Nyerere wrote:

> A National Movement which is open to all—which is identified with the whole nation—has nothing to fear from the discontent of any excluded section of society, for there is then no such section. Those forming the Government will, of course, be replaced from time to time; but this is what elections are for. . . . And, since such a National Movement leaves no room for the growth of discontented elements excluded from its membership, it has nothing to fear from criticism and the free expression of ideas.[76]

In March 1965, this position was narrowed slightly in the president's Commission on the One-Party State, which stated:

> To insist on a narrow ideological conformity would clearly be inconsistent with the mass participation in the affairs of the Party which we regard as essential. On the other hand, if membership involves no political commitment of any kind, T.A.N.U. would become co-extensive with the Nation and cease to function as a political Party in any serious sense. . . . A Party based on these principles [in TANU's constitution, article 2] and requiring adherence to them

75. Bienen, pp. 77–78.
76. "Democracy and the One-Party State," pp. 24–25.

as a condition of membership would be open to all but an insignificant minority of our citizens and would, we believe, be a truly national movement.[77]

At the time the TANU constitution required members to support a government devoted to, among other things, "encouraging private enterprise where this is directed towards the benefit of the whole country.[78] However, in the constitution adopted in June 1965, this clause was dropped and, among others, clauses were added that called for active state intervention in the economy to ensure economic justice and "effective control over the principal means of production."[79]

Party membership was further tightened following the nationalization of major businesses in 1967. Part Four of the Arusha Declaration noted:

> The National Executive Committee feels that the time has come for emphasis to shift away from mere size of membership on to the quality of the membership. Greater consideration must be given to a member's commitment to the beliefs and objectives of the Party, and its policy of Socialism.
>
> The Membership Clause in the TANU Constitution must be closely observed. Where it is thought unlikely that an applicant really accepts the beliefs, aims and objects of the Party, he should be denied membership.[80]

The party has now emerged as a more distinct unit from the masses. The ideas and attitudes of party leaders (average members are largely unaffected) receive closer scrutiny. This policy reflects the favorite slogan of one cabinet minister who regularly reminds his friends, "You can't build socialism without socialists." As the data reported in chapters 3 to 5 indicate, there were a number of Tanzanians whose socialist commitment was fairly weak. Since TANU membership has become an important, if till recently perfunctory, qualification for many positions in the public sector and even private business (part of which, of course, has now been nationalized), loss of TANU membership is a real and serious threat. Even greater conformity to the party's creed and rules for debate can therefore be expected. As one M.P. explained, "Your political career will pretty well be finished if you're sacked from TANU, and it will probably even

77. *One-Party State Report*, pp. 15–16.
78. From article two of the constitution of TANU, reprinted in ibid., p. 35.
79. *Interim Constitution of Tanzania, 1965*, pp. 42–43.
80. *The Nationalist*, February 6, 1967, p. 8.

hurt your business contacts." [81] The significance of this tighter party authority was manifested dramatically in late 1968 when the seats of nine members of the National Assembly were declared vacant after they had been expelled from the party.[82]

Thus, the Tanzanian political system has evolved a set of rules proscribing debate on differences over "fundamentals," relegating disputes over "minor issues" (such as priorities or timing) to private debate and leaving only "constructive criticism" and "helpful suggestions" to be aired publicly.[83] Although the privacy of the NEC is the principal arena for the acceptance or rejection of policy decisions, such major policies as the Arusha Declaration require broad support built through a hierarchy of expanding groups.[84] When widespread public support is sought, the discussion of policy is urged upon larger groups, not by the vanquished seeking to transfer the debate to a more favorable arena but by the victors in a preemptive move to have it ratified at all levels. Conflict is still minimized.

Although the one-party system seems to require this minimizing of conflict through emphasis on unanimity,[85] shortcomings and economic

81. Interview with M.P. No. 88, June 28, 1966.

82. Two of these men lost their seats due to continued absence: Anangisye, who was in preventive detention, and Oscar Kambona, who fled the country in 1967. The seven others were Chogga, Kaneno, Masha, Kibuga, Bakampenja, Kassella-Bantu, and Mwakitwange. See *The Nationalist, December* 6, 10, and 31, 1968, p. 1.

83. Nyerere and others have frequently urged greater public discussion of this third kind. The presidential commission, in the *One-Party State Report,* p. 21, states: "We consider that TANU has every right to insist that members of Parliament remain loyal to the basic principles of the Party. Subject to this, however, we believe that there should be complete freedom of discussion in the National Assembly and the right of members to criticize and question should be acknowledged by Government and Party alike." The president has regularly urged all Tanzanians to criticize the government without fear, as, for example, at a meeting of elders in Dar es Salaam reported in *The Standard* (Tanzania), June 19, 1965.

84. The basic elements of the Arusha Declaration, as worked out by Nyerere, were presented to the following groups for approval: first, the party central committee (12 members of whom Nyerere is one and appoints 8 of the remaining 11); second, the regional commissioners' conference (17 men appointed by Nyerere); third, the NEC (40% of whom are either regional commissioners or members of the central committee); fourth, the National Assembly (including 23 members of the NEC); and finally, a special national conference of TANU (which includes all of those in previous groups, plus representatives from the district level).

85. The behavior of a small-town school board described by Vidich and Bensman strikingly resembles the way in which conflict is limited in Tanzania. The board members

problems are usually faced forthrightly. The candidness of Nyerere's speeches is quite refreshing.[86] However, his political frankness masks the fact that he has no organized critics and that reporting of conflict among national political leaders, both as to the nature of the issue differences and the identity of antagonists, is firmly condemned. There is a feeling evidenced in Nyerere's speeches and in conversations with elite members that it is difficult to work with or trust someone with whom you have basic policy differences. Thus, the conflicts placed in the open are always those that will unite the vast majority of the population against enemies such as ignorance, exploitation, or imperialism. These conflicts displace political divisions along other, lesser issues—such as the priorities for developmental allocations—and prevent conflicts from creating any permanent divisions or alignments within the country. By deciding what political conflicts may become public, the political elite has maintained unity in a party and nation whose institutionalization is fragile, especially at lower levels. In contrast, in American and European politics, competing political groups regularly calculate the benefits of transferring conflict from a small to a larger arena, and large numbers of people often get involved on opposing sides of an issue. The rules by which the conflict may be fought, however, are rather well established in the memories and traditions of the populace. It is precisely because such rules are weak in Tanzania that conflict is avoided. In defending the need of preventive detention, Nyerere remarked:

> Our Union has neither the long tradition of nation-hood, nor the strong physical means of national security, which older countries take for granted. While the vast mass of the people give full and active support to their country and its government, a handful of individuals can still put our nation into jeopardy, and reduce to ashes the effort of millions.[87]

"attempt to minimize or avoid crises, and this leads to further demands for unanimity and concealment." Arthur J. Vidich and Joseph Bensman, *Small Town in Mass Society* (Princeton: Princeton University Press, 1958), p. 173.

86. See, for example, J. K. Nyerere, "President's Address to the OAU Emergency Meeting of Foreign Ministers" (Dar es Salaam: Information Division of Vice President's Office, 1964), which discusses the army mutiny, and "Principles of Development" (Dar es Salaam: Government Printer, 1966), an address to the NEC, June 8, 1966.

87. "President's Speech at the Opening of University College," p. 17.

Nyerere and the party leadership have used their control of the country to define politics in such a way as to prevent those conflicts likely to divide the public from becoming open disputes.[88]

Actions by Nyerere and other leaders have shaped the expectations of the major political actors in Tanzania. From the interaction of expectations and behavior there has emerged a set of informal norms or rules that govern political life in Tanzania. These rules are varied and complex; they differ in the degree to which they are recognized, accepted, and valued. Moreover, individuals hold different priorities for the rules regulating political action. In chapters 4 to 6, I discuss some of these rules.

The pattern of decision making under these rules varies according to the issue and personalities involved. However, the general style of political participation is fairly clear. The ideal actor is open-minded, he attends the meetings at which decisions are to be made, he listens to arguments and has a chance to present his own views, and then a decision is announced when there is sufficient support for one position. At this point each individual is expected to stop further discussion or promotion of alternatives and abide by and implement the decision. The British principles of cabinet responsibility and party discipline have been altered and extended to promote a consensus among national political actors.

The manner in which these men understand their own roles and those of other major political actors is an important factor in determining the "modern" political culture as it affects those who participate in the modern institutions of government. The balance of this book is an investigation of the Tanzanian elite political culture and some of the political norms that govern elite behavior.

88. For a discussion of the regulation of conflicts and its importance to politics, see E. E. Schattschneider, *The Semi-Sovereign People* (New York: Holt, Rinehart and Winston, 1966), p. 68. He writes, "Political conflict is not like an intercollegiate debate in which the opponents agree in advance on a definition of the issues. As a matter of fact, *the definition of the alternatives is the supreme instrument of power;* the antagonists can rarely agree on what the issues are because power is involved in the definition. He who determines what politics is about runs the country, because the definition of the alternatives is the choice of conflicts, and the choice of conflicts allocates power."

2. Political Roles and Political Institutionalization

One of the basic problems in politics is order. In new states change seems to occur frequently and unpredictably. Institutionalizing politics so that change becomes orderly and occurs within the bounds of a set of rules may be the foremost task facing leaders in newly independent states. A major difference among polities is that the parameters or relatively fixed conditions of political systems in "developed" states are variables in those systems that are less institutionalized. Change in the latter tends to be disorderly and occurs not according to the political formulas that contain the rules for political action and specify mechanisms for change, but rather by a struggle over the rules themselves. In political systems of this type, the lack of institutionalized procedures and behavior encourages disorder and the resort to coercive tactics by political contenders. Without discipline, a Hobbesian world in which violence becomes the dominant strategy emerges, for as Samuel Huntington concludes, "discipline and development go hand in hand." [1] Securing the conformity of people to regular patterns of political action is therefore an immediate problem facing newly independent nations.

In Africa, nationalist leaders inherited at independence an autocratic bureaucracy and a newly established set of institutions, such as a parliament, elections, and a cabinet organized according to the expectations of the metropolitan country. It has been the task of members of the elite in these nascent political systems to create and institutionalize a set of role expectations that contain the rules of politics which will accommodate the demands and pressures on the system and accord with the value patterns of the society. In one country after another in Africa, the original set of inherited rules governing the balance of power and interests has been overturned. In a dozen countries since 1960, military coups have occurred. In most of the others major constitutional revisions have been made. The inherited rules have been seen as unworkable, producing cor-

1. Samuel P. Huntington, *Political Order in Changing Societies* (New Haven: Yale University Press, 1968), p. 24,

rupt or ineffective office holders, inhibiting economic development, and reinforcing political divisions.

Since independence in 1961, Tanzania has avoided many of the political and social tensions common to so many other countries. By 1965 a pattern of closed politics emerged which, except for the army mutiny of 1964, has inhibited serious instability. As a principal basis for my study of the emergence and consolidation of this political pattern in Tanzania, I will analyze some of the major political roles as they evolved from ongoing political activity after 1961.

INSTITUTIONALIZATION AND POLITICAL CHANGE

New approaches to comparative politics in recent years include an emphasis on political culture, attention to changes in social and economic patterns, and structural-functional analysis.[2] Nearly all these approaches recommend a multivariate analysis that examines a wide range of social and psychological processes, such as motivations, attitudes, culture, demographic factors, social structure, technology, and individual skills and resources. A study of the institutionalization of political roles allows us to focus on a single process that organizes many of these variables.

My basic assumption is that environmental and historical constraints, cultural values, and personal leadership, acting as independent variables, shape the norms for political roles within a political system. Expectations about the legitimate behavior for leaders occupying these roles are contained in the political culture of a society.[3] As defined by Lucian Pye, political culture is "the set of attitudes, beliefs and sentiments that give order and meaning to a political process and that provide the underlying assumptions and rules that govern behavior in the political system."[4] In order to understand how a political culture operates not only to regulate overt activity but also to influence the pattern of ideas and subjective behavior,[5] I have focused on political roles as the key agents of translation

2. An excellent summary of the changes in thinking about comparative politics is Harry Eckstein, "A Perspective on Comparative Politics, Past and Present," in Harry Eckstein and David Apter, eds., *Comparative Politics* (New York: The Free Press, 1963), pp. 3–32.

3. The importance of political culture is discussed in Gabriel A. Almond and Sidney Verba, *The Civic Culture* (Princeton: Princeton University Press, 1963); Lucian W. Pye, *Politics, Personality, and Nation-Building* (New Haven: Yale University Press, 1962); and Pye and Verba, *Political Culture and Political Development.*

4. Pye, *Aspects of Political Development,* p. 104.

5. See Pye and Verba, p. 517

between the broad characteristics of culture and the discrete acts that constitute the political process.

Each role in a political system has a set of boundaries or parameters which, if violated, are likely either to alter the system or to remove the role occupant from his position. A president who fails to satisfy the demands and expectations of those in lesser political positions may find himself removed by coup, election, or otherwise. Similarly, lesser political figures may be forced out, probably in a more mundane fashion, for breaches of the political rules. While some role expectations are always ad hoc and issue centered, others are of a general nature, defining the boundaries of political roles, prescribing certain acts that are clearly wrong in the minds of most influential individuals. The institutionalization of roles in the political system is evidenced by a structured and interrelated set of norms for role behavior. Where these norms are weak or ambiguous, institutionalization not only of political roles but of the political system itself is at a low level.

Institutionalization as System Development

It is important to distinguish institutionalization of political roles from political development.[6] Political development is a normative concept. The writer using it should explicitly specify a set of criteria or values he deems necessary to development.[7] These criteria may refer either to certain valued properties supplied by a system, such as wealth or justice, or to characteristics of a system that he deems instrumental to promoting other values, such as recruitment by merit. The institutionalization of a system, however, refers to a different dimension of distinguishing among polities than is usually included by those who discuss political develop-

6. A number of alternative definitions of political development can be found in the literature. For some writers this term simply refers to legal changes in the direction of statehood, while for others it is synonymous with nation building; that is, the creation of national identities, Western values, and modern economic and social practices. There is yet another group of writers who use the idea of political development to refer to the relative establishment of certain specified political qualities such as equality, capacity, and differentiation, or security, welfare, justice, and liberty. These lists of development criteria are reviewed and specific ones recommended in Pye, *Aspects of Political Development*, pp. 45–48; and J. Roland Pennock, "Political Development, Political Systems, and Political Goods," *World Politics, 16* (April 1964), 420–34.

7. Harold D. Lasswell in "The Policy Sciences of Development," *World Politics, 17* (January 1965), 288–309, analyzes and suggests characteristics for an adequate model of political development, reminding the reader that "models of political development should be explicitly preferential."

ment or political modernization. In order to distinguish this from other characteristics by which political systems differ, I shall refer to it as "system development." System development or institutionalization has occurred when there is a stable and coherent set of expectations about how decisions will be made and order maintained, such that random shocks or the deviant behavior of a few men cannot alter the basic pattern of political life. This situation requires that the actions of individuals in politically important roles be regularized and predictable. The institutionalization of political roles serves to increase the pressures for continuity and conformity in the behavior of these individuals and hence both promotes and can serve as an indicator of more general system institutionalization. This view draws upon systems theory and the concept of a social system as a complex network of roles and actions. While institutionalization in a political system is empirically related to the phenomenon of political stability, which is often considered desirable, institutionalization itself is not necessarily a desirable quality. Moreover, it is a property attributed to a system but not necessarily to the individuals who are its members. Their lives may be quite insecure and unpredictable though the system itself is stable and institutionalized.[8]

A political system's institutionalization is normally affected by the stability of its environment. For instance, in Africa prior to European colonization, economic and social conditions changed rather slowly in most cases; in this period, a number of the traditional political systems in Africa were well established. These systems generally had a stable set of rules for allocating decision-making authority and effectively satisfying the limited demands that were placed upon them. There was dependable coordination of the efforts and expectations of tribal members to the

8. The ideas about political systems discussed here are based largely on the works of Karl W. Deutsch and David Easton. See Karl W. Deutsch, *The Nerves of Government* (New York: The Free Press, 1963), pp. 124–25, and David Easton, *A Framework for Political Analysis* (Englewood Cliffs, N. J., Prentice Hall, 1965), pp. 103–35. This definition of institutionalization is considerably narrower than Huntington's and explicitly rejects the view that an institutionalized system is developed politically. I find Huntington's four criteria of institutionalization take a much broader view, one that involves, for instance, aspects of modernization, democracy, equality, and stability. Huntington made a similar point at the American Political Science Association meetings in New York, September 2, 1969. His criteria or continua of institutionalization include complexity (which relates to the modernization aspects of role specificity), autonomy (which includes a notion of equal access to a political system for groups), and adaptability (which is assessed by persistence and the absence of coups and violence, and hence seems to imply stability).

attainment of their few societal goals. Although these systems clearly lacked the qualities of modernization that men like Weber and Almond have identified,[9] and although the majority of members in most of these societies had neither a share in decision making nor a very secure physical existence, many of these political systems were developed, in the sense that the policies and actions that occurred corresponded to what most members expected and accepted.[10] Similarly, the Soviet Union in the 1930s and 1940s, it might be argued, was a developed system. From the viewpoint of an individual member, particularly one who was politically active, life could be insecure and powerless. Nevertheless, there was a regularity and predictability about the way in which power was exercised and goals pursued.[11]

Thus a political system that is institutionalized is not necessarily politically modern or democratic, nor does it necessarily make its members happy or satisfy any list of analytically derived functional requisites.[12]

9. These qualities are associated with Weber's rational-legal ideal type and Parsons' "pattern variables," and include orientations that are secularized (affectively neutral), universal and not particular, specific and not diffuse, and achievement based and not ascriptive. See Max Weber, *The Theory of Social and Economic Organization,* ed. Talcott Parsons (New York: The Free Press, 1964), pp. 56–77 and 115 ff.; Talcott Parsons, *The Social System* (New York: The Free Press, 1964), especially pp. 101–12; and Gabriel A. Almond and G. Bingham Powell, Jr., *Comparative Politics: Developmental Approach* (Boston: Little, Brown, 1966), pp. 299–332.

10. See Lucy Mair, *Primitive Government* (Baltimore: Penguin Books, 1962), and M. Fortes and E. E. Evans-Pritchard, *African Political Systems* (London: Oxford University Press, 1940), for an account of many of these traditional political systems. Among the Baganda, for example, a political system existed that was capable of major persistence and adaptation in the face of British colonial power. In the 1860s, however, this system offered neither security nor power sharing to political aspirants. When Kabaka Mutesa came to power, for instance, he instantly burned to death some 60 of his brothers as an *expected* and *accepted* precaution against rebellion. See David E. Apter's account of the historical persistence of this kingdom in *The Political Kingdom of Uganda* (Princeton: Princeton University Press, 1963). Alan Moorehead in *The White Nile* (New York: Dell Publishing Co., 1960), pp. 55–63, gives some of the odious details of this kingdom as observed by the explorer Speke.

11. See Nathan Leites, *Operational Code of the Politburo* (New York: McGraw-Hill, 1951) and *A Study of Bolshevism* (Glencoe: The Free Press, 1953).

12. I am avoiding deliberately the problems in a structural-functional approach such as are outlined by Marion J. Levy, Jr., "Some Aspects of Structural-Functional Analysis and Political Science," in Roland Young, ed., *Approaches to the Study of Politics* (Evanston: Northwestern University Press, 1958), pp. 52–66.

"Development" occurs in a political system as its active members perceive and accept as authoritative a set of rules or norms governing the patterns of behavior that comprise the system. Thus the political system is conceived of as a set of interacting parts, linked by communication nets, pursuing the preservation of certain learned values by predictable procedures and patterns. It may be that the circulation of actors in power roles regularly occurs by nonlegal or violent means, as for example in Guatemala or Argentina, but if this procedure is an accepted and expected pattern, then the system may be institutionalized.

A political system may also embrace members with widely different goals, who consequently refuse to play the political game according to any set of institutionalized rules. In such a case, civil war, social revolution, or chaos is likely, as occurred for example in Spain in the 1930s, Cuba in the 1950s, and the Congo (Kinshasa) in the 1960s. While it is difficult to specify at what point a system undergoes deterioration or negative development, it is evident that some system decay has occurred in each country that has experienced rapid change, disintegration, and eventual transformation and reinstitutionalization.[13] System development, then, is a quality of a political system measurable in degrees of institutionalization and is similar in some respects to Samuel Huntington's idea of development and Talcott Parsons' notion of institutionalization in social systems.[14]

13. System change or decay and the subsequent establishment of a new system pose a difficult analytical problem. In part, one's analysis depends on the time period within which change is measured. See Easton, *Framework*, pp. 82–101. Easton apparently would argue that these systems persist only in a changed form, since political systems possess "the capacity to transform themselves, their goals, practices, and the very structure of their internal organization" (p. 99). Deutsch also stresses that the ability of systems to change their goals and internal patterns is characteristic of growth and "healthy" systems (*Nerves*, pp. 219–44, 248–54). My view is that in the case of these three countries, Spain, Cuba, and the Congo, clearly the people or entire system, i.e. the "social system," has persisted. Further, some modification of a major subsystem, the political system, has occurred such that the norms that characterize authoritative decision making for the society are different. Whether this is a new political system arising from the ashes of the old or simply a changed system is a question worthy of scholasticism. What is significant is that these systems underwent a period in which expectations, normative order, and the roles of politics disintegrated.

14. See Huntington, *Political Order*, pp. 12–39, and "The Change to Change"; and Parsons, *The Social System*, pp. 39 ff.

The Institutionalization of Political Roles

Roles are basic analytical units of political systems.[15] Political roles consist of a pattern of expected behavior for individuals holding particular positions in a system. These may range from the most general, such as citizen, to the fairly specific, such as president. The role concept links personality to social structure, and role expectations form the normative structure for system behavior. In a political system, role expectations contain the rules that regulate members' political actions—actions involving influence, decision making, or the authoritative allocation of values. A political system's institutionalization may be assessed according to the degree of acceptance and commitment among the active system members to a set of norms for orienting and guiding their political acts. In such a system, there is widespread agreement among expectations, and there is a commitment to these expectations. Moreover, political role expectations are shared and valued, most importantly by those actors who either perform important political roles or serve as alters to these roles, that is, the political elite.[16] Consensus of role expectations among members of the elite in a political system, then, is a possible measure of system institutionalization. The greater the acceptance of a compatible set of role expectations for major political roles—such as legislator, president, administrator, and citizen—the more the political system may be said to be institutionalized. Political role institutionalization, then, is here defined as the creation of a set of shared role expectations among significant actors in a state that effectively shape their behavior.

The study of elite roles and those who play these roles is particularly relevant to understanding politics in new states where leadership can have a very significant impact. Changes in elite composition, anxiety among elite personalities, and visions of the future held by elites have all been productive focuses for studying politics in new states.[17] Thus, our analysis of the institutionalization of roles based on a study of the

15. See Parsons, *The Social System*, and Easton, *Framework*, pp. 39–57.

16. An alter to a particular role has regular contact and interlocking duties with that role occupant.

17. See Marshall R. Singer, *The Emerging Elite: A Study of Political Leadership in Ceylon* (Cambridge: M.I.T. Press, 1964); Wendell Bell, *Jamaican Leaders* (Berkeley: University of California Press, 1964); James A. Scott, *Political Ideology in Malaysia* (New Haven: Yale University Press, 1968); and Frederick W. Frey, *The Turkish Political Elite* (Cambridge: M.I.T. Press, 1965).

background and attitudes of the Tanzanian elite may provide a test of this combination of analytical approaches as well as some understanding of the dynamics of Tanzanian politics.[18]

THE ANALYSIS OF POLITICAL ROLES: CONSENSUS AND CONGRUENCE

The institutionalization of norms or rules shaping durable political roles involves a system-level or macro process. These norms determine the style (democratic or authoritarian) and stability (peaceful succession) of politics in the system. Judgments about the degree to which a set of roles is institutionalized for an entire system require comparative standards. Unfortunately, no basis for cross-national judgments about the institutionalization of political roles exists, since attitudinal and other data for such purposes have not been generated or collated.[19]

My research, however, focused heavily upon individuals and what has been termed microscopic role analysis.[20] Carefully examining the roles of a few major political actors allowed me to combine a micro-analysis of roles, in which the behavior of individuals can be studied, with a macro-political analysis, since the norms that operate to constrain these elite actors are major components of the political culture and constitute some of the "rules of the game." If these rules are institutionalized they will be effective in shaping behavior and, therefore, will represent parameters of the political system. In order to investigate both the political rules that have emerged and the extent to which they are institutionalized, it is necessary to focus on a selected set of roles and on particular aspects of these roles.

The Role Process

A political role is the cluster of behavior *and* norms associated with a particular political position, such as chief, policeman, or president. Several

18. For the purpose of this study, the elite is defined as those who hold seats in the National Assembly or upper-level civil service positions. Although this excludes a number of important party officials not holding government posts, as well as a few important businessmen, journalists, etc., the bulk of those who share in influencing national decisions are included in this definition. See Singer, *Emerging Elite,* who uses a similar rationalization and limits his elite to parliamentarians, excluding civil servants.

19. Of course, cross-national data on instability and violence as a measure of institutionalization are now fairly widely available, but would be at best a second-order measure.

20. See Neal Gross, Ward S. Mason, and Alexander W. McEachern, *Exploration in Role Analysis* (New York: John Wiley and Sons, 1958), chaps. 10–12.

distinctions and definitions of a role have been offered by other scholars.[21] Essentially, these alternative views of the role concept are based on differing operational measures. The three major types of definitions describe a role in terms of (1) role expectations, (2) role orientations, and (3) role behavior, all of which are encompassed in my definition.

Role expectations refer to the norms or demands made by members of society upon all individuals occupying a particular position. Individuals who frequently interact with the occupant of a political position, as legislators do with a president, are the principal sources of these social norms. The concept of norm, as developed by Sherif, Newcomb, Festinger, and others, refers to communicated responses that produce conformity by prescribing behavior and offering associated sanctions.[22]

Role orientations refer to the individual role occupant's own ideas as to how he ought to behave when he is in the role situation. These ideas reflect the learned or internalized norms of those around him as well as his own personality and selective perception.[23]

Role behavior refers to the actions of an individual as the occupant of his particular position, "a patterned sequence of learned actions or deeds performed by a person in an interaction situation." [24] The focus here is upon the empirical rather than the normative aspects of role. Role behavior is differentiated from other behavior by the interaction situation in which it occurs. Because it is necessary to infer the role to which an act or set of actions belongs, an investigator must stipulate some external

21. See the collection of essays and extensive bibliography in Bruce J. Biddle and Edwin J. Thomas, *Role Theory: Concepts and Research* (New York: John Wiley and Sons, 1966). Clarifications of the definition of role may be found in Theodore M. Newcomb, *Social Psychology* (New York: Dryden Press, 1950); Gross, et al., pp. 11–18; Daniel J. Levinson, "Role Personality and Social Structure in the Organization Setting," in Seymour M. Lipset and Neil J. Smelser, *Sociology: The Progress of a Decade* (Englewood Cliffs: Prentice-Hall, 1961), pp. 300–02; and Lionel J. Nieman and James W. Hughes, "The Problem of the Concept of Role—A Resurvey of the Literature," *Social Forces, 30* (December 1951), 142–47.

22. Sanctions would include both rewards and punishments. This process is carefully described in Ragnar Rommetveit, *Social Norms and Roles* (Minneapolis: University of Minnesota Press, 1955), pp. 18–30. Law and courts would be examples of formal norms and sanctions, etiquette and ostracism examples of an informal nature.

23. Sargent, for example, uses this definition. See John H. Rohrer and Muzafer Sherif, eds. *Social Psychology at the Crossroads* (New York: Harper, 1951), p. 360: "A person's role is a pattern or type of social behavior which seems situationally appropriate to him in terms of the demands and expectations of those in his group."

24. T. R. Sarbin, "Role Theory," in Gardner Lindzey, ed. *Handbook of Social Psychology, 1* (Cambridge: Addison-Wesley, 1955), 225.

criteria for identifying the role to which an individual's behavior is related. Moreover, relevant behavior theoretically includes not only overt actions but motivations, beliefs, feelings, attitudes, and values.[25] As a result, role behavior is usually studied in practice only when outward and obviously role-related activity is distinguishable. Davis, for example, limits role to "how an individual *actually performs* in a given position, as distinct from how he is supposed to perform." [26]

Role expectations, role orientations, and role behavior present three aspects or observational standpoints for analyzing role events. By not assuming consensus of expectations or congruence among the various aspects of role, but treating the degree of consensus and the extent of congruence as variables to be empirically examined, it is possible to assess the institutionalization of a role within a political system.

Six points of possible observation for assessing a particular role are illustrated by figure 2.1. The "role process" is composed of the following six stages:

1. The expectations actually held by others with respect to the rights and duties of the role
2. The norms "sent" to the role occupant by the actions, verbal and otherwise, of role alters by means of personal interaction and also via communications media
3. The received norms—the perceptions and ideas of the role occupant as to what "society" expects of him
4. The definition of the situation by the role occupant and his personal views as to how the role "ought" to be played
5. Overt behavior of the role occupant relevant to the norms or prescriptions of the role held by others or himself or both

25. Certainly role expectations contain prescriptions involving the proper attitudes or motivations for playing a given role. See David Krech, R. S. Crutchfield, and E. L. Ballachey, *Individual in Society* (New York: McGraw-Hill, 1962), p. 311. In my research I asked, "If an M.P. wished to be recognized and liked by ministers and other important people, what would he do?" Nearly 20% of those interviewed initially rejected the legitimacy of this motivation saying that "this is wrong" or "he wouldn't care about that."

Robert K. Merton also makes a twofold distinction that seems to parallel the definitions suggested here, in *Social Theory and Social Structure* (New York: Free Press of Glencoe, 1957), p. 392. "Role refers to the manner in which the rights and duties inherent in a social position are put into practice; orientation as here conceived refers to the theme underlying the complex of social roles performed by an individual."

26. Kingsley Davis, cited in Gross et al., p. 14. Similar uses of the term may be found in Parsons, *The Social System*, p. 25.

6. The perceptions of the role behavior that will be scanned and compared with expectations by role alters. Subsequent appraisal of the behavior will reinforce or undermine expectations and result in further actions at stage 2, which may be either sanctions with respect to violated expectations or altered norms with respect to future role behavior. This stage completes a cycle of feedback and adjustment.

This role process is an ongoing dynamic aspect of social life. Individuals and roles change over time as roles become more clearly defined (and

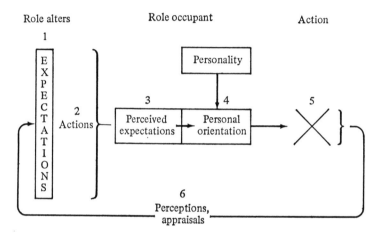

Figure 2.1. A Role Interaction Process

consensus increases) or they are learned better (and congruence increases) or individuals change roles—even create new ones—by their behavior.

Role behavior encompasses the activities that comprise the interrelated workings of a political system and that maintain or change the system. Ideally, the actions of people are channeled into patterns that will simultaneously satisfy some of their personal motivations or drives.[27] In an actual system, however, one may expect to find roles that are dysfunctional to the polity, to the role occupant, or to both. In appraising the "development" of a political system, therefore, it is important to examine both the attitudes and the behavior related to the roles in the system.

27. Melford Spiro, "Social Systems, Personality, and Functional Analysis," in Bert Kaplan, *Studying Personality Cross Culturally* (Evanston, Ill.: Row, Peterson, 1961), pp. 100–04.

Since the institutionalization of a political system is a function of the clarity and compatibility of role expectations, the system deteriorates when expectations and behavior are incongruent, and behavior loses its predictability.[28] Herbert Simon makes clear the importance of expectations in an analysis of power relationships.

> A political regime prescribes appropriate behavior roles to its participants; these roles include appropriate actions to constrain any participant (or small group of participants) who departs from his role. But the constraints will be applied only if the remaining participants (or most of them) continue to play their roles. . . . Hence, estimates of the stability of a political structure depend not only on observation of the distribution of actual power, or of the capacity of sub-groups for coordinated action. . . . Every observation of a power relationship makes an assumption, whether explicit or implicit, as to the pattern of expectation and of group coordination. Such an observation will have predictive value, in general, only so long as this assumption holds.[29]

Thus, when political roles are unclear to role occupants or to those who are in immediate contact with the role, or when conflicting expectations are held about boundaries of role behavior, political instability and disintegration may be expected, in the most severe instances in the form of coups, rebellions, or revolutions.[30]

We may envisage a continuum between full institutionalization of roles and its opposite, "the absence of structured complementarity of the interaction process," which Parsons at one point labels anomie.[31] Anomie occurs when discrepancies arise between role expectations and role behavior and when traditional norms no longer serve as effective guides to need-reducing role playing.[32] When anomie (or normlessness) increases, Par-

28. Huntington, for example, stresses the quality of "coherence" among and within political groups as an important element in political stability.

29. Herbert Simon, *Models of Man* (New York: John Wiley & Sons, 1957), p. 72.

30. Chalmers Johnson in *Revolutionary Change* (Boston: Little, Brown, 1966) proposes that disequilibrium of this sort between normative expectations and structural performance in the presence of a catalytic "accelerator" leads to revolution.

31. Parsons, *The Social System*, p. 39.

32. Merton suggests that social structure may lead to anomie or "normlessness" reducing social predictability and producing neurotic personalities. *Social Theory*, pp. 131–94. "It is clear that imperfect coordination of the two [the goals-and-means phases of the social structure] leads to anomie" (p. 159). A state of complete anomie in which there were no role expectations is unlikely in any contemporary society.

sons suggests, a particular system might "lose its identity, or it might be transformed into one which is drastically different."[33]

In the study of political systems in newly emergent states, examining the interrelations among role expectations, role orientations, and role behavior can provide important indications about the relative institutionalization of the system. There are a number of aspects and measures of political roles that might be investigated. Two strategies for research that should yield the most economical and significant results are (1) examination of the boundary characteristics of a political role, or the limits to which the occupant of a role may publicly assert his influence; (2) determination of the degree of consensus among role expectations and the extent of their congruence with actual role behavior. In focusing on these two aspects of role analysis, many other aspects must be excluded or ignored.

There is a hierarchical character to the set of role expectations or norms surrounding any given role. Some "prescribed" behavior may be fairly unimportant, peripheral, or optional. With respect to the role of legislator, for instance, attending social events may be unimportant, writing articles for magazines peripheral, and traveling among constituents optional. Even more central expectations, such as attending legislative sessions, may be violated on occasion without being negatively sanctioned. Thus, there are norms not only for types of behavior but also for the frequency with which it is demanded. Role attributes might be ranked from a pivotal attribute, the sine qua non of the role, down through less restricting and more incidental attributes contained in role expectations.[34] This latitude of behavior with respect to lesser role expectations provides a range from which individuals may select those behaviors most compatible with their own patterns of needs and motivations. In measuring role expectations, therefore, we should avoid studying norms where the "ranges of permissible behavior"[35] are so wide as to have little predictable effect on behavior. This elasticity of norms provides a major reason for examining role situations related to public and central, or boundary, role actions.

33. Talcott Parsons and Edward Shils, eds., *Towards a General Theory of Action* (Cambridge: Harvard University Press, 1951), p. 204. Parsons' analysis refers to society in general, that is, "social systems," but should be equally applicable to a political subsystem.

34. S. F. Nadel, *The Theory of Social Structure* (Glencoe: Free Press, 1957), pp. 31–35.

35. Samuel A. Stouffer, "An Analysis of Conflicting Social Norms," *American Sociological Review, 14* (December 1949), 717. This conclusion is based on one of the best experiments done on norms and roles, in which it was found that a range of role expectations existed that shifted according to how "exposed" a hypothetical act was.

A second area of role analysis excluded from investigation is personal roles.[36] In contrast to cultural roles, personal role behavior is unique to an individual or group and is often a differentiated subset of a major cultural role. A legislator, thus, may play a special aspect of his general role in different ways in relation to certain fellow legislators, a pressure group, or his constituency. This is similar to playing the role of friend a bit differently depending on which friend one is with. The more publicly exposed behavior is, the less particularistic it is likely to be. In general, cultural roles based on the role expectations (not necessarily in agreement) of all relevant individuals are more suited for studies of political systems, while personal roles may be of particular interest for investigating small subsystems, such as a legislative system.[37]

Roles are usually defined in relation to other roles, such as mother-child, teacher-student, and are interlocking or complementary to them.[38] The role set depicted in figure 2.2 focuses on a single role in Tanzania, that of the president. Several such interaction models, one for each political role examined, could be constructed. However, only one is necessary to illustrate propositions about the institutionalization of political roles. It should be noted that figure 2.2 represents a limited model. The expectations of ordinary citizens have been excluded both to narrow the scope of research and because the category of significant alters is exhausted once the elite has been considered. Elites in this model include what Lazarsfeld refers to as "political influentials" or what Dahl labels the "political stratum." [39] Other variables that might have been included have been

36. See Roland L. Warren, "Social Disorganization and the Interrelationship of Cultural Roles," *American Sociological Review, 14* (February 1949), 83–87; Rommetveit, *Social Norms,* pp. 35–38; and Robert K. Merton, "The Role Set: Problems in Sociological Theory," *British Journal of Sociology, 8* (June 1957), 110–13.

37. John C. Wahlke, Heinz Eulau, William Buchanan, and Leroy C. Ferguson, in *The Legislative System* (New York: John Wiley and Sons, 1962), pp. 3–28, 245–414, examined in four state legislatures various subroles of legislators, both personal (as in relation to other legislators) and cultural.

38. Merton, "The Role Set," pp. 110–20; Newcomb, p. 285; and Krech et al., p. 311.

39. See Elihu Katz and Paul F. Lazarsfeld, *Personal Influence* (Glencoe: Free Press, 1955) and Robert Dahl, *Who Governs?* (New Haven: Yale University Press, 1961), pp. 319–25. This distinction seems even more relevant to political systems in underdeveloped areas. This is not to indicate that the problem of anomic behavior based on disjointed role relationships and ineffective socialization among "common citizens" should be ignored, except in this context. Indeed the latent possibility of system change by revolution or other means based on mobilizing a small but unstable portion of the citizenry is an important component of the dilemma of change and stability in African politics.

either simplified or eliminated. Distinctions between the leader's perceived role expectations, role orientations, and role behavior, for instance, have been collapsed into role behavior, although his expectations and orientations could be inferred from speeches or other remarks. Likewise, the effect of social structure on expectations is not represented: possible different expectations and relationships among the elite are ignored. The role process depicted in figure 2.2, however, serves to illustrate the major variables for analyzing the institutionalization of a major political role in a new political system.

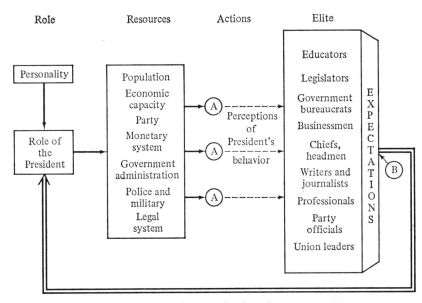

Figure 2.2. Diagram of the President's Role Process in Tanzania

Resources are the sum, distribution, and quality of the instruments available to the role occupant for implementing role-related decisions.[40] For President Nyerere, various government agencies and the party apparatus constitute the principal instruments for executing his will. The loyalty and efficiency of these instruments affect their reliability and/or usefulness. Other resources, less readily controllable by the leader—such as population, industrial capacity, and rate of social change—also cir-

40. It should be added that resources are of an "external nature." It would be conceivable for some analytic purposes to treat the skills and personality of the leader as resources. This does not seem a very useful way of grouping variables here, however.

cumscribe and define possible behavior for the head of government. Resources, while quite important, need only be examined descriptively in analyzing role behavior.[41]

Expectations should be studied both as independent and dependent variables. In the case of the president, role norms may be examined as the elite's expectations (at point B in figure 2.2). These norms define (1) the personal attributes desirable for the role, for example physique, intelligence, or ancestry; (2) the political demands to which the role occupant is expected to respond; and (3) the style of behavior appropriate for processing these demands. I have studied only the last type, and only among the "political" elite. Expectations about procedures are particularly relevant to the style of politics that may exist in a political system. Procedural expectations affect the ability of individual actors, such as a legislator, administrator, or the head of government, to pursue personal or group interests, and they govern the channels and methods by which demands are handled. Thus they contain the norms of the elite political culture, which in part determines the "style" of the political system.[42]

Figure 2.3 shows more clearly how rules for politics emerge from the recursive process of role interaction. At the beginning of the process (T_1)

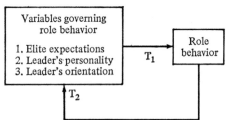

Figure 2.3. The Interdependent Character of Role Variables

the initial expectations of the elite create and define the role of the president. Recruitment into this role brings the second and third variables, the personality and role orientations of the leader, into the picture. As

41. While it would be interesting to assess whether a role occupant felt resources placed important limits on his ability to perform the role, subjective evaluations about resources were not incuded in my interviews among Tanzanians.

42. Using role expectations may avoid measuring system "style" based on, for example, sentiments about "democratic principles" which, as Prothro and Griggs have shown, have an artificial consensus in the United States. The focus on procedures should reveal the operational "rules of the game." See James W. Prothro and Charles M. Griggs, "Fundamental Principles of Democracy," *Journal of Politics*, 22 (1960), 276–94.

the leader begins to act, responding to the demands placed upon him with the resources at his command, a dependent variable, role behavior, emerges. At the next point in time, T_2, these actions of the president can be considered as the independent variable, shaping elite expectations, his own personality and role orientations, and the control and scope of resources available to him in his presidential role. This interaction of role behavior and role expectations may serve to strengthen or weaken consensus among elite expectations.[43] If the president's behavior is consistent with expectations, the role model presented here suggests that this will reinforce those expectations to which it conforms and modify divergent expectations, thus narrowing gaps among role expectations. On the other hand, role behavior that contravenes elite expectations would, it is predicted, lead to greater deviations, both among expectations and between expectations and basic attitudes of elites, and hence diminish the stability and institutionalization of the role.

Consensus and Congruence

Agreement among role expectations may generally be referred to as *consensus*. Consensus may be assessed among the aggregate of role alters, such as all political elite, or even all citizens, or it may be examined in one or another subgroup, such as among legislators. *Congruence* refers to the degree of matching or similarity between two sets of role expectations. For instance, we might examine the congruence between the expectations of legislators and administrators, or of an individual and a group. In the latter case, we could discover how deviant the expectations of an individual member of the elite were concerning a given role compared to the pattern of expectations among all elite members. Dissensus and incongruity lead to ambiguity and conflict and indicate strains upon the individuals and the system.[44] The more central the aspects of the political role and the greater the strain, the more we can expect either system change, a change of role personnel, or feelings of insecurity among

43. In the interviews, people often based their answers about expectations toward the president on Nyerere's past actions and fully expected him to continue behaving in a similar fashion.

44. Ambiguity would describe a situation where alternative expectations are about evenly distributed. In a conflict situation, incompatible expectations are held by important groups; when a role incumbent perceives the dissimilar expectations, he experiences role strain. On these points see Gross, chap. 15, and Robert L. Kahn, *Organizational Stress: Studies in Role Conflict and Ambiguity* (New York: John Wiley and Sons, 1964).

the actors. An example may make these distinctions clearer. If a Tanzanian M.P. (*Mbunge*) raises opposition to a government policy in the National Assembly when the majority of political elite feel such an action by creating a controversy over established government policy is wrong, this would be incongruence that created role conflict. If the relevant elite were divided in its views about the legitimacy of such criticism, however, lack of consensus would be indicated.

It would be possible also to analyze strains arising from conflict among different elite groups or between other groups, conflict resulting from multiple roles played by the same man, conflict endemic in competing but widely accepted roles, such as traditional authority versus modern leader, or discrepancies of communications between expectations, orientations, and behavior. The analysis of political roles and role strain obviously is not clear and simple, but rather is quite complex.[45]

In any concrete situation some strain will always be present. The essential problem is to determine the thresholds at which ambiguity or conflict produces serious strain and results in behavior likely to change established processes. Strain in itself is not negative; indeed, it indicates the possibility for change. The problem is to regulate strain to prevent an overload likely to be destructive.

Consensus on expected role behavior among relevant alters and congruence between the mean role expectations and those held by an individual role occupant are the primary indicators of role institutionalization used here.[46]

The creation of suitable measures of consensus and congruence is a difficult problem. It is easy enough to specify the individual role and the

---

45. For a discussion of the complex variables involved in role analysis, see Biddle and Thomas, *Role Theory*, pp. 29–45.

46. The existence and importance of consensus and congruence in role expectations can be assessed in several ways. Respondents might be asked if they have experienced role conflict or role strain. However, direct inquiry about a respondent's experiencing of role conflicts requires a high ability on his part to conceptualize the conflict situation, as well as overtly to admit conflict if it *was* experienced. Neither quality appeared widespread among the civil servants with whom the interview was pretested, and this tactic was therefore discarded.

Other related aspects of political role expectations could also be examined, though less systematically. These would include their clarity or coherence, that is, the degree to which different roles interlock smoothly, their specificity—including the range of permissible behavior—and their intensity, for example the severity of sanctions attached to the violation of expectations. I have specifically measured only consensus and congruence, although I occasionally discuss the other aspects of role expectations.

relevant groups or populations whose role definitions will serve as the basis for measurement. But the selection of the actual instrument to tap expectations demands the weighing of marginal costs and gains. As Gross has pointed out:

> There are at least two procedures that can be used to secure data for the analysis of consensus on role definitions. The first is to focus on the degree of agreement among role definers on which one, or which range of alternatives, among a set of available alternatives the incumbent of a position should adopt in a particular situation. The second is to focus on their consensus on a single evaluative standard that might be applied to him.[47]

While Gross chose the second alternative for "operational" reasons, I used the former procedure for practical reasons.[48] Questions about the expected response of the president, M.P.'s, and administrators in hypothetical problem situations were created and pretested among university students. A list of alternative responses was drawn up and then elite respondents were asked to comment on or evaluate the results of the students' expectations. After rejecting several approaches to quantifying the interview data, I decided to use responses that could be ordered along a continuum of role strength (the degree to which the role occupant is expected to react strongly or assertively in a given situation) to calculate both role consensus and individual congruence. Variance of responses (V), which indicates the extent to which expectations cluster about a mean or central point, has been employed as a measure of consensus within individual items, while standard scores (C, for congruence) provide a measure of the degree to which a particular respondent's expectations conform to the central tendency or norm.[49]

47. Gross et al., p. 101.

48. A brief pretest among civil servants indicated that the rapport of the whole interview was destroyed when I used a series of political expectation questions of an open-ended type (more than five or six produced reluctance in the interviewee to continue) or a single proposed role behavior to which responses along a single continuum were sought. The field situation required careful consideration of any question related to "politics," as a number of the elite respondents exhibited extreme sensitivity to being questioned on concrete political topics. Thus, a more informal and less structured procedure was chosen. Unfortunately, categoric responses of alternative role expectations do not lend themselves easily to statistical analysis.

49. The specific items for these measures and the formula for their calculations are explained in the appendix.

Roles and Personality

In an analysis of the roles of a political system, the personality of role incumbents is also important. Personality refers to, among other things, the habits and traits of an individual that provide continuity to his actions and are related to his unique person. Any study of roles must consider the effect of personality, since role behavior is a product of both social expectations and personal motives. However, the complexities of personality analysis are beyond the scope of this book. Beyond this discussion of the relationship between personality and roles, I shall describe only limited aspects of the impact of personal attributes on role expectations and behavior.

Role conflicts may affect personality and personality may have effects on role behavior. Moreover, modal personality features are likely to be useful in predicting future tendencies in political systems. The effects of interaction between role and personality will vary according to the comprehensiveness of the role—whether the role carries prescriptions for a large number of situations (for example a legislator) or for just a few situations (for example a voter); the psychic importance of the motivations and unconscious needs, or contrarily the indulgences and deprivations tied to the role performance; and the degree of discrepancy between perceived role expectations and the role orientations of individual role players. As each of these variables increases, the potential effects of role and personality interaction will increase.

In a rapidly changing social or political system, socialized attitudes and goals of childhood may not be relevant to the roles of adulthood. Consequently, potential discontinuities between individual motivation and social expectations for role behavior may change both personality and role behavior. The role of the political administrator in Tanzania is a good example. The president appointed several important TANU politicians to the newly created posts of regional commissioner and area commissioner. This resulted in many appointees suffering acute role strain because they perceived conflicting expectations: one set was derived from their own past experience, another from civil service subordinates, and a third from the public, many of whom expected TANU leaders, as previous champions of popular causes—often opposed to colonial government policy—to continue to sympathize with demands that challenged existing policies. The colonial legacy for the commissioner's post was shaped by the former British provincial and district commissioners, whose houses, servants, and powers (with a few exceptions) were transferred to the new political appointees. In some cases, the radically different requirements of this government role as compared to that of party organizer undermined the self-confidence and identity of the role occupant. Nevertheless, most politicians continued to play these roles, although since 1964 former civil servants rather than politicians usually have been appointed.

The negative consequences of such strains were apparently offset by the existence of latent as well as manifest rewards. An individual may continue to play a difficult role, even demand to do so, because of unconscious rewards rather than consciously accepted reasons. Sometimes rewards are obtained through role-related behavior that is unconnected and even counterproductive to essential role performance. For some regional commissioners, for example, the administrative duties were particularly burdensome, but duties such as entertaining visitors and making public speeches were enjoyable; other fringe benefits were greater access to sexual gratification and economic gain.[50]

By examining personality as an independent variable we can see three effects on roles. First, personality affects role recruitment through self-selection. Displaced private motives and cathected objects will make some roles seem desirable, others undesirable, depending upon the motives the person has acquired. Second, personality will affect the selection of role behavior within a range of permissible action. Even when a consensus of role expectations exists, there will be a latitude of available rights and demanded duties among which an individual can pick and choose in performing his role. This latitude of acceptable behavior contributes to the difficulty of assessing the effects of consensus of role norms. When role conflicts exist, in the form of conflicting expectations held by significant alters, the personality may reduce dissensus by determining which set of expectations is "legitimate."[51] For instance, President Nyerere has rejected expectations that the government has any special responsi-

---

50. One commissioner stated about his work, "Sometimes I hate it," and another said, "No one really understands how difficult it is. We work hard and have much responsibility; we deserve these things—a big car and house." William Tordoff has described some of the role conflict problems in regional administration in his article, "Regional Administration in Tanzania," *Journal of Modern African Studies, 3* (May 1965), 63–90.

51. Gross et al., pp. 285–95, discuss this selection of "legitimacy" in conflict situations. Another alternative, compromising among conflicting expectations, would also reflect personality influences.

bility to African citizens. Non-African citizens have been "officially" afforded the same opportunities and treatment as Africans. In part, Nyerere was able to promulgate this policy because two opposing sets of expectations were held: that he should be president of all the people and build a nonracial society and that Africans deserved preferred treatment. The choice among such conflicting views, where neither set of expectations was clearly dominant, was made by the president on the basis of his own ideas and values.[52] Finally, in situations of ambiguity, personality traits and private motives are more important in structuring roles, both for the self and for others. In an unstructured situation, such as a disaster, an "emergency social system" may arise as social interactions and individual decisions about behavior literally create roles and role relationships.[53] Some fascinating instances of this may be found in the nascent and developing political systems of newly emergent states. Many Tanzanians, my interviews revealed, were consciously aware that they were creating role norms and precedents. The influence of one or a few leaders upon the norms and behavior of a political system is much greater in new states where constitutionalized patterns are just being established. The impact of Ataturk, Mao, and Nyerere on their respective states, for instance, has been notable.

Role as an independent variable shaping personality may have three effects. First, the political system, through the recruitment process, which selects role incumbents on the basis of skills or some other attributes, will thereby reward or punish these skills. These should lead to the reinforcement or extinction of traits linked—positively or negatively—to the selection criteria as seen by the individual. Nyerere, for example, has always been respected for his habit of hard work, a trait he has not only exemplified but also has demanded from his countrymen in a fashion distinctive among African politicians. A "maverick" elected to the National Assembly may continue in his volatile style of behavior, even if this style loses him both party support and the respect of his colleagues, provided he thinks his behavior will help re-elect him.

Second, a role will shape the attitudes and values of the role incumbent[54] in varying degree according to the context of the situation in

52. Nyerere has argued forcefully in public for nonracial policies (see for example the account in Listowel, *Making of Tanganyika*, pp. xvii–xix).

53. See Allen H. Barton, *Social Organizations Under Stress: A Sociological Review of Disaster Studies* (Washington, D. C.: National Academy of Sciences, 1963), pp. 19–72.

54. The length of time a role is played will be important in determining the extent

which the role is enacted.[55] This proposition is empirically similar to theories concerning the effects of reference groups on attitudes.[56] In Tanzania, for instance, M.P.'s who hold government positions give fewer critical speeches in the National Assembly ($r = .39$).[57] The role incumbent may adopt not only norms related to role behavior but also a whole set of peripheral attitudes and norms. Even new problems may be analyzed in terms of the role. Many Tanzanian civil servants, for instance, have had their ideas about dress, politics, even life goals shaped by their previously developed set of attitudes. British-modeled education and periods of apprenticeship at lower civil service posts selected and molded the outlook of some of the civil servants I interviewed to fit an "administrative" role. In such cases, it is very difficult to separate out the influences of role orientation and personality on each other and on behavior.[58]

Finally, role-structured interaction may lead an individual to acquire new tastes and motives. Experience in a role permits a variety of unconscious psychic conflicts to be resolved, perhaps allowing them to be displaced or acted out in role behavior in socially useful ways. In this sense, a political role can channel and articulate latent personality predispositions.[59]

It must be remembered that many personality features will not be intrinsically related to role behavior. I have chosen to examine only four attitudes related to personality traits—anomie, authoritarianism, faith in people, and belief in democratic practices—in an attempt to illustrate how the pattern of elite political culture and the role norms it supports involves the interaction between roles and personality.

---

of role influence. Lieberman, in an investigation that supports this proposition, found that only a few months or a year was sufficient time to effect significant attitude changes after role recruitment. See Seymour Lieberman, "The Effects of Change in Roles on the Attitudes of Role Occupants," in Seymour M. Lipset and Neil J. Smelser, eds., *Personality and Social System* (New York: John Wiley and Sons, 1963), pp. 264–79.

55. Stouffer, "Conflicting Social Norms."

56. Merton, *Social Theory*, pp. 225–386.

57. See table 5.9.

58. Lane, "Political Personality" (unpublished monograph, New Haven, 1965), pp. 6–7, has noted this point: "In practice it is not easy to distinguish role determined behavior when a person is acting out his concept of appropriate role behavior, or, worse, when he has accepted the values and beliefs associated with a given role and performs accordingly."

59. Harold Lasswell and Arnold Rogow, *Power, Corruption and Rectitude* (Englewood Cliffs, N.J.: Prentice-Hall, 1963), point out that recruitment to the role of the presidency has altered personality patterns, promoting patterns of rectitude, for instance, in the case of President Arthur.

3. The Elite: Background and Attitudes

The attitudes and expectations of the Tanzanian political elite form the political culture within which modern politics, to a large extent, is carried on. Childhood experiences, levels of education, and political responsibilities and other background factors provide possible explanations for differences in elite attitudes and expectations. The purpose of this chapter is to describe the background and attitudes of the elite who were interviewed as well as to provide some idea about the universe from which they were drawn.

The Tanzanian political elite, as it is defined here, consists of two groups: members of the National Assembly and government administrators. Influential persons from other areas, such as business, labor, military, and education, are not included because (1) very few Africans hold high positions in these areas, (2) such people do not play specifically *political* roles, (3) data on these people, especially the military, are difficult to gather,[1] and (4) the relationship between a high position in the private sector and political influence is weak.

Published lists, the *Government Directory* (March 1966) and the *National Assembly* (printed directory, February 1966), were used to construct a universe of 185 legislators and 157 upper-level administrators.[2] A random sample from each group was drawn and interviews were conducted during April to July 1966, with 58 M.P.'s and 51 administrators. These interviews lasted about two hours and covered a wide range of topics, including personal history, political and social attitudes, and expectations about political role performance.[3] Before discussing the information gathered by the interviews, it is important to describe and define the elite positions studied.

1. About the only data source available for elites in general is *Who's Who in East Africa 1965–1966* (Nairobi: MARCO Publishers, 1966). This volume, however, is not complete.

2. In fact, there were only 184 members at any one time in the National Assembly between December 1965 and June 1966, but one member, a regional commissioner, was replaced in March 1966, and both the original M.P. and his predecessor are included in this universe.

3. For a more detailed description of the sampling and interviewing procedures see app. B.

THE ELITE

The Administrator

The administrative officer played a crucial role in British overseas administration. Whether posted in a remote region as district commissioner or assigned to a ministry in Dar es Salaam, he generally was a versatile bureaucrat with important responsibilities for decision making and leadership.[4] In areas that were cut off from Dar es Salaam for months on end the district commissioner *was* the colonial government. Since the period of German rule, a relatively small corps of administrators, spread thinly across the country and concentrated at the heads of departments in Dar es Salaam, has maintained law and order, supervised services, and guaranteed at least minimum central control throughout the country. Although, following independence, politicians have been appointed to the top positions both in the regions and districts and in the ministries in Dar es Salaam, basic responsibilities for organization and management of the civil service, as well as for some important policy matters, have remained in the hands of the administrators. The total number of administrative officers at succeeding periods in the development of the Tanzanian political system varied from 79 in 1914 to a high of 184 in 1931; the number fell to 169 by 1946 and then rose to 397 in 1961. Following the exodus of European administrators at independence, the actual number of people in these posts has declined (see table 3.1). The number of administrators compared with population has always been small and its size has increased relatively little over the years.

Until 1956 few Africans had penetrated the upper levels of the civil service. Prior to this time Africans had been largely excluded from the administrative level of government by educational barriers and by a system of "junior civil service." Only eight were appointed to the administrative cadre between 1949 and 1954. By 1956 24 Africans had been admitted, 23 serving as assistant district officers—the lowest level. During the remaining five years of colonial rule the number of African administrative officers was expanded to provide Africans with necessary experience. Following independence the trend to Africanization or "localization" has continued even more sharply.

4. See John C. Cairns, *Bush and Boma* (London: J. Murry, 1959), the memoirs of an administrative officer. Also Robert Heussler, *Yesterday's Rulers: The Making of the British Colonial Service* (Syracuse: Syracuse University Press, 1963).

TABLE 3.1. Composition of Administrative Posts, 1956–1965

Year	European	African	Others	Total	Percent Local
1956	244	24[a]	5	273	11
1959	267	55[b]	5	327	18
1961	287	96[c]	4	387	26
1963	78	185	4	267	71
1965	20	275	4	299	93

a. From among this group of 24 have come the head of EACSO, two regional commissioners (both appointed from high civil service jobs), two principal secretaries, one acting principal secretary, three holding the second position either in a ministry or para-statal body, four administrative secretaries, the only Tanzanian judge among the nine full judges in the country, and two lower magistrates (one a "district" and the other a "senior" magistrate). The remaining eight had either died or retired by 1966.

b. Whereas in 1956 only one man was in the upper ranks of administration, in 1959 there were five. Of the 32 who joined between 1956 and 1959, two became ministers, two principal secretaries, three administrative secretaries, ten are principal assistant secretaries, and three became foreign service officers, including one ambassador.

c. The new appointees between 1959 and 1961 included by 1966 the head of the National Bank, two principal secretaries, the ambassador to the U. N., the chief education officer, six principal assistant secretaries, two administrative secretaries, plus a number of officials who, though entering at the same level, have not advanced very far.

Source: Staff List (Dar es Salaam: Government Printer, 1956, 1959, 1961, 1963, 1965). Figures include all officers in provincial administration (1956–61) or regional administration (1963–65), and those in establishments.

By five years after independence only a handful of expatriate administrative officers remained, and most of them were waiting for retirement while serving in teaching or advisory posts. Their African successors have assumed direction of the central government's machinery. Table 3.1 documents this change over the 1956–65 period. Africans have moved more slowly into the more general civil service category of "middle and high grade" positions. In 1961, for such positions (4,452), 26 percent had been "localized" compared to 26 percent among administrators. In 1963, 49 percent of all the middle and high grade civil service posts were localized, compared to 71 percent among administrators. And by 1965, the general figure was 66 percent compared with 93 percent.[5]

The universe of administrators studied differs in some respects from the catalog of administrative posts used to prepare table 3.1. First, some administrators not specifically attached to the "administrative cadre" were included in the research universe. Thus ambassadors, foreign service

5. Tanzania, Second Five-Year Plan, vol. 1: General Analysis (Dar es Salaam: Government Printer, 1969), p. 24.

officers, and staff officers (often principal secretaries) were included. Many of them had been administrative officers and each of their positions involved high-level administrative responsibility. A second criterion used in creating the universe was to include only high administrators, thus eliminating from the universe approximately the lower half of those in administrative positions, including assistant secretaries in ministries and area secretaries (who are the head civil servants in each district). Table

TABLE 3.2. Comparative Composition of High Administrative Elite

	Total (N = 157)		Sample (N = 51)		Sample as Percent of Total (33)
	%	N	%	N	
Principal secretaries, ambassadors	20	32	26	13	41
Commissioners, adm. secretaries, directors, counselors	29	45	28	14	31
Principal asst. sec., sr. asst. sec., other administrators	51	80	47	24	30

3.2 gives a breakdown of the universe and sample according to positions of similar status.

The range of the basic salaries of these administrators is given in table 3.3. These figures are for 1965 and do not reflect the pay cuts that were

TABLE 3.3. Salaries of Administrative Elite, 1966

	Sample (N = 51)		Total (N = 151)	
	%	N	%	N
£2400 or above	28	14	15	22
£1900–2400	16	8	21	32
£1300–1900	37	19	44	67
£1300 or below*	20	10	20	30

* Nearly all salaries were above £1000. £2400 was the basic salary for principal secretaries and a few other positions.

made in October 1966 amounting to as much as 10 percent in the highest pay bracket. These two tables indicate that administrators at the highest level, largely principal secretaries, have been oversampled, mainly because principal secretaries were easier to contact and more willing to be interviewed.

The Legislator

The National Assembly is an historical outgrowth of the Legislative Council created in 1926. Over the years this body has increased in size, changed in racial composition, and altered the mode by which members are selected. Table 3.4 presents the composition of the Legislative Coun-

TABLE 3.4. Evolution of the Tanzanian National Assembly

	Membership			Racial Divisions[b]		
Year	Total	Officials	Unofficials	Europeans	Asians	Africans
1926	23	13	7	5	2	—
1935	23	13	10	7	3	—
1945	27	15	12	7	3	2
1947	28	15	13	7	3	3
1954	29	15	14	7	3	4
1955	61	31	30	10	10	10
1957	67	34	33	11	11	11
		Nominated	Elected			
1959	53	28	25			
1961	80	9	71	14	12	54
1965	184	77[a]	107	3	4	177

a. The 77 nonelected members in 1965 break down as follows: 10 nominated, 20 ex officio, 32 appointed from Zanzibar, and 15 national members.

b. These figures are for "Unofficials." Official members were all European prior to 1959.

Sources: The figures for 1926–59 are from J. P. Moffett, ed., Handbook of Tanganyika (Dar es Salaam: Government Printer, 1958) and Tanganyika's Parliament (Dar es Salaam: Government Printer, 1961) as cited in Friedland, "The Evolution of Tanganyika's Political System" (Program of East African Studies, Syracuse University, Occasional Paper No. 10), p. 48.

cil/National Assembly for the various years in which changes have occurred.

As a result of the new constitution adopted in 1965 and the elections held in September of that year, the Assembly composition changed considerably. Six categories of membership were created. In addition to elected members, there are national members, nominated by seven national institutions and elected by the Assembly itself, and four types of nominated members: regional commissioners, appointed by the president, who serve ex officio; ten members whom the president may nominate; up to 32 members from Zanzibar's Revolutionary Council; and up to 20 other Zanzibaris whom the president, in agreement with the president of Zanzibar, may appoint. All categories of membership except those from Zanzibar were filled by mid-1966. Table 3.5 compares the sample

TABLE 3.5. Total and Sample as Percent of Members of the National Assembly

	Total (N = 185)		Sample (N = 58)		Sample as Percent of Total (32)
	%	N	%	N	
Elected	58	107	71	41	38
National	8	15	9	5	33
Nominated	5	10	3	2	20
Zanzibar nominated	8	14	3	2	14
Zanzibar Revolutionary Council	10	18	2	1	6
Regional commissioners	11	21*	12	7	33

* There are only 20 regional commissioners, 17 from the mainland and 3 from Zanzibar, but the universe included two regional commissioners for Tabora region (see note 2).

of legislators with total membership in the Assembly. Members from Zanzibar are underrepresented in the sample because of the reluctance of some of them to be interviewed.

The National Assembly elections of September 1965 were the first in which nearly all voters had an opportunity to choose between two Assembly candidates (Zanzibar and six mainland constituencies were the exceptions). In the previous elections, 1958/59 and 1960, most of the candidates had been "elected" unopposed, thus eliminating the need for balloting. The 1965 election also demonstrated that important leaders could be turned out of office. Among those defeated were two ministers, six junior ministers and eight M.P.'s. Only 48 percent of the 31 incumbent M.P.'s who stood for election were successful, only 39 percent, or 9 of the 23 NEC members were victorious, and only 29 percent, or 9 out of 31 TANU officials were elected. The most successful group in the elections was civil servants, 16 of 22, or 73 percent, of whom were elected.[6] Although a number of important political leaders were defeated, most of the elections were not particularly close; over half the candidates were elected by a two-to-one margin or better and only 16 percent were in

6. See Belle Harris, "The Tanzanian Elections," Mbioni, 2 (Dar es Salaam: Kivukoni College, 1965), app. 2.

close contests (in which their opponent received 43 percent of the vote
or more).[7]

BACKGROUNDS OF ELITE SAMPLE

The legislative and administrative elite has undergone a variety of
educational and personal experiences. It is difficult to find for this elite—
as one could for their British predecessors—a homogeneous culture and
ideology in their backgrounds. A number have had long experience serving in junior posts in the colonial administration. A good many others
were secondary school teachers. In recent years, an increasing number
have entered politics or administration directly after completing their college education and are still quite young. A sizable percentage of legislators have been civil servants, some of whom have retained civil service
status after their appointment to "political" posts;[8] among the administrators, there are only a few former politicians. In general, these elite
are men with different levels of education and ambition, different identifications and ideologies, and different expectations and habits of action,
who are engaged with varying degrees of harmony in the major tasks of
government.

Most members of the elite were born and raised in either a rural village or a small rural center containing a church, a dispensary, or some
small shops. Their descriptions of their early years in this rural environment seemed quite ordinary for African society. About three fourths of
them remembered herding cattle or goats as youngsters. Much of their
time was taken up with farming or household chores or looking after
younger brothers and sisters; 85 percent said their childhood was "happy."
In general, they did not come from the poorest families. Each was asked
whether he considered his family average, below average, or above average
in terms of wealth in the community. The majority described their
families as "above average."

Their pattern of family life differed widely. Most came from rather
large families, with 66 percent having five or more brothers and sisters,
and 32 percent being born in a family where the father had more than

7. For all the figures see the *Report of the Third General Election of Members of the
National Assembly and the Second Presidential Election in Tanzania* (Dar es Salaam:
Government Printer, 1966).

8. For example, after 1965 several regional commissioners, the attorney general, and
the principal secretary in the president's office all became M.P.'s and also were (or retained
the status of) civil servants.

one wife. Most but not all came from patrilineal systems. In order to learn about the images of authority acquired at an early age, these interviewees were asked about their parents or other senior family members. The paternal image usually was that of a strong, harsh figure. A third described their fathers as "kind," helpful," or "loving"; while two thirds described their fathers as *"kali"* (fierce, tough), "strict," or "a strong disciplinarian." But the male's role was not seen generally as one of absolute authority in the family. Only 46.4 percent of their fathers were seen as the sole decision maker in the family (56.6 percent of administrators' fathers and 38.5 percent of legislators' fathers).[9]

TABLE 3.6. Early Environment of Elite
(in percentages)

Size of Community	Administrators (N = 50)		Legislators (N = 58)	
Rural village	32		17	
Rural center	42		67	
Urban area	26		16	
Traditional Status	Administrators* (N = 51)		Legislators* (N = 58)	
	%	N	%	N
High status (Parent was chief or member of royal clan)	8	4	28	16
Middle status (Parent was headman or elder)	24	12	15	9
Low status (Parents had no traditional status)	69	35	57	33

* Chi-square is significant at $p < .05$ level between the two groups.

Traditional status was also an important factor in their backgrounds. Men from families of traditional nobility were often given special attention by the colonial government, with improved educational opportunities

9. Owing perhaps to the important role older siblings play in the training and care of African children, and also the extended family environment in which many of the elite were raised, few indicated any special respect or admiration for their mothers. The most common descriptions of mothers were "hard-working," "faithful," and "reserved." Not untypical is the remark of one administrator when asked to describe his mother, "She was an ignorant woman but very kind." Less than half (45%) saw the mother as an important force in the family.

and a government position and salary. High traditional status, therefore, was examined as a possible influence on attitudes and behavior. Such status, because of the wide variety of traditional systems in Tanzania, is difficult to compare, but some general qualities make a crude categorization possible. Traditional authority was generally ascriptive and conservative in nature. Consequently, it seemed likely that an authoritarian outlook, a distrust of democratic procedures, and a disenchantment with socialist policy might be associated with traditional status. In table 3.6, the elite sampled are categorized as high status if they or their parents were members of a royal family, as middle status if their parents were headmen or local nobility, and as low status if they had no special standing in traditional society. More legislators than administrators come from a high-status background. The high traditional status of some M.P.'s may have been helpful in their election, but it apparently was less important in the selection of administrators.

Education was the crucial factor in the careers of most elite respondents. It differentiated them from the majority of their kinsmen and made possible their later attainment of modern elite positions. The educational system, particularly at the primary level, was characterized by strict discipline and occasionally harsh punishment. After primary school, as a rule at the age of ten to thirteen, most left home to live at a boarding school. Life at these upper primary and secondary schools was a new experience; at the secondary level teachers were often European and authority was exercised over a wide range of student activity by a system of prefects. As respondents described their impressions and memories of their schooling, the importance of discipline and stern authority, especially in the earlier years, was revealed.

> There was, I think, much more discipline in our school than these days. Teachers used to cane liberally and there were ex-military sergeants who imposed semimilitary discipline in the schools. (A minister describing his primary school experience.)

> Life was tough here; in the school we still did farm work. Discipline was very strict and teachers were Africans with some Italians and a Swedish headmaster. (Elected M.P. describing his secondary school.)

> In 1944–45, I went to a mission school. We slept on the floor and had to cook our food and do manual work. . . . I liked secondary

school because there was more respect for students than primary school where beating as a method of making a pupil understand was used. (Senior assistant secretary.)[10]

The government secondary school at Tabora was modeled on a British public school, and during the British colonial period it was considered the best school in the country. A principal secretary described it as "a very good school—the best. Our teachers were Europeans and very good." A student who did well in the highly selective territorial examinations and was accepted at Tabora found himself in a special environment. "Life was better here than before; we had food, blankets, and even a bed and sheets." Respondents who have attended Tabora are able to recite a half-dozen names of prominent Tanzanians who were their classmates, including President Nyerere for those who attended around 1940. Forty-five percent of the administrators and 21 percent of the legislators attended Tabora.

For those who went on to college the educational experience was less regimented. "It was a good change from secondary school. On our own, we could manage our own affairs, and we were responsible for our own actions," recalled one principal secretary.

Thirty-seven percent of the legislators and 55 percent of the administrators in the sample have had the opportunity to study overseas. Lasting sometimes for only six months or a year, these overseas educational experiences were very important for many. Often they helped administrators prepare or qualify for their present positions and responsibilities. M.P.'s who went abroad claimed the experience helped give them a new perspective on their country and motivated them to assume leadership in bringing about change. The level of education attained by elite members is presented in table 3.7.

Although a sizable percentage of the administrators were appointed directly after finishing their education, most had experience in some prior occupation. Some, possibly following in their fathers' footsteps, entered local government or the junior civil service. Some took up a commercial career, often as a trader or transporter. A number went into teaching. Farming was the most common occupation of their parents, but relatively few, all of whom were legislators, pursued this vocation.

10. These quotations, like others included in the book, have been randomly selected from the interviews as representative responses except where otherwise noted.

TABLE 3.7. Education of Elite: Highest Level Attained
(in percentages)

	Administrators		Legislators	
	Sample (N = 51)	Total (N = 127)	Sample (N = 58)	Total (N = 162)
1 to 4 years	0	0	9	8
5 to 8 years	0	3	12	14
Some secondary	10	12	21	20
Completed secondary*	11	11	19	15
Post-secondary or special training	29	28	21	26
University (3 years or degree)	26	25	14	14
Postgraduate	25	22	5	4

* For younger respondents this would be Standard XII, for older respondents who attended school in the 1930s and early 1940s, Standard X.

Sources: A number of sources were used, including Who's Who in East Africa 1965–1966 (Nairobi: MARCO Publishers, 1966) unpublished materials, and informants. The N for each total represents the number of elite in the universe for whom data could be gathered.

Table 3.8 gives a breakdown of the occupations of the elite immediately prior to their entering politics or the administrative cadre. The percent who were former teachers is higher than the figures indicate, since a number left teaching for other jobs or for further education before entering their elite position. Although legislators are less well educated, they have a wider range of occupational backgrounds and training than administrators. Neither group is well educated by Western standards, or even in comparison with the educational attainment among the elite in many less developed countries. For the most part these are the first generation to move from a traditional rural environment.

Two other background characteristics of the elite that may be important and could possibly be used to explain differences in attitudes and behavior are age and religion. These variables among elite are summarized in table 3.9. Although the average ages of administrators and legislators are nearly identical (39.8 compared with 39.9 years), legislators tend to be more widely dispersed throughout the adult age brackets while administrators are concentrated between the ages of 30 and 45. An exposure to Christianity, particularly Protestantism, was a frequent experience for elite (see table 3.9). Where more direct evidence was not available, training

TABLE 3.8. Prior Occupation of Elite and Fathers' Occupations
(in percentages)

	Administrators			Legislators		
	Total (N = 123)	Sample (N = 51)	Fathers (N = 50)	Total (N = 163)	Sample (N = 58)	Fathers (N = 58)
Student	29	33	0	3	3	0
Teacher	20	20	8	18	10	5
Civil service, jr. civil service, local govt.	34	29	20	26	24	19
Farmer	0	0	28	6	2	29
Manual worker	1	0	14	6	7	12
Commerce, trader	3	4	14	11	12	12
Service worker (health, sanitation, police)	9	10	8	7	12	2
Cooperative or union official	0	0	0	17	19	2
White collar (including pastors)	4	4	8*	7	10	19

* All but one of the fathers were in religious work.

in a Protestant, Catholic, or Koranic school has been used as an indicator of religion, reflecting at least religious experience and training.[11] This does not indicate personal commitment, since securing an education often necessitated attending a missionary school. Moreover, there are differences among Protestant and Catholic sects (as well as among Muslims) that make it difficult to draw inferences from such gross attributions. Few Muslims, compared with the total, were in the National Assembly interview sample because of the underrepresentation of Zanzibaris, nearly all of whom are Muslim.

Table 3.10 presents the major tribal affiliations among the elite and compares these with tribal percentages among the total population. The figures suggest that the National Assembly reflects, in a rough fashion, the tribal proportions found in the nation, while the administrative elite

11. When a respondent specifically declared himself a nonbeliever, he was classified as having no religion. The percentage of nonbelievers within the universe is probably undercalculated, since noninterviewed elite were automatically not afforded this opportunity.

TABLE 3.9. Age and Religion of Elite
(in percentages)

| | AGE | | | |
| | Administrators | | Legislators | |
	Sample (N = 51)	Total (N = 153)	Sample (N = 58)	Total (N = 173)
30 or under	10	6	16	17
31 to 35	26	27	19	19
36 to 40	28	24	21	23
41 to 45	24	23	26	17
46 to 50	6	14	10	10
51 to 60	8	7	5	10
Over 60	0	1	3	5

| | | RELIGION | | | |
| | | Administrators | | Legislators | |
	Nation*	Sample (N = 51)	Total (N = 119)	Sample (N = 58)	Total (N = 167)
Protestant	11	61	57	45	38
Catholic	14	26	29	24	23
Muslim	31	12	13	26	37
None or other	43	2	1	5	2

* In 1957.

are highly overrepresentative of such tribes as the Haya, the Chagga, and the Nyakusa, and underrepresentative of others such as the Sukuma, the Makonde, and the Hehe.

One of the remarkable features of Tanzania is the variety of tribes, none of which constitutes an active political force. The fact that each tribe represents but a small fraction of the population is one explanation for the absence of tribal political organizations. Another reason is that assertions of independence by tribal leaders were suppressed initially by the colonial government and more recently by TANU. Shortly before independence a few modern tribal institutions arose, such as the Chagga Democratic Party, but these have proven abortive.

Nevertheless, three tribes in Tanzania are noteworthy for their progress, economic development, and educational attainment. The strongest demands for education have come from these groups and some tendencies

TABLE 3.10. Tribal Group
(in percentages)

		Administrators		Legislators	
	Nation	Sample (N = 50)	Total (N = 116)	Sample (N = 58)	Total (N = 137)
Sukuma	12.5	2.0	4.3	12.1	10.2
Nyamwezi	4.1	4.0	3.4	8.6	5.8
Makonde	3.8	0.0	0.9	0.0	0.9
Haya	3.7	18.0	20.7	1.7	5.1
Chagga	3.6	14.0	17.2	6.9	3.6
Gogo	3.4	0.0	1.7	0.0	2.2
Ha	3.3	0.0	0.0	1.7	2.9
Hehe	2.9	0.0	0.0	5.2	2.2
Nyakusa	2.5	8.0	7.8	3.4	3.6
Luguru	2.3	2.0	0.9	0.0	0.0
Bena	2.2	4.0	2.6	1.7	2.2
Turu	2.2	0.0	0.0	0.0	0.7
Sambaa	2.2	10.0	4.3	3.4	3.6
Zaramo	2.1	4.0	1.7	1.7	2.2
Iramba	2.0	0.0	0.0	0.0	2.9
Yao	1.6	0.0	0.0	1.7	1.5
Mwera	1.6	0.0	0.9	0.0	0.7
Mbulu	1.5	0.0	0.0	1.7	0.7
Zigua	1.5	2.0	2.6	1.7	2.9
Pare	1.4	4.0	2.6	0.0	1.5
Ngoni	1.1	0.0	0.0	6.9	2.9
Nyasa	0.8	4.0	7.8	3.4	2.9
European	0.2	0.0*	0.0*	1.7	2.2
Asian	0.8	0.0	0.0	6.9	2.9
Arab	0.2	0.0	0.9	0.0	1.5
Other	47.9	24.0	20.6	29.6	30.9

* Three Europeans were included in the universe and one was interviewed, but since all were noncitizens they were excluded from the study.

toward autonomy from central control have emerged.[12] These groups are the Chagga, the Haya, and the Nyakusa. Their interest in a tribal language, as opposed to English or Swahili, might be an indicator of rising

12. The dissident activities of the Bukoba Council, the rise of a Chagga political party, and the defeat of a minister among the Nyakusa in the 1965 elections were evidence of these tendencies.

nationalism as it has been historically elsewhere.[13] This, along with economic and social similarities, has made these groups both distinctive and
somewhat alike.[14] To establish the importance of tribalism in elite attitudes, these three groups have been compared against all other tribal
memberships among elite. This variable was compared with other variables by treating membership or nonmembership in these three groups
as a dichotomous "dummy" variable. The results of these calculations are
labeled "Tribe" in table 3.13. The relationships of this variable with
background characteristics, such as traditional status and career length,
and with differences in economic views are low. The conclusion is that
tribalism is not important as a factor for reinforcing economic or social
cleavages among the elite.

The final two background characteristics of elite respondents that were
examined are their period of entry into civil service or politics and the
time of their initial membership in TANU. It was assumed that long experience in the colonial administration or the nationalist movement prior
to the attainment of independence was important in shaping the attitudes
and behavior of the elite. It seemed likely that such experience would
shape attitudes and expectations that would reflect the values and styles of
action within these institutions. The correlations in table 3.13 suggest that
these prior role experiences were important, especially for administrators.
Table 3.11 shows the percent of the elite who entered the civil service or
politics at various historical periods. About 40 percent of the legislators
did not become active in "politics" until after independence, while over
88 percent of the administrators were in the civil service before independence and thus received at least some training by British colonial

13. See Karl W. Deutsch, *Nationalism and Social Communication* (Cambridge: M.I.T.
Press, 1953), pp. 25–30, 131–37.

14. W. H. Whitely has stated about these groups: "After the 1939–45 war, changes in
the previously uniform pattern [spread of Swahili language and culture] became discernible, particularly in three areas: Haya, Chagga and Nyakusa. Such changes did not
occur immediately nor at any one time, and had probably been taking place over a
long period. There are signs of interest in language from Nyakusa in 1951, and Chagga
interest dates also from this time, with the appointment of Mr. T. Marealle as Paramount
Chief. However, all the areas have something in common: all are great centres of Mission
work, all are border areas (Nyasaland, Kenya and Uganda) and all are wealthy (Nyakusa
from maize, rice and coffee and the other two from coffee). In addition Haya was one
of the few areas where an indigenous tribal authority was recognized by the Germans,
and there are those who may see in the banana eating habits of the Chagga and Haya
the cult of the national dish." W. H. Whitely, "Language and Politics in East Africa,"
Tanganyika Notes and Records, Nos. 47 and 48 (June and September 1957), pp. 159–73.

officers. As one might expect there is a relationship ($r = .48$) between age and the time that respondents began civil service or political careers. However, since age "explains" only about a quarter of the variance, factors such as ability and interest are probably also reflected in the timing of initial involvement in politics or administration.

TABLE 3.11. Date of Entry into Civil Service/Politics
(in percentages)

	Administrators	Legislators
Before 1945	10	2
1946–50	14	2
1951–54	20	9
1955–58	16	35
1959–61	29	14
1962–66	12	40

Note: The date was supplied by the respondent and represents his personal view of when he began his political career.

The other important historical event in an elite member's career is the period in which he joined the party. Table 3.12 gives the percent of administrators and legislators joining TANU at three major stages in its historical development. The first period, 1954–57, marks the historical rise of the party; the second, 1958–61, its consolidation of power; and the

TABLE 3.12. Date of Joining TANU
(in percentages)

	Administrators ($N = 43$)	Legislators ($N = 57$)	Total ($N = 150$)
1954–57	16	47	41
1958–61	12	35	31
1962–66	72	18	28

Note: The chi-square between administrators and legislators is significant at $p < .05$ level. TANU includes ASP, founded in 1956, for Zanzibari respondents.

last, 1962–66, the post-independence period. Although civil service regulations prevented administrators from joining TANU (or any political organization) between 1953 and July 1964,[15] a number of administrators professed that they joined the party clandestinely before 1964.

15. See Establishment Circular No. 7, July 10, 1964, which rescinded the regulation forbidding membership in political parties.

The background characteristics of the elite, then, indicate that more legislators than administrators come from families with traditionally high status. This was the only significant difference not readily explained by differences in their career obligations. Other differences are that administrators are better educated, more heavily Protestant, and less representative of the tribal proportions in the country. Administrators have been involved in their careers as civil servants for a longer period than elite members pursuing political careers, but legislators have been active as party members for an even longer period, due in part to the legal restrictions on civil servants' participation in TANU.

ATTITUDES OF ELITE

The foregoing summary of the characteristics of the elite sample was intended to make more meaningful their responses to the attitude questions in the interview. Twenty-one forced-choice attitude items, most selected from scales developed in the United States, were administered.[16] These items were used to form four attitude scales. Questions on citizenship, leaders, qualities of leaders, democracy, and African socialism were also included in the interview. Answers to these questions provide some important insights into the elite political culture, concerning both the type of attitudes held and the structural relationships among them.

In order to examine the relationship between and among background indices and attitude measures, correlations were calculated among the variables examined in this research. The three matrices in table 3.13 present, first, correlations among all elite and then similar correlations among administrators and legislators.[17] The correlations underlined have a prob-

16. The items were drawn from a longer list of 42 attitude questions, because they seemed to have prima facie validity and were not obviously culture-bound. This initial list was administered to 120 Tanzanian students at the three campuses of the University of East Africa in March–April 1966, as the first part of a questionnaire designed to pretest questions for the elite interviews. An item analysis of student responses was the basis for the 21 items used in the elite study. Nine of these items were included in the main body of the interview, and twelve items, typed on a separate sheet, were administered at the conclusion of the interview. See app. A for a more complete description of the interview.

17. Boldface correlations are significant at the .05 level. Significance of individual correlations was tested using the statistic $r^2(N-2)/(1-r^2)$, which has an $F_{1,N-2}$ distribution (Hubert Blalock, *Social Statistics* (New York: McGraw-Hill, 1960), p. 304); see pp. 309–10 for the procedure for testing significant differences.

Several of the variables in the matrices (5, 6, 8) are simply trichotomous measures. It is unlikely that these variables satisfy the requirements of interval scale and normal dis-

ability of .05 or less of having occurred by chance if there were no relationship. The correlation patterns of M.P.'s and administrators are
rather different; this had not been anticipated so a two-tailed test of differences among correlations was made and those correlations that are
significantly different at the .05 level or less have been starred.[18]

An examination of the correlation matrices was made, with two questions in mind, in order to interpret my findings: what relationships
emerge between background factors and attitudes, and what factors surprisingly appear not to be interrelated? Most of the propositions discussed
are drawn from my field experience and/or the literature on attitudes.
Since the actual formulation of hypotheses and propositions emerged from
the analysis of the data, that is, without prior prediction, two-tailed tests
of significance were used, as they were on all relationships in this study
(unless otherwise specified).

The questionnaire responses of 120 Tanzanian university students are
also reported in this chapter. These students, enrolled at the three
campuses of the (then) University of East Africa, completed written
questionnaires in February and March 1966. Respondents were chosen
primarily from those enrolled in social science courses. They answered
the same attitude and role questions as political elite interviewed.[19] Since
university students in Tanzania comprise a nascent elite, as many of their
careers will lead to important economic and political posts, their responses
provide a useful comparison with those from members of the elite.

---

tribution for the product moment correlation significance tests. But in order to simplify
and standardize discussion of variable relationships, using a single summary measure of
association, the product moment correlation has been used. For some relationships that
seem important in our discussion and where it was questionable that the variable measure
adequately met parametric assumptions, appropriate nonparametric tests were made. In
all cases where r was significant ($p \leq .05$), Tau C and Gamma, statistical measures of
association for ordinally grouped data, were also significant.

18. There are a number of pitfalls in using correlations to analyze and summarize
data. Because correlations may be misleading, the analysis of deviant cases can also be
important. In general, I have relied upon correlations because of their ease of presentation,
wide familiarity, and comparability. However, I have also extended the analysis on occasion to examine deviant cases. Moreover, I rely only in part on significance tests to
interpret results. See Edward R. Tufte, "Improving Data Analysis in Political Science,"
World Politics, 21 (July 1969), 641–54. Tufte also recommends regression analysis and
graphing of data, which I did not undertake.

19. For a more detailed discussion of the student questionnaire, which also included
a number of items not used with the elite, see Raymond F. Hopkins, "Political Roles
in a New State" (Ph.D. dissertation, Yale University 1968), app. 2.

Table 3.13. Correlations of Backgrounds and Attitudes

	(1)	(2)	(3)	(4)	(5)	(6)	(7)	(8)	(9)	(10)	(11)	(12)	(13)
1. Auth'ism													
2. Anomie	**24**												
3. Faith in people	−09	**−20**											
4. Dem. pract.	−06	**−29**	09								ALL ELITE		
5. Af. soc'ism	**25**	11	04	−14									
6. Commit. to econ. eq.	08	−16	17	08	−04								
7. Trad. status	13	**26**	−11	−10	10	−06							
8. Wealth	02	−12	−04	−08	17	−00	**30**						
9. Father figure	**21**	−03	−07	09	−09	01	−02	05					
10. Education	**−43**	**−39**	19	04	**−21**	13	−15	18	−10				
11. Newspapers	**−29**	−14	17	10	**−25**	−05	−04	08	13	**41**			
12. Career length	09	05	−17	−11	03	−11	00	12	04	−07	08		
13. Age	11	14	−13	−05	−07	01	12	**23**	13	−25	−09	**48**	
14. Tribe	**−30**	−06	06	−03	−01	−10	−07	08	**−32**	**31**	10	18	07

	(1)	(2)	(3)	(4)	(5)	(6)	(7)	(8)	(9)	(10)	(11)	(12)	(13)	(14)
1. Auth'ism														
2. Anomie	04													
3. Faith in people	00	06*												
4. Dem. pract.	−09	**−33**	23							ADMINISTRATORS				
5. Af. soc'ism	15	20	−02	**−29**										
6. Commit. to econ. eq.	22	25	−24	−02	**−26***									
7. Trad. status	18	**36**	00	**−38***	17	−17								
8. Wealth	02	09	−08	−24	13	−09	**28**							
9. Father figure	21	−04	−15	−01	−08	−08	−18	−07						

	(1)	(2)	(3)	(4)	(5)	(6)	(7)	(8)	(9)	(10)	(11)	(12)	(13)	(14)	(15)
10. Education	−21	−26	−06	13	−26	08	−26	−17*	−09		07*	**−50***	**−40**	**30**	16
11. Newspapers	−04*	09	**−37**	15	−22	06	09	−05	29			**−37***	**−27**	08	−10
12. Career length	**33**	19	07	**−31**	07	−15	22	21	05				**68**	07	11
13. Age	**28**	07	−02	**−31**	−02	01	21	33	11					**31**	18
14. Salary	17	−07	03	−25	−15	05	−09	05	25						11
15. Tribe	−16	08	−11	−01	−11	−08	24	23	**−36**						

LEGISLATORS

	(1)	(2)	(3)	(4)	(5)	(6)	(7)	(8)	(9)	(10)	(11)	(12)	(13)	(14)	(15)
1. Auth'ism															
2. Anomie	**37**														
3. Faith in people	−14	**−42***													
4. Dem. pract.	−00	−24	−07												
5. Af. soc'ism	**39**	02	09	−02											
6. Commit. to econ. eq.	**37**	−09	10	**10***	17*										
7. Trad. status	−03	17	−15	10	10	01									
8. Wealth	04	−26	02	04	21	07	**34**								
9. Father figure	20	−04	01	17	−09	08	06	14							
10. Education	**−50**	**−41**	**29**	−06	−29	−26	02	**34***	−08						
11. Newspapers	**−48***	**−33***	22	03	**−30**	−14	06	15	02	**57***					
12. Career length	−01	05	−05	−06	−07	−06	−01	04	08	−10*	**47***				
13. Age	−03	18	−05	17	−11	01	07	19	14	−18	03	**42**			
15. Member gov.	**−35**	−22	**26**	04	09	02	08	09	−01	24	**59**	**48**	09		
16. Tribe	**−37**	−13	**25**	**27**	06	−09	−17	−13	−25	22	25	03	−02		**35**

* Indicates a significant difference ($p < .05$) between administrators and legislators. For ease of presentation, decimal points have been deleted.

Authoritarianism

Authoritarian qualities, especially traits of submission and dominance, have been noted in several underdeveloped states.[20] Four items from the F-scale and one item from scales used by Doob in East African research were employed to measure authoritarianism.[21] Table 3.14 gives the per-

TABLE 3.14. Elite Responses to Authoritarian Items
(in percentages)

	Agreement		
	Administrators (N = 51)	*Legislators* (N = 57)	*Students* (N = 120)
1. Obedience and respect for authority are the most important virtues for children to learn.	78	83	83
2. What this country needs most, more than laws and political programs, is a few courageous, tireless, and devoted leaders in whom people can put their faith.	53[a]	75[a]	78
3. Most people who don't get ahead just don't have enough will power.	47	63	63
4. Superiors should say just what is to be done and how to do it if people are going to do a good job.	16[b]	28[b]	53[b]
5. Laws should always be obeyed.	26	30	37

a. Chi-square is significant at $p < .05$ level between legislators and administrators.
b. Chi-square is significant at $p < .05$ between elite and students.

centage of agreement for administrators, legislators, and the Tanzanian university students on each of these items. Administrators are notably

20. See, for example, Robert Levine, "Political Socialization and Culture Change," in Clifford Geertz, ed., *Old Societies and New States* (New York: Free Press, 1963), pp. 289–303; Donald N. Levine, "Ethiopia: Identity, Authority and Realism," in Pye and Verba, eds., *Political Culture and Political Development*, pp. 250–56; Pye, *Nation Building*, pp. 183–86; and James C. Scott, *Political Ideology in Malaysia*.

21. See T. W. Adorno, Else Frenkel-Brunswick, Daniel J. Levinson, and R. Nevitt Sanford, *The Authoritarian Personality* (New York: Harper, 1950). The fifth question has been used by Leonard W. Doob and may be found in "Leaders, Followers and Attitudes toward Authority," in Lloyd Fallers, ed., *The King's Men* (New York: Oxford University Press, 1964).

the least authoritarian. Since higher education would presumably be related to lower levels of authoritarianism, it is surprising to find that students appear about equally as authoritarian as legislators, most of whom are less well educated. Doob, for example, on question five, found only 21 percent agreement among Makerere University graduates whom he felt were leaders, contrasted with 68 percent among "followers."[22] And a recent study in the United States indicates that so-called "working-class authoritarianism" may be largely the product of educational differences.[23] Indeed, the whole concept and measurement of authoritarianism may be largely a product of differences in either education or intelligence. Since it is an important concept in understanding a political culture, I tried to assess authoritarianism among the elite using a five-item Guttman scale.[24]

An examination of the correlations between authoritarianism scores and indices for many of the demographic background variables suggests that, indeed, higher education is associated with weaker authoritarianism. The correlation is $r = -.50$ among legislators and $r = -.21$ among administrators, and for all elite, $r = -.43$. The rather weak association among administrators, however, and the fact that, even among legislators, education explains only about 25 percent of the variance in authoritarianism, suggests that other factors influencing authoritarianism are worth investigating.

Elite who described their fathers with terms such as domineering or *kali* (fierce) seemed to be more authoritarian (whether they recalled this parental relationship with misgivings or high praise). The correlation among M.P.'s and administrators is about the same and for all elite, at $r = .21$, is significant. This proposition mirrors similar conclusions found by other researchers.[25] Individual differences in family experience may

22. Doob, "Leaders," p. 122.

23. Lewis Lipsitz, "Working Class Authoritarianism: A Re-evaluation," *American Sociological Review, 30* (February 1965), 109. Lipsitz points out that higher authoritarianism among the working class may be explained almost solely on the basis of lower educational levels than the middle class.

24. For a complete discussion of the scaling procedures and their results for this and other attitude scales, see app. C.

25. Frenkel-Brunswick, for instance, found differing parental images among high- and low-scoring authoritarian types, and Robert Levine found that Nuer, who are more egalitarian, remembered their fathers as warm and supportive compared to Gusii men, from a more authoritarian society, who remembered their fathers as distant and harsh. See Adorno et al., *The Authoritarian Personality,* pp. 359 ff., and Levine, "The Internalization of Political Values in Stateless Societies," *Human Organization, 19* (1960), 51–58.

be related to different social patterns based on lineage and tradition, but there was no way to test this possibility with such a diversity of tribal backgrounds in my sample.

Since the British colonial administrative service was elitist and paternalistic, experience by Africans over a number of years in the colonial system seemed likely to promote tendencies and attitudes reflecting this environment. Among administrators, career length was significantly correlated ($r = .33$) with authoritarianism. Older administrators are most likely to have had longer careers and age is therefore also related. The fact that older administrators probably experienced a more rigid and discipline-oriented educational system is another likely factor in this relationship. In general, it seems that longer experience in an authoritarian government institution is likely to lead to greater authoritarianism. The only other background characteristic correlated significantly with authoritarianism is the extent of newspaper reading ($r = -.29$ for all elite),[26] which appears to be related independently of the effects of education.[27]

Anomie

Feelings of anomie among the elite were also investigated. Questions were designed to probe feelings of political uncertainty, loneliness, and discontinuity with the future. Two of the four items (one and three) reported in table 3.15 are taken from Leo Srole's five-item anomie scale. Other questions from his scale that seem related to qualities such as powerlessness and general depression (eumania) were rejected as inap-

---

26. The index of newspaper reading consists of a four-point scale running from those who seldom or occasionally read local papers to those who regularly read local and overseas papers. The relationship, although "significant" among elites, seems to be due solely to that among M.P.'s ($r = -.48$ while $r = -.04$ for administrators). The correlations of authoritarianism with education and newspaper reading are much lower among administrators. One possible explanation is that education and newspaper reading vary less among administrators than among legislators. Since educational levels and patterns of reading are rather similar among administrators, they are likely to have less effect on variations in authoritarianism. Richard Christie makes this same point in explaining differences in correlations with authoritarianism between two groups. See his "Authoritarianism Re-examined," in Richard Christie and Marie Jahoda, eds., *Studies in the Scope and Method of "The Authoritarian Personality"* (Glencoe: Free Press, 1954), p. 171.

27. The hypothesized model is that education leads both to higher newspaper reading and low authoritarianism and that the correlation between newspaper reading and authoritarianism is really zero; however, the partial correlation is −.14. See Blalock, pp. 330–57; also Blalock, "Spurious Versus Intervening Variables: The Problems of Temporal Sequences," *Social Forces, 40* (May 1962), 330 ff.

TABLE 3.15. Elite Responses to Anomie Items
(in percentages)

	Agreement		
	Administrators (N = 51)	Legislators (N = 57)	Students (N = 119)
1. It is hard to tell nowadays who a person really can count on.	22	32	56*
2. Fundamentally, the world we live in is a pretty lonely place.	8*	28	23
3. Nowadays a person has to live pretty much for today and let tomorrow take care of itself.	12	12	20
4. Things are changing so fast these days it is hard to tell what will happen or who will cause things to happen.	24	17	66*

* Chi-square is significant at the $p < .05$ level between students and elite on items 1 and 4 and between administrators and legislators on item 2.

propriate.[28] Two other items were used to measure anomie: one from Rokeach's dogmatism scale (item two), which seems to tap feelings of isolation and loneliness,[29] and one (item four) designed by the author specifically to reflect normlessness. These four items formed a seven-point anomie scale based on the sum of the item scores.[30]

Students, it appears, are more anomic than the elite. Differences on the fourth question are particularly striking. Politics is apparently unpredictable for university students. They also see the political process as closed to them. Seventy-seven percent agreed with the statement that "despite what constitutional arrangements may exist, major political decisions are always made by a few men in secret." Only one of the 120 students indicated a desire to become a politician. Most students anticipated future occupations as civil servants or teachers, which were careers explicitly encouraged by the government. Since students constitute the basis for the next generation of elite, their feelings of normlessness repre-

28. See Leo Srole, "Social Integration and Certain Corollaries: An Exploratory Study," *American Sociological Review, 21* (December 1956), pp. 709–16.

29. See Milton Rokeach, *The Open and Closed Mind* (New York: Basic Books, 1960), pp. 413–19.

30. A Guttman scale with a reproducibility of .86 was also formed but was not used, since this failed to meet the criteria suggested by Guttman and others.

sent an interesting harbinger of the possible weakening of institutionalization as they come to play important roles in the future.

Their view that the political world is unpredictable was not shared
by most of the political elite respondents. One M.P. stated in answer to
item four, "I suppose an outsider might feel this way, but we know
where we're going and there's no uncertainty." Less than a quarter of
the elite agreed with the two statements suggesting uncertainty and
lack of predictability in life. Thus anomie, at least as reflected in responses
to these questions, does not appear to be a serious problem for the elite.

Two background factors seem important in promoting anomie—traditional status and education. The correlation of the anomie scale with
high traditional status ($r = .26$) suggests that individuals in modern roles
from families with high traditional status are likely to experience anomie.
This is particularly the case among administrators ($r = .36$).[31] Higher
education, on the other hand, is likely to lead to weaker anomie. Among
legislators, $r = -.41$, while for administrators, $r = -.26$. In a rapidly
changing world, greater education and a better understanding of social
forces can instill greater confidence in one's ability to control and manage his life. Among the Tanzanian elite this relationship seems to hold
true.

A person who felt uncertain, lonely, and unsure about what might
happen in his country would probably view strong leaders favorably and
place a high priority on obedience. Thus it seemed likely that anomie
would be related to authoritarianism. Research in the United States found
a correlation of .59 between anomie and authoritarianism.[32] However, in
Tanzania it was only .24—well below the size expected although still significant. Among administrators it was .04, compared to .37 for legislators.
These weaker relationships in Tanzania may indicate measurement error
due to the small number of items and the cross-national setting. However,
it may also indicate, at least in part, weakly structured attitude patterns

31. Since many high-status administrators entered the civil service early compared with
other administrators, it seemed possible that career length was an intervening factor for
administrators between high status and anomie. The sharp transition from a long period
under British tutelage to the TANU government could have generated anomic feelings.
However, career length does not act as an intervening variable, as the partial correlation
of traditional status and anomie controlling for the effects of career length is .33. Since
.33 is far from 0, we may reject the null hypothesis that career length is an intervening
variable.

32. Herbert McCloskey and John Schaar, "Reply to Srole and Nutter," *American Sociological Review, 30* (October 1965), 765.

compared to those found in cultures in which there is not a large gap between modern and traditional sectors.

Faith in People

Two questions were used to measure faith in people. Adapted from
a scale by Morris Rosenberg, these items and the percent of elite agreement with them are reported in table 3.16.[33] Compared with the elite,

TABLE 3.16. Elite Responses to Faith-in-People Items
(in percentages)

	Agreement		
	Administrators (N = 51)	Legislators (N = 57)	Students (N = 120)
1. Most people are fundamentally cooperative and inclined to help others.	82	91	68
2. Most people can't be trusted.	16	32	47

students have a lower opinion of people's trustworthiness and cooperative-
ness. The greater anomie among students is thus matched by a relatively
greater distrust of human nature. In contrast, the elite seem to have confidence in their fellow man. Cross-national studies using similar questions
to probe faith in people suggest that members of the political elite in
Tanzania are more optimistic about their fellow man than the average
citizen of the United States or the United Kingdom. Since openness and
trust have been shown to be important associates of democratic cultures,
the high proportion of elite with this attitudinal quality could indicate
that an important psychic support for democratic procedures is present in
Tanzania.[34]

33. Morris Rosenberg, "Misanthropy and Political Ideology," *American Sociological Review*, 21 (December 1956), 690–95.

34. See Almond and Verba, eds., *Civic Culture*, pp. 267 ff. for the figures on faith in
people for the five countries they studied and a discussion of the relevance of this attitude
trait to politics. The Tanzanian elite was above the national sample in all five countries.
If one reverses item 2 in table 3.16, 75% of the Tanzanian respondents presumably would
agree that most people can be trusted, compared with 55% in the U.S. (the highest) and
only 7% in Italy (the lowest). Others who have noted the relationship between faith in
people and strength of democratic attitudes are Harold Lasswell, *Power and Personality*
(New York: Viking Press, 1948), pp. 148–73; Lane, *Political Ideology*, pp. 163 ff.; and
Rosenberg, "Misanthropy," pp. 690–95.

A faith-in-people index, based on the two items, was used for the correlation analysis. In general, it failed to correlate highly with most other variables. Since faith in people is likely to be related to widely accepted cultural views of human nature or to personal experiences, it is not surprising that differences are not statistically associated with most demographic traits.

However, education has been cited as an important factor in shaping trustful attitudes toward others. Almond and Verba, for example, found that "confidence in the human environment tends to increase among the better educated and economically more privileged elements of the population" in all five of the countries they studied.[35] The correlation among legislators provides some support for this proposition, but, surprisingly, among administrators education has a small negative correlation with faith in people $(r = -.06)$. Consequently we must conclude that faith in people, at least among administrators, is not promoted by higher education. But one factor was associated with trust in others for administrators: career length. A correlation between career length and faith in people $(r = -.37)$ suggests that longer experience in authoritarian government institutions is likely to lead to less faith in people.

In relation to the other attitude scales, faith in people appeared to be unrelated to authoritarianism $(r = -.09$, surprisingly low), and inversely associated with anomie $(r = -.20)$. Administrators, again, did not exhibit expected relationships. In fact, there was a significant difference between the correlations of anomie and faith in people for administrators and legislators.[36]

Democratic Practices

Three questions probing attitudes toward different democratic practices were asked. These questions touch on the legitimacy of disagreement

35. Almond and Verba, eds., *Civic Culture*, p. 268.

36. In an effort to account for the small positive relationship $(r = .06)$ among administrators, the interview transcripts of those who scored high on both anomie and faith in people were reexamined. It would appear that many of these people had a general faith in individuals but were tense or uncertain about social relationships. For example, one administrator disagreed on the item, "Most people can't be trusted" but qualified his response with, "Of course some of the people I know can't be trusted." A distinguishable minority of administrators tended to have positive feelings toward people in general while

with the government, the value of competition for leadership, and the dependability of voting for choosing good leaders. The results of these questions are given in table 3.17. There were no great differences be-

TABLE 3.17. Elite Responses to Democratic Practices Items
(in percentages)

	Agreement		
	Administrators (N = 51)	Legislators (N = 57)	Students (N = 119)
1. Laws are wrong which prevent disagreement with a government from being expressed.	77	74	77
2. Competition for leadership in open elections undermines a country's unity and purpose.	16	14	20
3. Giving people the power to vote a leader out of office can be dangerous because the average voter is not competent to choose good leaders.	8	16	37

tween elite and students on these items, although students seemed slightly less committed to democratic procedures. Comparing elite responses with responses on similar questions asked in the United States, it appears that the Tanzanian elite more fully supports democratic practices. For example, 28 percent of U.S. "influentials" agreed that "most people don't have enough sense to pick their own leaders wisely," while only 12 percent of the Tanzanian elite agreed that the average voter is not competent.[37] The democratic commitment of the Tanzanian elite seems particularly strong in contrast to democratic attitudes found in four West Indian states. For instance, 92 percent of the elite interviewed felt that democracy was the "best form of government" for Tanzania, compared to 28 percent among the West Indian elite. On another question only 12 percent felt the average voter was not competent, contrasted with

feeling uncertain or anomic toward their immediate acquaintances. As a result, they appeared to have both anomic *and* trusting outlooks.

37. Herbert McCloskey, "Consensus and Ideology in American Politics," *American Political Science Review, 58* (June 1964), 361–82.

72 percent of the West Indians.[38] The West Indian study was conducted at the time of independence, while Tanzanian attitudes were measured five years after independence. Had there been serious competition among parties, as for instance occurred in Zanzibar or in some of the West Indian countries, support for democratic practices evidenced in the responses of Tanzanian elite might have been considerably lower.[39]

The sum of the scores for the three items was used as a scale of belief in democratic practices. Fifty percent of the elite received the highest possible score. There is reason to believe that, particularly among legislators, their responses often reflected "accepted" views rather than firmly held personal convictions. Some respondents revealed ambiguous views on democratic practices although their scale scores suggested complete support. Two responses will illustrate this: (1) "Everybody is competent [as a voter]. In the last election only a few made a mistake and voted against the president"; (2) "Any leader must be elected by the people. If not, the leader may not be liked by the people and, therefore, they may not follow what he directs them to do." Voting was thus seen more as a means for securing support than as a way to insure popular control. The two M.P.'s who made these remarks scored high on authoritarianism, indicated they had little faith in people, but appeared democratic. Their responses to these questions, therefore, may indicate greater commitment to democratic practices than in fact exists.

The case for weakly held beliefs in the value of democratic practices is also supported by the fact that expected relationships with other attitude variables did not emerge. Looking at relationships among all elite, no background variable was significantly correlated. Among administrators, however, two interesting correlations appeared: career length ($-.31$) and traditional status ($-.38$). These results prompt the following proposition: administrators with longer experience in an authoritarian government institution or from higher traditional status are likely to believe less strongly in democratic practices. Traditional status was related to

38. Charles C. Moskos, Jr., and Wendell Bell, "Attitudes Towards Democracy Among Leaders in Four Emergent Nations," *British Journal of Sociology,* 15 (December 1964), 320.

39. Interviews with three Zanzibaris—incomplete and therefore not analyzed in our data—revealed great cynicism and distrust for democratic practices. Two individuals specifically mentioned the 1963 Zanzibar elections in which the ASP party had a majority of the popular vote but failed to capture political power owing to population inequalities in the electoral districts. One of these Zanzibar politicians, in response to the question whether he thought M.P.'s might be elected from Zanzibar, replied, "Never."

support for democratic practices in a significantly different way as between administrators and legislators. The correlation for the latter is $r = .10$, suggesting a positive relationship.[40]

Only the correlation of democratic practices with the anomie scale ($r = -.29$) is large enough to justify any proposition about interrelationships between attitudes. This expected inverse correlation was present among both elite groups, but statistically significant only among administrators. Anomic individuals, cut loose from social anchors, could be expected to distrust the overt credos of their present environment.

What is more interesting about this measure of belief in democratic practices is that it is not correlated with either authoritarianism or faith in people. Remembering Rosenberg's finding that faith in people is correlated with belief in democratic practices, it seemed probable that these attitudes would be closely related; however, it was only .09. It is statistically possible that there is no relationship between these attitudes. It also seemed likely that support for democratic practices would be negatively correlated with authoritarianism, since individuals who are highly authoritarian would be less likely to support democratic principles. In addition to other studies indicating that these attitudes are related,[41] the very questions used in constructing the authoritarianism scale seemed to tap attitudes likely to be tied to distrust in democracy—for example, "Leaders should always be obeyed." Consequently, when no structural (interactional) relationship appeared in the correlations—among all elite it was −.06—it seemed probable but strange that these attitudes were not directly related.

The nonemergence of these relationships, found in attitude studies elsewhere, is partly a product, I believe, of exaggerated statements of faith in democracy. The responses of some highly authoritarian and distrustful elite indicating strong support for democratic practices perhaps reflected official views on democracy or represented answers thought to please the interviewer. Even considering the possibility that a number of these re-

40. It seems possible that at least part of this proposition is not true. High-status individuals who feel positively about democracy may have been more likely to choose political careers, while those who were fairly content with traditional patterns and colonial rule may have chosen civil service careers. Such an early self-selection among high-status individuals who have now arrived in elite positions may account for this quite different attitude relationship between legislators and administrators.

41. See Adorno et al., chap. 7, on the relation of authoritarianism and antidemocratic feelings, and Lane, pp. 400–12.

sponses were superficial, however, support for democratic procedures must be considered strong among the Tanzanian elite.

But whether this "support" means the same thing in Tanzania as it does in Western nations is doubtful. It could well indicate allegiance to the official position of Tanzania in claiming to be democratic; an expression, then, of nationalist sentiment rather than political commitment. If so, these positive attitudes toward democracy may be brittle. They appear unsupported by interrelated attitudinal networks and hence susceptible to rapid change under pressure from latent though potent authoritarianism emerging from the stress of disruptive public events.

One other prominent feature in the pattern of correlations was the differences between relationships among administrators and legislators. These differences, highlighted in table 3.18, suggest that the attitudes of each group respond to different influences and are affected by different types of background factors. Different patterns of recruitment and motivation may account for these variations. In any event, elite attitudes, as repre-

TABLE 3.18. Differences in Attitude Correlations
of Administrators and Legislators*

	Administrators	Legislators
Education with		
Authoritarianism (A)	−.21	**−.50**
Anomie (An)	−.26	**−.41**
Faith in people (FP)	−.06	**.29**
Democratic practices (DP)	.13	−.06
Newspapers with		
Authoritarianism (A)	−.04	**−.48**
Anomie (An)	.14	**−.33**
Faith in people (FP)	.09	.22
Democratic practices (DP)	.15	.03
Career length with		
Authoritarianism (A)	**.33**	−.01
Anomie (An)	.19	.05
Faith in people (FP)	**−.37**	−.05
Democratic practices (DP)	**−.31**	−.06
Traditional status with		
Authoritarianism (A)	.18	−.03
Anomie (An)	**.36**	.17
Faith in people (FP)	.00	−.15
Democratic practices (DP)	**−.38**	.10

* See note 17. Boldface correlations are significant at $p < .05$ level.

sented by the four scales, are not consistent among administrators and legislators. If these patterns extend throughout the elite and downward to middle-level civil servants and party personnel, changes in the backgrounds of those recruited to these two elite groups will also produce changes in attitudes. For instance, as the level of education rises among legislators, authoritarianism may be expected to decline; and as administrators with low traditional status are recruited increasingly, they may become less anomic and more democratic in outlook. However, changes in educational level among administrators or in the level of traditional status among legislators may have little or no impact on political attitudes.

Economic Attitudes

In chapter 1 the important though largely private conflict over economic policy was discussed. Since occasional public comments indicated that economic controversies were important, two questions on attitudes toward economic issues were asked the elite. The first was, "Do you agree that, above all else, the government must create economic equality among people?" Responses generally fell into three categories. Some agreed completely with this statement. For instance, one administrator said, "Yes, this is our present policy to move from capitalism toward this goal." Others expressed reservations of some kind but did not disagree. Two responses illustrate this, one from a "national" member of the Assembly, the other from a principal secretary: (1) "I'd love to have that. But not even in the most socialist countries does this exist. I think all the government can do is agree to bring up the level of the lower group"; (2) "I don't like this idea, but yes, the government is ruling hard to get us to this. Certainly the wealth of people must be shared." A third group was in disagreement, often expressing capitalist sentiments. The answer of another principal secretary to this question was: "Never; if you start two people out equally, soon one will be up and another down." Many answers contained rather mixed reactions, which created difficulty in coding. Very few actually challenged economic equality as an ideal. A number responded that this was an important goal but that development was a more important task. Others felt economic equality was impossible or impractical. The answers to this item, therefore, as presented in table 3.19, must be considered unreliable and only a rough approximation of the differences of opinion that existed.

One clear finding revealed by this question was a substantial disagree-

TABLE 3.19. Elite Views on Economic Questions
(in percentages)

Question	Answer	Administrators (N = 50)	Legislators (N = 57)	Students (N = 120)
Above all else, the government must create economic equality among people.	Agree	44	40	71
	Qualified agree/uncertain	20	33	3
	Disagree	36	26	26
How about the pace of change these days, do you think things are changing about the right speed, too slow, or too fast?	Too fast	24	16	
	About right	57	66	
	Too slow	20	19	

ment over economic goals. While 42 percent of the respondents unreservedly agreed that the government should intervene in the economy to create economic equality, a rather large portion, 31 percent, did not agree. This disagreement may also account for a number of inconsistent attitudes. For example, one principal assistant secretary who heartily agreed that the government should put a high priority on furthering economic equality added, "This is an important step toward a mixture of capitalism and socialism."

An attempt was made to explore relationships between attitudes on economic equality and other attitudes and background variables. The correlations in table 3.13 indicate that in general there were no strong relationships. Only among legislators were there any significant correlations: .37 with authoritarianism and −.26 with education. Thus, economic views did not seem strongly dependent upon or related to the backgrounds or other attitudes of the elite respondents.

A high percentage of students agreed with the statement about economic equality, 71 percent compared to 42 percent among the political elite. This was quite unexpected since, in replies to questions about their support for Marxian economic views or in reaction to government action to limit their future incomes, students were noticeably disenchanted. With regard to "scientific socialism," for example, only 13 percent expressed support, while a bare 3 percent thought of themselves as "Marxists." High support for economic equality may reflect a different interpretation of the question by students than by the elite.[42]

The second question relating to economic attitudes followed a question about future development. Respondents were asked, "How about the pace of change these days? Do you think things are changing at about the right speed, too slow, or too fast?" The majority expressed satisfaction at the pace of development and change occurring, frequently citing progress in construction, agricultural output, and Africanization. The response of one principal secretary is typical of the optimism generally expressed: "We're moving at the right speed generally, though in some spheres, too fast. But we're really moving. A lot of us are sleeping through key changes and only notice things five years later."

Although most elite respondents were satisfied with the existing pace of change, important minority elements expressed dissatisfaction, maintaining either that things were moving too fast or that the pace of progress was too slow. The latter group mentioned that there was a growing imbalance between demands for progress and the government's ability to respond. Not surprisingly, those who felt things were changing too fast tended to score high on the anomie scale ($r = .24$). Tribal affiliation, as indicated by membership in one of the three "progressive" tribes, was not related to either economic issue. Thus tribal differences do not appear to translate themselves into differences over economic policies.

These attitudes toward economic issues indicate majority agreement on the desirability of government intervention in the economy, the need for some economic leveling or "closing the gap," and the adequacy of the speed of change and development. However, agreement was considerably lower than on questions indicating support for democracy. The political struggle in Tanzania seemed to revolve to a large extent around the question of what specific economic goals the government should pursue. Of the various decisions of nationhood,[43] this was one that had not been re-

42. In a conversation with a few students I discovered that they had interpreted economic equality to imply that privileges of politicians should be ended and that equal economic rewards for equal ability (evidenced by education) should be established, that is, equality among elite. If such an interpretation was widespread, the meaning of student support for the proposition of economic equality would have to be understood in very different terms than was true for elite respondents.

43. For a discussion of the decisions facing political elites following independence see Wendell Bell and Ivar Oxaal, *Decisions of Nationhood: Political and Social Development in the British Caribbean* (Denver: University of Denver Press, 1964).

solved for many members of the elite and was a controversial and difficult subject.[44]

African Socialism

African socialism has been an important ideological concept among many African elites. Leaders in a number of African countries have expounded theories and programs for socialism, African style.[45] In 1962, Nyerere outlined his views in a speech entitled "Ujamaa." One of the central tenets of African socialism, particularly as Nyerere outlined it, is the avoidance of self-interest conflicts.

> True socialism is an attitude of mind. It is, therefore, up to the people of Tanganyika—the peasants, the wage earners, the students, the leaders, all of us—to make sure that this socialist attitude of mind is not lost through the temptations to personal gain (or to the abuse of positions of authority) which may come our way as individuals, or through the temptation to look on the good of the whole community as of secondary importance to the interests of our own particular group.[46]

The basis frequently invoked for African socialism was the social relationships of traditional society, which were generally seen as in harmony with this philosophy. Nyerere stated, "We in Africa have no more need of being 'converted' to socialism than we had of being 'taught' democracy. Both are rooted in our own past—in the traditional society which produced us." [47] Since African socialism seemed to be such an important concept in the political ideology of Nyerere, as well as other African leaders, respondents were asked their reaction to this term and how they would define the concept. Table 3.20 contains a breakdown of responses. The majority expressed reservations about the concept, finding it unclear and confusing; a number even suggested it was misleading or wrong. A sampling from the interviews indicates the wide range of responses evoked.

44. The Arusha Declaration of January 1967 and the subsequent nationalization of industry, have no doubt altered this picture.

45. See William H. Friedland and Carl G. Rosberg, Jr., eds., *African Socialism* (Stanford: Stanford University Press, 1964).

46. Ibid., p. 243. Chandler Morse points out that "under idealized socialism there is thus no conflict of economic interest, no competitive struggle of man against man, sector against sector." "The Economics of African Socialism," ibid., p. 44.

47. Nyerere, "Ujamaa," ibid., p. 246.

I don't believe in African socialism as a term. There is much confusion over this idea. (A first term M.P.)

We have clearly told the world we want African socialism and that it is not copying the East or the West. Now we are awaiting a committee which will tell us exactly what this means. (Regional commissioner)

Personally I have no idea. No one has convinced me that Nyerere has explained it really. African socialism is just an undiscriminating term. Really the socialist aim is to form a classless society—the problem is we want to control the means of production and this is the right thing. (Junior minister)

I don't like the word "African." Socialism is the same in every country, but we're trying to find out what it means in this country. We're supposed to have a commission sometime to examine this idea. (A principal secretary)

It is not revolutionary; it is not new; we have been with it and it is with us, and it will still remain with us. It is a spirit of togetherness, it is a spirit of *ndugu yangu,* that is, my relative, which is used to describe the extended family. (An administrative secretary)

Africans have had their culture, have had certain obligations among themselves, for example, helping each other so that everybody lives. It is the translation of this culture into the framework of modern life or modern way of living which is African socialism. It is not communism, and although it has not been defined, Africans have had this socialism for some time. (A principal assistant secretary)

As one administrator remarked, "this is a very controversial subject." Definitions of African socialism (shown in table 3.20) were of two types. The first argued that African socialism was an outgrowth of traditional culture and practices and that it reflected an extension of communal obligations into modern society. The majority of administrators and legislators took this position, and most felt that as such, it was a "good thing." The second definition was that African socialism is simply real socialism or scientific socialism, which is based on control of the means of production and the evolution of a classless society. Of those who understood this to be the definition of African socialism, the majority approved it or felt it was a good thing, but a sizable minority disapproved. For example, one M.P. who disliked African socialism claimed that "This means the same thing as Marxism in the backs of the minds of our leaders, and they use it to sway people in that direction." Another M.P., who supported scientific or Marxist socialism, took just the opposite view of

TABLE 3.20. Elite Views on African Socialism

	Percent Who Chose		
	Administrators (N = 48)	Legislators (N = 48)	Students (N = 120)
African socialism as a concept:			
Dislike, wrong, misleading	17	27	
Uncertain, unclear, confusing	38	33	
Like, good, expresses our experiences	46	40	51*
African socialism defined:			
Real socialism, scientific socialism— Good thing	19	33	
Based on tradition, brotherhood, communal obligations of African society—Good thing	58	49	
Real socialism, scientific socialism— Bad thing	19	9	
Based on tradition, brotherhood, etc.— Bad thing	3	9	

* The students responded to African socialism in a close-ended question. They either expressed support for African socialism or they did not.

African socialism. His response—"Humbug! I don't support it." There is a strong tendency for those who reject the philosophy of African socialism, regardless of whether they define it as based on tradition or scientific principles, to dislike it as a concept. Seventy-seven percent of those who liked the concept defined it in traditional terms, and of these 91 percent thought it was a "good thing."

Reactions to the term "African socialism" (like–dislike) were also included in the correlational analysis. The correlations suggest that *those who liked this term tend to be authoritarian, less well educated, and less likely to read newspapers extensively.* Among administrators, the belief in democratic practices was negatively related to approval of the African socialism concept. Those who were content with the concept of African socialism, therefore, appeared somewhat less likely to exhibit the syndrome of attitudes and background typical of a participant and democratic personality.[48]

The Arusha Declaration, proclaimed in January 1967, about six months after the interviews were completed, may have clarified or reshaped some elite attitudes on this subject. The uneasiness with which they viewed this term as a concept is perhaps reflected in the fact that nowhere in the Arusha Declaration was the term "African socialism" used. Likewise, nowhere were traditions such as communalism and brotherhood mentioned. Instead, a new term, "true socialism," was introduced, consisting of: (1) the absence of exploitation, (2) control of the major means of production, and (3) democracy. The Arusha Declaration preempted the need for the promised presidential commission on socialism which, had it followed the practice set by previous commissions of holding public meetings and soliciting wide public comment, could have opened the issue of defining socialism to public controversy and debate. A second accomplishment of the Declaration was the synthesis accomplished by Nyerere, in part two, which blends the egalitarianism of "scientific socialism" with a strong emphasis on the need for self-reliance and rural development, stressing individual initiative and hard work.[49] The Arusha Declaration perhaps settled some of the controversy and uncertainty that many of the respondents mentioned. If so, this is a further example of Nyerere's skill in articulating national policy so as to satisfy, at least minimally, all major attitude groups among the elite. His ability to perform this function is a crucial feature of Tanzanian politics, without which unity and the practice of closed politics might not be possible.

Leadership

Respondents were asked to mention leaders—anywhere in the world—whom they admired and the qualities for which they admired them. Table 3.21 lists the leaders most often named by administrators, legislators, and students and the percent (among those mentioning at least one leader) who mentioned each leader. The popularity of Nyerere, although expected, is still striking. Only among the students was there a noticeable

48. See Lane, *Political Ideology;* Lasswell, *Power and Personality,* and "The Selective Effect of Personality on Political Participation," in Christie and Jahoda, especially pp. 202 ff.

49. My analysis of the style of the document, along with news commentary on its authorship, suggests that Nyerere was responsible for parts two and three.

TABLE 3.21. Leaders Admired by Elite

Percent Mentioning Each Leader

	Administrators (N = 47)	Legislators (N = 55)	Students (N = 114)
Nyerere	100	96	86
Kennedy	26	40	68
Kaunda	23	22	11
Nkrumah	15	26	28
Obote	15	6	5
Touré	6	13	11
Kenyatta	15	4	9
Kawawa	4	11	1
Nehru	4	11	10
Nasser	2	9	5
DeGaulle	6	6	4
Karume	2	7	1
Gandhi	2	7	15
Mao Tse-tung	2	6	4
Wilson	2	4	22
Khrushchev	2	2	6
Selassie	4	2	1
Kambona	0	2	4

minority which failed to include Nyerere's name among those admired. President Kennedy, interestingly enough, was the second most frequently named leader. Nkrumah, despite his overthrow a few months prior to this study, was still highly popular. Kaunda, the president of Zambia, was easily more popular than either Obote or Kenyatta, the leaders of Tanzania's two partners in the East African Common Market. Kenyatta, in particular, was a target of bitter remarks from a few M.P.'s who were disillusioned with his actions since Kenya's independence. No Tanzanian leader other than Nyerere was mentioned with any frequency. Kawawa and Karume, the two vice-presidents, were named by a few of the elite, while Kambona, the former secretary-general of TANU, was the Tanzanian leader mentioned second most often among students.

The most frequently mentioned qualities of leadership were strength, humility, ability, and correct political views (such as believing in country, peace, or nonalignment). Among legislators, humility was the commonest attribute cited, while administrators most frequently mentioned principles, convictions, and high ideals. Legislators more often based their views of leaders on their policies and political outlook, while administrators emphasized characteristics such as ability and firmness. The two qualities most often associated with Nyerere's name were humility and principle.

Nyerere was highly popular both among economic conservatives—those who felt things were changing too fast or who disapproved of the policy of economic equality as a realistic or desirable goal—and among strong socialists, who at times disapproved of government policy and felt that economic equality was not being achieved or that the government was moving too slowly. The few comments about other Tanzanian leaders praised (or occasionally condemned) them for their reputed policy views. One leader was admired because he "is the only true socialist in the cabinet." Another was mentioned because he "is not one of those who wants us to be Chinese." These lesser leaders seemed to be liked on the basis of their identification with important issues. This highlights Nyerere's position as a leader who stands above policy disputes. He was admired not because he necessarily shared the ideology of the particular elite member, but because it was felt he had a direct, down-to-earth approach to leadership and a strong, sometimes religious, commitment to acting on principle. As one administrator expressed this feeling, "Nyerere is someone you can trust to do the right thing." Support for Nyerere, which appeared nearly universal, constitutes an important unifying factor in Tanzanian politics. His leadership, however, has more than symbolic consequences. For example, potential cleavages among the elite on economic issues, such as were indicated by the responses on African socialism, were anticipated, perhaps resolved, by Nyerere's forceful leadership in promulgating the Arusha Declaration and quickly pushing its implementation.

A Citizen's Rights and Duties

The rights and duties of the citizen are an integral part of the reciprocal role relationships between the governed and the governors in a political system. In an effort to ascertain what ideas the elite held about the responsibilities of citizens and what rights they felt citizens deserved, respondents were asked to list the most important rights and duties of a "good or ideal citizen." Table 3.22 gives the percent of administrators, legislators, and students mentioning various types of duties and rights. Most frequently mentioned by the elite were government output functions, in terms either of services, such as education, or of police and legal

TABLE 3.22. Elite Views on a Citizen's Rights and Duties

	Percent Mentioning Each Right		
Rights	Administrators (N = 50)	Legislators (N = 54)	Students (N = 105)
1. Government services, especially education	24	35	3
2. Government protection and administration of justice	28	32	17
3. Civil liberties: speech, press, religion	28	17	62
4. Human rights—vague	12	13	15
5. Freedom of action—not harmful to others or as allowed by the state	14	8	6
6. Political liberties: vote, criticize, assemble	14	15	46
7. Economic liberties: own property or make profit	8	9	8
8. Career opportunities: choose job, advance	8	7	6
9. Freedom to move about	4	6	1
Duties			
1. Understand and participate in nation building	65	64	43
2. Loyalty to the nation	39	40	20
3. Defend country (physically)	8	4	22
4. Help neighbors, sacrifice for others	33	22	8
5. Be honest, responsible	8	4	7
6. Obey laws	31	29	33
7. Pay taxes	12	13	15
8. Fight corruption, cooperate against crime	4	4	5
9. Vote, exercise rights	6	15	9

protection, which guarantee justice for the community. In clear contrast to these emphases, students were most concerned with civil liberties, particularly freedom of speech and of the press. They also emphasized political liberties, such as the right to vote and to criticize the government. Political liberties were mentioned by less than 15 percent of the elite. Thus, a clear conflict emerges in defining the role of a citizen: the elite stresses obedient subjects and the students focus on active participation in the system.

The most important citizen duty, as seen by administrators, legislators, and students, was to understand nation building and be willing to participate in it. The term "nation building" (*jenga ya taifa*) was frequently used to connote the broad goal of modernizing society. The citizen was expected to share this goal and work actively toward it. Loyalty to the nation was the second most frequently mentioned duty; obeying the law, the third. The obligation to participate by joining the party, voting, or engaging in other political activity was frequently suggested only by the elite. Students infrequently mentioned these activities, probably because they did not think of them as "duties."

The obligations to participate and to be politically competent have been discussed as important citizen norms in democratic cultures.[50] In Tanzania, however, only a minority expects a citizen to exercise his political influence or to make demands on the government for his own benefit. The majority defines his duties in terms of responding to governmental outputs, such as speeches that explain development plans and the need for greater efforts by citizens. A typical role definition given by an administrator was: "A good citizen is one who contributes to the achievement of the targets of planned development knowing why he does so." A cabinet minister outlined the role in a more personal and direct form. For him the good citizen should "understand his responsibilities to his neighbors; not be tribal minded; and be prepared to accept the national decisions, whether it is to his own economic benefit or not. In return, he deserves equal opportunities and the necessary protection against ill-treatment."

Some answers to this question suggested a sense of frustration and distance in the elite-citizen relationship, particularly among administrators. It was felt that citizens failed to understand the complexities stemming from the country's poverty and the need for major development if modern standards of living were to be extended to more than a few. The lag in economic development in Tanzania compared with industrialized nations of the West had been observed at first hand by a majority of the elite. For them, poverty, disease, and ignorance were serious problems, indeed "enemies" against whom battle had to be waged. But this view of

---

50. See Almond and Verba, chaps. 7 and 8, and Robert E. Lane, "The Tense Citizen and the Casual Patriot: Role Confusion in American Politics," *Journal of Politics,* 27 (November 1965), 735–60. Lane finds that norms of participation, however, are generally avoided or excused. See pp. 742 ff.

the situation seems to have brought a sense of loneliness to some elite respondents, who felt their view was not understood or shared by the masses of citizens. A few examples from interviews may illustrate this point.

> The greatest need is for a citizen to understand his country's problems and contribute to their solution. But unfortunately, only a few do this. (A principal secretary)

> His greatest responsibility is to know what is expected of him by his country, to do the things for the sake of his country. But there are very few who do this. In every person there is an element of self-interest. What is needed is that one must understand his obligations. (Principal secretary)

> All of them should be as the president. That is, each should regard every problem of the country as their own problem—to feel the problem as the president does. (A regional commissioner)

In general, what occurs to members of the elite when asked about the responsibilities of an ideal citizen are not the qualities of civic competence and participation often associated with the role of citizen in modern democratic societies, but the obligation to participate and share in the tasks of nation building, not only through hard work and increased individual effort but by sharing with the elite the psychic burden of the problems and difficulties of national development. Thus, the citizen is expected to be an important participant in the political process, but largely on the output side, accepting and furthering government programs and nation-building projects. His role as a critic and voter is seldom mentioned, and his proclivity to assert self-interest is condemned.

These attitudes do not necessarily imply undemocratic practices or a desire to manipulate people. Certainly tendencies to minimize criticism are found in democratic cultures. But the impact of these attitudes, coupled with a possible latent authoritarianism, could undermine the strong surface commitment to democracy. The widespread agreement with statements of democratic ideals and the expression of support for democracy as a concept may not indicate that the political process in Tanzania is going to follow procedures that are truly democratic. Since disagreements over issues of economics and socialism were not related to demographic cleavages, including tribal differences, they may not represent a deep-lying threat to political unity or democracy. However, the elite political culture, which appears democratic and unified, does contain several latent characteristics that might under stress provide support for patterns of political procedures that were neither democratic nor stable.

4. The Role of the Administrator

Administrators are responsible for the government's operation. They supervise the work of the bureaucracy and implement policy decisions. The expectations that shape their role performance help determine the style of administration in the political system and the extent to which bureaucrats participate in the decision-making process. These expectations and the pattern of administrative role behavior are examined now and their implications for future trends in politics are discussed.

ADMINISTRATIVE TYPES

Apter has suggested that career patterns are a crucial element of role performance in the politics of modernization.[1] The two career or background variables most strongly related to attitude differences among Tanzanian administrators were education and career length. Dividing administrators into those who had a college education and those who did not, and those who entered the service in 1959 or later and those who entered prior to 1959, I created three categories of administrators. I chose these two dichotomies because of the demonstrated statistical influence of these background factors on attitudes and the historical significance of the cutting points. Nearly half the administrators had had a college education. 1959 was the first year when independence was clearly foreseen and the rapid recruitment of African administrators began.

Those with high education and short government service are labeled "Moderns"; those with low education and long service are called "Veterans." These two groups constitute 78 percent of the sample of administrators. A third group, those with high education and long tenure, is labeled "Technocrats." All but one of the administrators in this third group had college degrees in technical fields such as engineering or veterinary science, and they had reached their present posts only after service in technical fields. A fourth group, recent entrants with less than a college education, contained only four cases, each representing rather

1. David E. Apter, *The Politics of Modernization* (Chicago: University of Chicago Press, 1965), pp. 140–78.

different circumstances; they were not included in my subsequent analysis.[2]

What other features besides education and length of service characterized these three groups? Table 4.1 presents information on six demographic characteristics. Most Veterans were over 40 years old while Technocrats and Moderns were younger. A Protestant background, common to 61 percent of administrators, was slightly more prevalent among Veterans, but religious differences among the three groups were slight. Membership in one of the three economically progressive tribes—the Chagga, Haya, and Nyakusa—was unevenly distributed among the groups; seven out of eight Technocrats came from one of these tribal groups while only 13 out of 38 (about one third) of the other administrative types were from these tribes. High traditional status (grouping all those whose families had at least minimal traditional social importance) was characteristic of 55 percent of the Veterans contrasted with only 25 percent (two out of eight) of the Technocrats and 6 percent of the Moderns. Thus a Veteran not only had longer experience and less education, but also tended to come from a high-status traditional background. The Technocrat, on the other hand, was not as old or as likely to have traditional status, but he was more likely to be a member of one of the three economically advanced tribes. On a percentage basis, Technocrats had higher salaries and held more responsible positions than either of the other administrative types. Moderns were younger, and fewer of their number were members of the "progressive" tribal groups. A relatively large portion of the Moderns received salaries in the middle range. An equal number of them (five) compared with Veterans were principal secretaries. These differences represent other importannt background characteristics associated with and further delineating each administrative type.

Attitudes of the administrative types were examined according to where each group falls on the four attitude scales discussed in chapter 3. In table 4.2, each scale has been dichotomized into high and low scores and the percent of each group falling in these two categories is presented.

2. The four eliminated administrators were: two secondary school teachers, one young and one old, who joined the administration in 1961 and have only recently been appointed to the upper echelons; a former businessman with high traditional status who joined the administration in 1961; and a younger man who has risen rapidly through his work in a specialized area.

TABLE 4.1. Backgrounds of Administrative Types
(in percentages)

	Veterans (N = 22)	Technocrats (N = 8)	Moderns (N = 17)	Percent of Total (N = 51)
Age				
35 or under	9	25	71	35
36–40	27	25	23	28
41–45	41	37.5	0	24
46 or over	23	12.5	6	14

Veterans/Moderns X^2 = 18.9*

	Veterans	Technocrats	Moderns	Percent of Total
Religion				
Protestant	64	50	59	61
Catholic	18	37.5	29	24
Muslim	14	0	12	12
Tribe				
Chagga, Haya, Nyakusa	32	87.5	35	41
Others	64	12.5	65	57
Traditional Status				
High	54.5	25	6	31
Low	45.5	75	94	69

Total X^2 = 10.7*   Veterans/Moderns X^2 = 8.2*

	Veterans	Technocrats	Moderns	Percent of Total
Salary				
Below £1300	23	0	12	20
£1300–1900	41	25	41	37
Above £1900	36	75	47	43
Position				
Principal secretary	23	37.5	29	25
Commissioner, admin. sec.	23	25	35	27
Principal & sr. asst. sec.	54	37.5	35	47

* These chi-squares are significant at the p < .05 level. The chi-square test requires that expected frequencies be at least five for most cells. This requirement was not met in a number of cases where differences led to "significant" chi-squares. The only alternative, in order to use the test, would have been to collapse categories, which either would have alleviated the problem of cell size or allowed Fisher's Exact Test to be used. Since the distinctions had analytical significance I did not collapse categories. I have presented the tables with only those associated statistics that did not violate minimal cell size requirements, although collapsing would have solved this problem in a number of cases. Subsequent tables will continue to alert the reader to this qualification where appropriate. See Sidney Siegel, *Nonparametric Statistics for the Behavioral Sciences* (New York: McGraw-Hill, 1956), p. 178.

TABLE 4.2. Attitudes of Administrative Types
(in percentages)

	Veterans (N = 22)	Technocrats (N = 8)	Moderns (N = 17)	Percent of Total (N = 51)
Authoritarianism				
High	68	37.5	35	53
Low	32	62.5	65	47
	Veterans/Moderns $X^2 = 3.0*$			
Anomie				
High	68	37.5	18	51
Low	32	50	82	49
	Veterans/Moderns $X^2 = 7.9*$			
Faith in People				
High	55	37.5	82	65
Low	45	62.5	18	35
Democratic Practices				
High	36	37.5	76.5	55
Low	64	62.5	23.5	45
	Veterans/Moderns $X^2 = 4.7*$			

Note: Each scale has been dichotomized into as nearly equal proportions as possible for the entire 109 elite.

* These chi-squares (X^2) are significant at the $p < .05$ level.

The differences between some groups are striking. Moderns, for example, scored the highest on democratic practices and faith in people and the lowest in anomie and authoritarianism. Technocrats were only slightly more anomic or authoritarian, but they had the greatest lack of faith in people and the least acceptance of democratic practices. Veterans, who were most often from families with traditional status, scored the highest on anomie and authoritarianism, and a majority of them were in the lower half of the democratic practices scale.

The attitudes of administrative types on issues of economics and socialism are presented in table 4.3. On the question of economic equality, Technocrats were the most conservative in their views, 71 percent disagreeing that this was the government's prime objective. Among Veterans, a plurality agreed with this statement, but over a third were in disagreement. Sixty-five percent of the Moderns accepted the notion that economic equality was the government's overriding responsibility. Since Technocrats generally rejected the notion of economic equality, it might

TABLE 4.3. Economic Views of Administrative Types
(in percentages)

	Veterans (N = 22)	Technocrats (N = 8)	Moderns (N = 17)	Percent of Total (N = 51)[a]
Economic Equality				
Agree	46	12.5	65	43
Qualified agree	18	12.5	18	20
Disagree	36	62.5	18	35
Technocrats/Moderns $X^2 = 6.9$[b]				
Pace of Change				
Too fast	32	12.5	18	24
About right	59	25	71	57
Too slow	9	62.5	12	20
Veterans/Technocrats $X^2 = 9.4$[b] Technocrats/Moderns $X^2 = 7.1$[b]				
African Socialism as a Concept				
Misleading	9	12.5	29	16
Uncertain	36	37.5	41	35
Good expression	50	37.5	29	43
African Socialism Defined				
True socialism—Good thing	9	12.5	23	14
African tradition—Good thing	55	12.5	29	35
True socialism—Bad thing	9	12.5	17	12
African tradition—Bad thing	4	0	0	2

a. Missing data are indicated where percentages do not add to 100%.
b. These chi-squares (X^2) are significant at the $p < .05$ level, but do not fully meet the requirements for minimal cell frequencies; see note to table 4.1.

have been expected that they would have been content with the slow pace at which economic change was then occurring, including, presumably, the leveling of economic differences. However, it was the Technocrats who were *least satisfied* with the pace of change. They were not simply unsympathetic to the government's commitment to economic equality, an attitude that would have made them critical of government efforts; they were also interested in development and rapid change in Tanzania, and thus dissatisfied with the speed at which change was occurring. Veterans and Moderns, in contrast, seemed generally satisfied with the pace of change, although about a third of the Veterans felt that things were moving too fast.

The reactions of these administrators to African socialism are also revealing. Veterans and Technocrats were the least critical of African socialism as a term. This suggested that approval of African socialism might be negatively related among administrators to approval of the goal of economic equality, since these two groups showed the least support for this goal. A test of this hypothesis tends to confirm it (Gamma $= -.35$, which is significant at $p \leq .05$ with a one-tailed test).[3] Sixty-three percent of those who disliked the term or found it misleading were Moderns. Thus the greatest negative feelings about "African socialism" were expressed by Moderns, not by Veterans or Technocrats, who were most unhappy about the goal of economic equality. It is apparent that different interpretations underlie attitudes toward African socialism. The vagueness of the concept serves to conceal differences in economic attitudes and allows those who, like some Veterans and Technocrats, oppose policies of socialism—such as the promotion of economic equality—to appear united with others in support of "African socialism." This superficial and deceptive quality of the concept is the reason that many, especially Moderns, regarded it with distrust or uncertainty.[4]

The definitions given for African socialism further support this conclusion. Only 32 administrators gave classifiable definitions. Among these, however, two tendencies are clear. First, Veterans predominantly defined African socialism in traditional terms and, with this interpretation, supported it. The majority of Moderns whose responses were codable defined it as having continuity with Western or Eastern socialism, including such goals as the control of the means of production and a classless society. Seven, or 58 percent, of the Moderns gave this definition; of these, however, only four considered it a good thing.

Although few of these differences were statistically significant, some tendencies can be distinguished. Veterans were uncertain about their acceptance of economic equality, accepted the pace of change as either "about right" or "too fast," and looked with benign equanimity on African socialism. Technocrats seemed economically progressive but not committed to socialism. Moderns were the most socialist-minded and the most con-

3. Goodman and Kruskal's Gamma is a statistical measure of association appropriate for ordinal grouped data and has some properties similar to the correlation coefficient. See Leo A. Goodman and W. H. Kruskal, "Measures of Association for Cross-Classifications," *Journal of the American Statistical Association, 49* (December 1954), 732–64. The significance of the numerator S was tested using its normal approximation.

4. See Fred Burke's discussion of "Ujamaa," in Friedland and Rosberg, *African Socialism.*

tented with the pace of things; they appeared, thus, to be the administrators most likely to get along with the TANU regime.

The greatest reluctance to discuss overt political issues was found among
Veterans, who were also the most critical of politicians. One, for instance,
volunteered in response to a query about his views on African socialism:
"I'm very emotional on this subject. I'd better not say anything though;
I might get into trouble discussing my views." Some of the Veterans felt
ambivalent about their reserve on political issues; one, after being particularly cautious about stating his views, compensated by offering the
use of his desk and any files that I wanted. In the center of his desk
in capital letters was the following typed note:

1. BEWARE OF SPIES, LOVE, BAR GOSSIP
2. BEWARE, SPIES ARE EVERYWHERE
3. PERSONAL SECURITY COMES FIRST

Related to such alternating moods of revelation and withdrawal may
be lingering tensions felt by civil servants who carry the onus of their
prior connections with the colonial government. A number of administrators felt fear and insecurity with respect to politicians, though for only
a few did this seem acute.[5] One Modern expressed the feeling—a feeling
he recognized but did not particularly share himself—in a discussion on
the removal of the ban against civil servants joining the party:

> In the sense that Tanzania is a one-party state and will be for a long
> time to come, this is all right. And the result has been to create a lot
> of confidence among those who are civil servants. Politicians were
> under the impression that civil servants were holdovers from the
> old colonial regime; their ideas were suspected. Politicians were say
> ing, "We fought for the country and the civil servants didn't." It was
> a fact that civil servants were alienated, even though they fully sup
> ported the party as did all thinking people. Now civil servants are
> accepted. . . . Since the change, in fact, civil servants may be a real
> threat to the career of politicians. The problem is to try to allay
> their suspicions and overthrow the idea that civil servants didn't fight
> for the country's independence.

5. In a pretest interview among lower-level administrators in a course of study at the
university, one administrator vehemently refused to be interviewed and with trembling
hands explained that the political nature of my questions made it impossible for him to
cooperate, although few of his colleagues shared this opinion.

Most politicians would have agreed with this analysis of the situation though they might have argued that little tension ever existed between themselves and civil servants. Some, however, were unhappy with the strength of administrators. One member of the government, discussing the promotion of civil servants into TANU posts, responded:

> No, it's not a good thing. There has been no change in the civil servants. These people simply can't change their colors. They don't trust politicians and they feel our ideas are no good unless we have a B.A. or something.

ROLE EXPECTATIONS

Official Expectations

The administrator's role as officially defined encompasses three types of responsibility.[6] First, there is the inherited function of maintaining the administrative system and level of government services. Independence has added two new responsibilities: expanding government activity to modernize society and adjusting and transforming the political power of the administrative structure. The practices inherited at independence have had to be revised to meet requirements of TANU leaders. Administrators have been obliged to internalize development goals, to participate at least nominally in the party, and to relinquish authority in policy making to political superiors.[7]

Development as one of the new responsibilities of administrators requires an altering of attitudes. The administrator is expected not simply to maintain existing levels of government activity but to promote greater efforts toward economic and social improvement through the coordination, planning, and supervision of development activity and through the choice of priorities related to development demands. The administrator is exhorted to greater effort on behalf of development, and in turn is expected to direct others toward this goal. For example, in a 1966 speech circulated to civil servants, Joseph Namata, then head of the civil service and Presi-

6. This summary is based on several sources. One is an official statement of administrators' duties prepared by the Central Establishment Division, *Professional Careers Guidebook* (Dar es Salaam: Tanganyia Standard, 1965), p. 51.

7. The required party membership is an informal expectation, not a legal dictate, except in Zanzibar.

dent Nyerere's principal secretary, outlined "The Role of the Civil Service
in a One Party State."

> Here [in Tanzania] the civil servant is expected to be committed to
> development for the masses. . . . In our conditions, it is essential that
> good civil servants understand the politics of the country, the objec-
> tives of the party, and that they share the basic philosophy of the
> nation. . . . Once a policy decision has been made, and a particular
> project is adopted, the civil servant in the field can—with the con-
> currence and cooperation of his Area Commissioner—work directly
> with the people. . . . The civil servant can suggest that such meetings
> [of cell leaders] would be useful, they can brief their Party colleagues,
> and have it known that they are available for questioning.[8]

Thus, administrators are expected to act as conscious agents of national
development sharing "the basic philosophy of the nation."

The second new role responsibility, the acceptance of political (TANU)
control over government administration, increased tensions between politicians and administrators. In a number of cases, administrators have
been given orders by TANU leaders that required action exceeding their
authority or financial resources. These conflicts were resolved by restraining overzealous TANU leaders, clarifying chains of command, and transferring unresponsive administrators.[9] Prior to independence, administrators had been the effective policy makers. Despite a chain of command
from the colonial office and the governor in Dar es Salaam through senior
civil servants, provincial commissioners, and district commissioners to
field officers, the administrators were the real "politicians," the men who
ran things.[10] In fact, the telegraphic address of provincial administration
headquarters throughout the territory was simply "Political."

Although few Africans ever reached the highly political position of district commissioner, let alone provincial commissioner or permanent secretary, many with long experience in the colonial government were familiar
with and accepted the political role exercised by administrators. But since

8. J. A. Namata, "The Role of the Civil Service in a One-Party State," *Civil Service
Magazine*, No. 7 (July/August 1966), pp. 8, 12, 20.

9. See Tordoff, "Regional Administration," and Dryden, "Local Administration," passim.
Namata also points out that sometimes differences have occurred, and when serious "then
one or other person is moved to a different job." Namata, p. 12.

10. A description of the power of administrators in the pre-independence period is contained in Chidzero, *Tanganyika*, pp. 53–60.

independence the scope and prerogative of administrators' decision-making ability has been redefined. Control of the government by the party was emphasized repeatedly. Although administrators have been expected to play a "positive" political role, by joining and participating in local party affairs and by promoting "understanding" of development among the citizenry, there still must be a "distinction between the work of a senior civil servant and the politician. The decisions on policy *have to be made by ministers.*" [11]

The positive role expected of the administrator urges him to criticize policy alternatives, within the ministerial framework, and to promote new ideas for development. It is his duty to cooperate with the politician and to understand and share problems and goals, but equally to accept a subservient position. The political and development functions of administrators were summarized by Namata:

> The good Tanzanian civil servant thus recognizes two things; firstly that the Ministers and other political officers are responsible for policy, and secondly that his role is to help the politician to achieve the national objectives by the full use of his brains, training and experience.[12]

Administrators' Role Expectations

How do the "official" role expectations outlined by the head of the civil service compare with administrators' own expectations? Do administrators hold similar or different views of their role, and what might explain differences that exist?

Administrators were asked, "How would you describe your work? What are the most important things you have to do?" Responses varied widely, not only in content but in richness of elaboration and the number of tasks mentioned in each job description. Practically all administrators mentioned some facet of their immediate work responsibility and often tended to elaborate on some special problem or task with which they were confronted. Nearly one out of five mentioned financial difficulties and the problem of inadequate funding for the programs for which they were responsible. Three types of responsibilities, however, were mentioned by a third or more of the administrators: (1) maintenance or control of ad-

11. Namata, p. 12 (emphasis added).
12. Ibid.

ministrative programs; (2) handling of personal relations; and (3) participation in policy making. After an administrator had ruminated about his job and its responsibilities as fully as he cared to, he was asked, "Recalling the different tasks that you are responsible for in your work, what would you say is the most important aspect of your job?" Table 4.4 gives

TABLE 4.4. Role Definition of Administrative Types
(in percentages)

	Veterans (N = 22)	Technocrats (N = 8)	Moderns (N = 17)	Percent of Total (N = 51)
Most important role responsibility				
Administration	36	87.5	29	45
Policy making	59	12.5	35	41
Personal relations	5	0	35	14

Veterans/Moderns $X^2 = 6.3$*

* This chi-square (X^2) is significant at the $p < .05$ level.

the responses to this question. The three alternatives mentioned relate generally to the three aspects of role expectations we noted in the "official" role definition. Administration or control of program involves both the traditional maintenance of government responsibilities as established in pre-independence Tanzania and, at least for some, a concern with development activity. Participation in policy making refers to the political aspect of the administrator's role and suggests a continuation of the traditional broad decision-making autonomy enjoyed by colonial administrators. Personal relations, on the other hand, indicates among other things a concern for the adjustments and required reshaping of role boundaries between politicians and administrators and, among administrators, the coordination of organizational procedures. The responses indicated that each of the administrative types tended to emphasize a different role responsibility. Nearly all Technocrats mentioned administrative tasks or the operation of physical programs as their main responsibility. The Veterans, with their long experience in colonial administration, emphasized decision making and policy making. And Moderns, perhaps because they were more receptive to the political forces working to reshape the administrative role, mentioned personal relations more often than either of the other groups; six of the seven who mentioned this aspect of the administrator's role were Moderns.

A few actual responses to this question may make clearer the role conceptions held by persons in each category. A Technocrat, a principal secretary, described his job:

> I'm in charge of the ministry. My job is to make sure the government has enough [specific area of his responsibility] and that [his ministry's work] in the towns is carried out. I still go down to the second floor and check on plans. . . . I wish I had more time for it.

A typical Technocrat is interested in getting the job done, in improving government performance and development.

Many Veterans felt that decision making was the most important aspect of their role. One Veteran explained, "Everything I do is important, but I can put aside routine work for important items such as deciding." Not all Veterans emphasized decision making; some mentioned their administrative responsibilities and the need to maintain programs. One emphasized that he tried to see that his men "have better buildings, housing, and we need transportation, communications—some places it's 150 miles to the nearest phone." But decision making was emphasized by the majority. Many responded like the principal secretary who stated, "[my most important task] is to develop an idea and have it accepted."

Moderns emphasized almost equally each of the three role aspects. But, as we noted, of those citing personal relationships nearly all were Moderns. One respondent emphasized relations with other civil servants to promote "coordination within the ministry" and to "secure efficiency for any system," while another felt "keeping the good relations among the staff" was important in itself. The posts held by some Moderns brought them into contact with politicians more regularly than was true for most administrators. Two who had responsibilities of this sort mentioned relations with politicians and political groups as the most important aspect of their work. One who dealt with legislative work emphasized this, while another, in foreign affairs, stressed his role as a "guide, friend, and philosopher" in relations between Tanzanian politicians and foreign representatives.

Role Consensus

An important source of conflict and strain in the administrator's role stemmed from the tendency of administrators to continue to view themselves as policy makers and as politically autonomous in spite of the redefinition of their duties by the political leadership. To learn how members of the elite viewed the decision-making functions of the administrator, two projective role questions were asked of administrators (in open-ended interviews) and of legislators (on typed cards).

The first question was: "If you initiated a policy which resulted in unforeseen bad consequences and brought hardship to a number of people, what would you do?" This question specifically went beyond such acknowledged administrative functions as regulation of staff, approval of forms and applications, or action to solve a problem for an individual citizen,[13] to indicate that the situation involved a *policy* which the administrator had initiated and for which he was responsible.

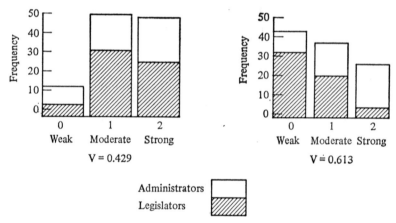

Figure 4.1. Distribution of Role Expectations for Administrators

Responses fell generally into three categories along a continuum from weak to strong. First, there were those who argued that once a policy had been laid down it could not be easily changed, or that it was not their duty or right to change policy. Such answers interpreted the administrator's

13. Unsystematic discussion with elite respondents made clear the general acceptance of these functions. In addition, a government brochure describing the administrators' officially sanctioned duties of this sort states: "Administrators organize and direct work of departments, including responsibility for the planning and accomplishment of the development plan for their departments. They consult with political heads of government and other government departments in matters of policy requiring definitions or decision, and make their own decisions where the policy so provides. They ensure that government policy is properly interpreted and applied by subordinates; consider officers for appointment; and build effective team operations through application of good management practices." *Professional Careers Guidebook*, p. 51.

role as a weak one with respect to policy making. Few gave this response, as figure 4.1 illustrates. Responses in the second category, which indicated moderate expectations for role assertiveness, implied that an administrator would report the negative policy effects and inquire into changes that might be made. He might even ask whether he could alter the policy or propose to his political superiors alternatives that might correct or alleviate the faults in the policy. As table 4.5 indicates, this response was the most prominent among Moderns and among legislators. A third type of response, most typical of Veterans and Technocrats, suggested rather strong action from an administrator, who was expected simply to change or abandon the policy.

Another problem in the transition of the administrator's role following independence has been his relationship with the party. It was not unusual, particularly after independence, for TANU officials to attempt to direct administrators even though they held no formal government positions. However, by 1966 such occurrences were infrequent. One Modern explained the situation this way: "This wouldn't happen. I suppose we had some trouble with this a while back, but it has been cleared up and lines of authority within the party and government were made clear to everyone." External evidence from several sources tended to confirm this judgment. However, clarifying lines of authority and restraining nongovernmental party officials from interfering with the administrative structure had not eliminated a residue of mistrust and hostility felt by at least some politicians and administrators toward each other.

Administrators were asked, "If a TANU official not holding a government post gave you an order, what would you do?" Responses to this question have been coded along a three-point continuum from weak to strong: (1) weak—accept the order; (2) moderate—equivocate, compromise, or attempt to adjust to the order; and (3) strong—refuse the order.

One Veteran seemed anxious to comply with a TANU leader's order. He replied: "If what the official asks is anything in my power, I will do it." Other administrators were much more reluctant to accede to an order. A Technocrat cautiously said: "With a knowledge of the constitution and of the party, I would investigate the order and tell him whether or not I will do it." The strong response was illustrated by the curt reply of a Modern: "I won't accept it. I am also a TANU member." Table 4.5 lists the percent of each administrative type falling into each of these three categories. It also

TABLE 4.5. Role Expectations of Administrative Types
(in percentages)

	Veterans	Technocrats	Moderns	Total Administrators	Legislators	Total Students	Students Approving
Responses to a bad policy:	(N = 21)	(N = 8)	(N = 17)	(N = 51)	(N = 56)	(N = 113)	(N = 64)
Can't act	14	12.5	18	10	7	19	59
See superior	29	25	47	45	54	38	90
Change it	57	62.5	35	44	39	43	85

Administrators/Legislators $X^2 = 3.7$ Elite/Students $X^2 = 47.7$*

	Veterans	Technocrats	Moderns	Total Administrators	Legislators	Total Students	Students Approving
Response to order by party official:	(N = 22)	(N = 8)	(N = 17)	(N = 51)	(N = 51)	(N = 111)	(N = 65)
Do it	32	12.5	18	40	54	7	71
Accommodate	32	25	35	35	35	6	100
Wouldn't do it	36	62.5	47	25	11	87	94

Administrators/Legislators $X^2 = 16.6$*   Elite/Students $X^2 = 14.1$*

* Significant at $p < .01$ level.

gives the responses for legislators and university students.[14] Technocrats' expectations were toward the strongest end of the continuum, Veterans formed the largest percent at the weakest end, and Moderns fell about midway between.

As figure 4.1 illustrates, only a small portion of legislators (11 percent) compared with administrators (41 percent) expected an order by a TANU official to be refused by an administrator. Equally striking is the contrast of elite with student expectations, 87 percent of the latter assuming that the administrators would reject the order. These results reflect a wide divergence of expectations and suggest that unresolved though probably latent role conflict existed between politicians and administrators with respect to the direct subservience of administrators to party directives. The answers to this question may reflect lingering tensions between some politicians and civil servants rather than merely the likely responses of administrators to a hypothetical and possibly remote situation.

The disagreements between legislators and administrators on the assertive behavior appropriate for administrators indicate weak consensus and a lack of congruence. Each group of elite respondents expected somewhat

14. These questions were given to legislators and students in written form. The students' responses were written on questionnaires; legislators' responses were verbally indicated choices among pre-coded alternatives, with the option of choosing an alternative not given. On the item concerning an administrator's reaction to a bad policy there are no large differences among responses of legislators, administrators, and students, although legislators are less likely to see administrators taking direct action (39% of the legislators compared with 50% of the administrators).

different behavior from administrators. Thus, consensus is greater among administrators and among legislators than it is among the elite as a whole. While the variance of responses did not indicate sharp conflict in expectations, a great deal of ambiguity was revealed.

Role Congruence

The emergence of normative patterns of role expectations, as discussed in chapter 2, is an important part of the political institutionalization process. Norms based on shared expectations serve not only to shape behavior but also to structure and thereby limit conflict. The distribution of scores among all elite on each of the administrative role strength items was transformed into standard scores (Z) in order to weight proportionately deviation from the mean response. The average of the absolute values of these two standardized item scores was used as a measure (C) of the congruence of an individual's role expectations. A similar calculation, based on the average for ten role expectation items (two are these administrative role items; the remaining eight refer to the roles of the legislator and president and are elaborated fully in subsequent chapters) was used as an overall measure (Average C) for the congruency of the expectations of each administrator with the elite sampled. This statistic, it may be recalled, measures the extent to which an individual's expectations conform to or deviate from mean expectations.

Since those with the most "moderate" responses received the highest C-scores for the administrator's role, it seemed possible that this measure was merely an artifact of my index construction. After all, those respondents who scored "high" in congruence were those who took a vacillating, or perhaps "balanced," position on these items. However, student responses tend to corroborate the view that responses closest to the mean were the most legitimate or accepted expectations in the political system. A portion of the students were asked after completion of their questionnaires to re-read each of their role expectation responses and to indicate whether the answer was in fact what they personally would do or approve. The percent of students who responded with a yes, or approval, for each particular response category is shown in table 4.5. These results indicate that the middle score, the one which in each case is closest to the mean for elite responses, was also considered legitimate or appropriate by the greatest proportion of students. Another counterargument to the possibility that the calculation for congruence is artificial is the fact that the continua on which it is based were created after the interviews were completed and are based on the discrete responses that emerged from the data. That is, "moderate" responses were uncovered by the analysis itself. The responses of a highly congruent Modern, a principal secretary, illustrate the "normative" expectations for administrators according to my analysis.

A BAD POLICY: First advise the minister why things have gone wrong. Then I would suggest laying out a paper before the cabinet. If the minister agrees, we could prepare one for moderating the policy.

A TANU OFFICIAL's ORDER: He can't give me an order. The machinery is well laid down. But he can request though, and I would see what could be done.

Expectations of the congruent individual, as determined by the pattern of expectations among the elite respondents, also agree with "official" role specifications. This indicates a congruency between different segments of the role process. The congruent administrator is willing to play a constructive but subordinate role in decision making and to be responsive to party requests, though expecting continued separation of party and administrative hierarchies.

The percent of each administrative type scoring high, medium, and low on administrative role congruence and on congruence for all role expectation items is given in table 4.6. Moderns are the most congruent, while

TABLE 4.6. Role Congruence of Administrative Types
(in percentages)

	Veterans (N = 22)	Techno- crats (N = 8)	Moderns (N = 17)	All Adminis- trators (N = 51)	Legis- lators (N = 58)	Total Elite (N = 108)
Administrative						
High	27	25	41	35	33	34
Medium	31	25	35	31	50	41
Low	41	50	24	33	17	25
Average						
High	18	12.5	53	34	33	34
Medium	41	50	29	36	36	35
Low	41	25	18	30	31	30

Veterans/Moderns $X^2 = 5.5^*$

* This chi-square is significant at $p < .10$.

Veterans and Technocrats tend to have low congruency scores. On congruency for the administrative role, Technocrats are the lowest, while for all items Veterans are the least congruent. The individual whose expectations are most congruent with those of other members of the elite is a Modern—younger, better educated, and probably more able to adjust to the changing role expectations fostered by political independence than those who are older and more conditioned by the colonial system.

Predicting Role Congruence

What characteristics among administrators are associated with role congruence, perhaps in a causal way? Possible explanations for congruence were sought in correlations of scores on individual role congruence with background and attitudinal variables. If a few indicators among these variables were related to congruent expectations, it might be possible, by examining the present trends in these variables, to speculate about whether to expect an increase or decrease in role congruence in Tanzania.

Correlations between a few background and attitude variables and two measures of congruence, administrators' congruence and average congruence, are presented in table 4.7. No correlation examined, including over

TABLE 4.7. Correlations of Backgrounds, Attitudes, and
Congruence Measures among Administrators
(N = 51)

1. Education							
2. Traditional status	−.25						
3. Career length	−**.50**	.18					
4. Democratic practices	.13	−**.38**	−.31				
5. Anomie	−.26	**.36**	.20	−.33			
6. Authoritarianism	−.21	.18	.23	−.09	.04		
7. Admin. congruence	−.16	−.09	−.09	.15	−.16	.01	
8. Average congruence	.09	−.02	−**.30**	.22	.03	−.01	**.50**

Note: Bold face correlations are significant at the .05 level.

25 not presented, appeared to be significantly related to administrators' role congruence. Position, an ordinal classification of administrators into three levels of job importance, shows some relation to administrative role congruence. When this congruence score is trichotomized (as in table 4.6) Goodman-Kruskal's Gamma is −.43, significant at the .05 level. This seems to indicate that the higher an official's position, the less congruent his ex-

pectations. However, controlling for the effects of education and tenure in the civil service by examining the relationship among Moderns and among Veterans suggests that this association is spurious, for among Veterans Gamma $= -.55$ and among Moderns Gamma $= .02$. Thus Veterans, trained under British tutelage, emerge as the real source of deviation and possible role strain. Correlations with average congruence yield several moderate correlations, only one of which is statistically significant. Career length has a correlation of $-.30$ with average congruence, again in line with the general finding that Veterans and Technocrats are less consensual. Thus those used to the old system are more likely to hold expectations incongruent with the consensus developing in a new system.[15]

CASE HISTORIES

Most of the relationships between administrative types and background, attitudinal, and role expectation variables are imperfect. Administrators are complex people; they are not adequately described by one or another summary statement or a few tables. No administrator categorized into one of the three types exhibited all of the dominant tendencies associated with that type. Experience in the colonial government, for instance, seems to have affected men differently. The ideas and values of British superiors were internalized in varying degrees, and there is no way to differentiate administrators according to the extent to and direction in which the colonial experience affected their attitudes, values, or outlook. Moreover, there is a whole range of personal and family experiences that could not be explored sufficiently with each respondent to allow an analysis of the effect of these aspects of an administrator's life upon his role expectations or his outlook on politics.[16]

A selection from the case histories of each type of administrator will

15. Notable though statistically insignificant correlations were also obtained in a positive direction with newspaper reading ($r = .27$), belief in democratic practices ($r = .22$), and attendance at Tabora ($r = .23$), while negative correlations were found between age ($r = -.21$) and tribe ($r = -.21$). The negative correlation with tribe suggests that those from the three most economically advanced tribes had somewhat more deviant expectations. However, the nature of this deviation was not consistent, in terms of interpreting the role in a stronger or weaker fashion than the "norm," as further analysis revealed.

16. In his study of political ideology in Eastport, Lane was able to relate these broader, at times more salient, life habits, routines, and relationships to the pattern of political attitudes of his respondents. But his respondents were lower-class individuals who were willing to talk in the presence of a tape recorder for a total of fifteen hours. See Lane, *Political Ideology*.

illustrate this diversity, the complexity of interaction between attitudes, backgrounds, and expectations, and the dominant qualities associated with each type. Each case history selected contains both dominant features of its type and variations on them. For instance, one of the two Veterans whose profile follows had quite weak views on administrative role strength, while most Veterans held strong expectations.

Fictitious names and the omission of easily identifiable characteristics such as birth date are used to preserve anonymity. The decile for each person on nine different measures precedes each case history, giving an idea of the relative standing of each administrator. Three of the measures, expectations about how strong the president's role should be and the congruence of the respondent's expectations for the roles of the M.P. and the president, are described in chapters 5 and 6.

Mr. Fundi: A Technocrat

AUTHRN	ANOMIE	FAITH IN PEOPLE	DEM. PRACT.	PRES. ROLE STRENGTH
5th	9th	8th	2nd	9th

ADM. CONGRUENCE	MP CONGRUENCE	PRES. CONGRUENCE	AVERAGE CONGRUENCE
9th	7th	3rd	6th

The most important aspect of his work, according to Mr. Fundi, is "to get the job done at the right time. That's what's most difficult and most important. . . . I enjoy seeing something get done and to look back and say that it is mine."

Mr. Fundi was born in a small town at the edge of an urban area. His father, a mechanic, originally wanted him to be a priest in the Lutheran Church. After Fundi ran away from boarding school and refused to return, his father gave up that notion. Although he recalls that "Daddy was sort of a terror," it was his father's work that aroused his interest in a technical field. As an industrious auto repair man, Fundi's father was able to make him feel "better than ordinary" as a youngster. "I had all the money I needed—I even had shoes before anyone else." Fundi did well in school—"I was never below second"—and recalls that "my studies were easy so that I had a lot of time for football." He went through Standard XII at Tabora and then to an overseas school, where he received a technical degree. After returning, Fundi moved rapidly toward the top of his ministry, aided perhaps by the fact that he was "the only citizen" among the upper-level staff in his ministry.

Fundi rises every morning about five o'clock to hear the morning news on the BBC. His wife, the daughter of a chief in their area and a former schoolteacher, looks after their seven children. He regularly reads the local English papers: "The *Standard* and a bit of the *Nationalist,* but none of the others." He finds he does not have much free time; when there is some he usually spends it at home, reading a technical book or maybe "a bit of a novel at bedtime."

In spite of his comparatively high salary and good position, Fundi is not sure that his life is much better than his parents'. "Financially better? Well, in number of shillings, yes. But father often sends us money." How does he do it? "He must have more." Did he feel that his present life was happier? "Perhaps. But I have too much to worry about—too many things I need." His uncertainty about the advantages of his life, however, is not reflected in his score on anomie.

In defining his work, Fundi nowhere mentioned decision making, dealing with other administrators, or working with politicians. For him, it is "the government that lays out policy." Although Fundi stated that he unofficially joined TANU in 1955 (his father was a local officer), his responses to role expectation questions indicated that he saw a strong or at least autonomous role for the administrator. In this view he is deviant (as reflected in his role congruence score above). He responded to the question, "What would you do if a party official not in the government gave you an order?": "Kick him out; I've kicked out many of them." And what if a policy went wrong? "I'd change it; I've changed many."

Fundi's views on economics and politics also separate him from other administrators. When asked about leaders he admired he replied, "I'd better think about it. I may be out of line with others and don't think I'd better comment." He was then asked, "Well, how about Nyerere?" and he responded, "Yes, he's one, but he's not at the top of my list." On economic questions Fundi expressed these views: "If I work for a house, then I have a right to it. The rights of possessing are mine. Not just a piece of paper, but property rights." On economic equality: "Never. If you start two people out equally, pretty soon one will be up and the other down." He rejects economic equality and would like faster progress. "It's fast, but we've got to catch up." Fundi supported democracy, scored high on the democratic practices scale, and accepted the one-party idea as "O.K.; if ideas are not imposed on people it's the only solution for a developing country, but you need the right to speak. If I were asked to keep quiet for the sake of keeping quiet, then life would be meaningless." But the idea of African socialism did not strike a responsive chord in Fundi. "What is it? I don't like empty slogans. I know politicians use empty words like this."

Fundi gave the impression of a man of action. His desk was cluttered with papers and his answers came unhesitatingly. But I also had the impression that Fundi would be happier working on projects of national development than handling the administrative affairs for which he was then responsible. He did not seem cynical about Tanzanian politics and supported civil servants joining TANU—"as long as there's no more than one party"—but his attitudes and answers on economic and social issues indicated disagreement with the slogans and some of the policies of TANU. As long as politics did not interfer with his job or eliminate the democratic practices that he strongly supported Fundi seemed prepared to be a loyal and dedicated servant of the government, and probably one of the most hard working.

Mr. Ndizi: A Veteran

AUTHRN	ANOMIE	FAITH IN PEOPLE	DEM. PRACT.	PRES. ROLE STRENGTH
1st	2nd	1st	10th	1st

ADM. CONGRUENCE	MP CONGRUENCE	PRES. CONGRUENCE	AVERAGE CONGRUENCE
10th	1st	10th	8th

Looking over a foot-high stack of folders marked confidential, Mr. Ndizi explained that he was one of the few children in his area to go to school. "People in my part of the country were not much interested in education; they feared it would undermine our Muslim faith." His teachers were "elderly Germans" who were "very harsh and demanded discipline. . . . I never disagreed with a teacher, and was one of the very disciplined students." His father, who sent him to school, was a prominent figure in their small village. He ran a small shop that employed several people. Many villagers, and "even the colonial government consulted my father," Ndizi recalls.

After finishing secondary school he joined the government service. For a decade and a half he slowly worked his way up the ranks of his particular ministry until, at the time of independence, he held an administrative rank. Ndizi described his current job as "advising the minister, giving the administrative point of view. And, of course, administering in the ministry, controlling the staff and finances." He was not in accord with the majority of Veterans who emphasized decision making or policy making. Asked what he would do if a policy he had initiated resulted in unforeseen bad circumstances Ndizi replied: "We are no policy makers. Politicians make policy and it is our duty to see that it is carried out. Therefore, my duty as a civil servant is to carry it out whether I like it or not."

He joined TANU reluctantly when it became legal because it "allows us not to fear politicians." He hoped to remain a civil servant: "I have reached the top and have no desire to be a politician." It was alternatively "the political world" or "civilization" that created the uncertain conditions of modern life that he felt existed. He viewed the administrator's role as weak, and attributed great authority to the role of president. His expectations included for example, that an M.P. "in a one-party state must agree with the president." He felt that leaders should always be obeyed because "this is essential with our African socialism. Once you obey a leader you are automatically obeying the government." And he approved of laws which "prevent disagreement."

With such attitudes, it is not surprising that he was unsure that democracy is the best form of government for Tanzania. In any event, he stated, "it is wrong to say that in a country like this we have democracy in any real sense. Democracy is very difficult to achieve. We have invented democracy so that, like religious differences, democracy differs from country to country. If you compare Great Britain and the United States, there are differences which are due to the country itself." He doubted that equal treatment of citizens is a part of democracy or "if it is, it is never practiced." Ndizi's distrust of democracy was further reflected in his doubts about the capabilities of citizens, most of whom he felt were not competent to choose good leaders. He did not have much faith in the press either, remarking at one point, "I only know what I read in the papers and one can't trust what goes into papers."

Ndizi's views are fairly consistent. His background and work in the colonial administration provide some explanation of his high score on authoritarianism and weak support for democratic practices. Ndizi was not cynical about democracy in Tanzania; his past socialization had simply not led him to place a high value on democracy, and he felt, therefore, no pressure to defend his rather undemocratic description of current political practices.

Mr. Masafi: A Veteran

AUTHRN	ANOMIE	FAITH IN PEOPLE	DEM. PRACT.	PRES. ROLE STRENGTH
1st	6th	6th	6th	2nd

ADM. CONGRUENCE	MP CONGRUENCE	PRES. CONGRUENCE	AVERAGE CONGRUENCE
3rd	2nd	10th	9th

Mr. Masafi had won the respect, if not the admiration, of all his colleagues. He was, as he aptly described himself, "a no nonsense civil servant." "If someone rings me up and asks a silly question, I give them a foolish answer right back. People think twice before they call me."

Masafi was among those with the highest possible score on authoritarianism. If he could answer a question yes or no, he did so. He clearly admitted that he had no philosophy of office—"I don't have time to think about things like that." When asked how he would describe his job, his initial reaction was that the interviewer should read the government directory. Answers as to how civil servants might be expected to behave could all be found in the *General Orders,* a body of codes and rules that prescribes lines of authority for the civil service. He described these *General Orders* as his "Bible." After some reluctance, however, he did discuss his work. His description emphasized administrative duties and his satisfaction in decision making. "I am in constant consultation, and therefore I do have a policy influence." Asked, "To whom are you responsible?" Masafi answered, "I don't think I'm responsible to anyone. Well, of course, there is [the civil servant above him] and the minister."

Masafi took a strong and aggressive view of his role, even on politically sensitive matters. He responded to the question about a TANU official's order by saying, "I won't do it; I'm no fool." His scores on role congruence are near the bottom. A further indication of Masafi's outlook is his scores on faith in people and democratic practices, both of which were in the lower half of the scales.

With these attitudes, what were Masafi's feelings about political questions? For him the good citizen was one who "does his work, pays his taxes, and causes little trouble." He did not want citizens who would rock the boat or be participants. For him, democracy was not a set of rules or rights.

I have studied [this question of democracy], but I'm not a politician. My own definition is that it is the feeling of the individual, the way the mind feels—if you feel the country is going properly, then it's democratic; if not, then it's something else.

Democracy ought to ensure equal treatment for people, he felt, but it is not necessarily the best form of government for Tanzania.

What experiences produced an administrator of this sort? Although Masafi refused to talk about his childhood, he described his father as a "very strict" man who made all the family decisions. He went to school at Tabora at a time when discipline was extremely stern. He never questioned a teacher or he "would have been expelled." After leaving Tabora, he joined the civil service as a clerk, and during World War II served in the army, becoming a noncommissioned officer. Returning after the war to the civil service, he had held half a dozen posts. The British selected him for a year's training in Britain and eventually he was promoted to the administrative cadre, where he helped manage the affairs of several districts prior to his assignment in Dar es Salaam. Masafi has few friends in the civil service and spends most of his free time with his family. For him, duty, discipline, and hard work are the keys to success. He likes no political leader because "People are people and not fit subjects for liking."

The coldness and correctness of his work relations with Englishmen, built on his background of a strict and authoritarian home life and school experience, produced this tough-minded administrator. It is doubtful the British he worked with were as rigid or authoritarian as he felt, but his contact was always limited to formal occasions. He was viewed by one English colleague with respect—an African who "gets a bloody lot of work done" and is not afraid to make decisions or take responsibility. He certainly had a reputation as a tough administrator. As Masafi said, "When I make a decision, it is the right one. After I make a decision, I never look back at it, never change it."

In spite of his authoritarian attitudes, his feelings toward democracy were not completely unfavorable. He seemed pulled in two directions. On the one hand, his British training taught him that democracy was right. Indeed he personally liked the idea of treating people equally, applying rules to everyone without "exception or favor." But on the other hand, a benevolent dictator might more easily fit his image of the desirable form of authority, a person who, like himself, would "love all, trust a few, and do harm to none."

Mr. Wazania: A Modern

AUTHRN	ANOMIE	FAITH IN PEOPLE	DEM. PRACT.	PRES. ROLE STRENGTH
10th	9th	2nd	2nd	6th

ADM. CONGRUENCE	MP CONGRUENCE	PRES. CONGRUENCE	AVERAGE CONGRUENCE
6th	4th	1st	2nd

Self-sacrifice and determination to be a "progressive" were two dominant themes that characterized Wazania's career. Born in a small village of 50 to 60 families, Wazania was the oldest of eight children. He was a sensitive child, reacting strongly to the needs, fears, and angers of those about him. To him, his father was a "hero." A transitional in a village of traditionals, his father was "very much respected by all the villagers." He worked as a driver; this took him away long distances, and when he returned he brought with him stories of the outside world, of "breakdowns and animal hunts and other excitement." In Wazania's eyes his father was "a progressive," with a "good temperament" and a quiet-spoken manner, and as a youngster he wished to emulate his father. "When I was very young I first thought of becoming a driver." But his career ideas changed as he advanced in school. "As I grew older, I thought of becoming a clerk, but this was ridiculed by my teachers," who saw ever larger responsibilities in store for him.

His sensitive character also emerged as he related his childhood experiences. For instance, he recalled with lingering guilt an incident when he carelessly struck his niece with a *panga* (machete). In school, he volunteered to stand punishment for one of his classmates. At thirteen he left home for boarding school where he recalls there was "a lot of praying." He continued to the university, where he was a popular student and was elected to offices in several organizations.

After several years' work in Dar es Salaam, he began a course of advanced study in a technical area. He soon felt that this new study was a waste of time so, traveling by bus and train across Africa, he arrived in newly independent Ghana. He considered attending the university there, but the belief that a really good education could be obtained only in Britain drove him on to London, where he arrived impoverished. After appeals home to the government and his father brought no money, he determinedly set out to work and study on his own. A year later, the Tanganyika government agreed to support his study and eventually he completed a degree. Since then he has held several posts in the government, including a period as temporary head of a ministry.

Wazania is a strong supporter of democratic practices. He is also a socialist. His interests in reading reflect a protean spirit and include works on "the theory of politics, capitalism, Marxism, and African socialism." His ideas are important to him, and he remarked at the close of the interview that he might someday like to "write them all down." He views himself as an agent of nation building and expects others to share his involvement in the national tasks. A good citizen, he stated,

> should be able to keep himself informed about what the state does so he can evaluate the essentials in any policy; he should cooperate with the government in the achievement of the essentials of the nation . . . and he should be able to stand his ground when the government is not doing the right things.

In discussing democracy, Wazania suggested four criteria by which the democratic nature of a country could be judged: (1) Do people like it; (2) can the people influence its actions; (3) can people change it without the use of force; and (4) is it based on neither color nor creed? To his mind, Tanzania easily met these tests.

Wazania was slender, athletically built, and quite articulate. His openness and enthusiasm set him apart from many of his successful colleagues, particularly those who were Veterans. Most civil servants are politicized in one fashion or another and Wazania was no exception, but his involvement was more in the realm of ideas than of policy making. It was his ideas that made him particularly interesting. For example, he volunteered the view that all civil servants in the upper salary brackets should take a voluntary salary cut, since their earnings were so much greater than those of the average Tanzanian. Six months later, with rather strong urging from the president, civil servants did just this. Wazania's ideas about socialism stressed the good of the community above that of the individual. But he was not doctrinaire, since he saw a role for both "public ownership" and "private enterprise." If one were to seek a spokesman among civil servants to articulate the official government position, at least as it stood at the time of the interview, Wazania would have been an outstanding candidate.

Mr. Masomo: A Modern

AUTHRN	ANOMIE	FAITH IN PEOPLE	DEM. PRACT.	PRES. ROLE STRENGTH
8th	4th	2nd	2nd	3rd

ADM. CONGRUENCE	MP CONGRUENCE	PRES. CONGRUENCE	AVERAGE CONGRUENCE
4th	3rd	4th	3rd

Mr. Masomo stared past scurrying messengers toward the harbor. Carefully he answered the question about democracy.

> The best men in history have thought about this idea. Personally, I think Lincoln's definition is the best, but history accommodates different people's ideas about this. You see, democracy reduces the area of acute disagreement in a society to manageable size. That's the beauty of it . . . and it is the best form of government anywhere.

Masomo was one of the few Tanzanians with a graduate degree. His career in the government had kept him in close contact with leading politicians. When he spoke there was authority in his voice. There were few major decisions since independence which he had not known about or participated in; some day he hoped to write a book about the first five years of independence. At the time he held a high position in the civil service in which "contributing to decisions is a real source of satisfaction." There was an air of confidence in his remarks. When asked about changes in Tanzania that might make it difficult to tell what was going to happen, he replied, "I can't relate this to Tanzania. I see myself as a player in a world chessboard."

Life may have seemed difficult to Masomo as a youngster walking seven miles to a Moravian mission school each day, but he remembered it as a "very happy childhood." His father, an average farmer, was like "what I am now—I became like him." His classmates at Tabora included a number of prominent politicians. His background and interests reflect a blend of politics and civil service experience that explains his interest in problems of institution building. The style of British colonial administration had little fascination for him. "What we need now are development administrators, not law and order men." In discussing qualities of leadership he quickly related these to the nation-building theme.

> We are building a nation from scratch, therefore we can build on our own good qualities. The president has integrity: he is not susceptible

to corruption. He supports the rule of law, he is firm in dealing with others, and he is not pompous—he is a man of the people. These are the qualities we want to build into our national life.

He supported the general political aims of TANU and considered himself a socialist who "doesn't like the word African added to the label. Socialism is the same in every country. But there is a Tanzanian way of getting at things, of having a revolution."

Masomo was seriously grappling with the problems his country faces, and he had little tolerance for those who could not or did not appreciate these problems. As he put it, "I don't suffer fools gladly." It is the citizen's duty to understand the country's problems, but alas, "only a few do this." Masomo felt that "most voters don't use their votes wisely, but voters should have the right to choose." He was something of an elitist, but his scale scores indicated neither authoritarian nor antidemocratic attitudes. I sensed in Masomo a strong will to see Tanzania develop. The priority of this goal shaped his rather outspoken views on politics and the kind of leadership needed among both politicians and administrators.

EMERGING NORMS

On the basis of the interview material and the analysis of role consensus and congruence it is possible to formulate a few emerging rules or norms that govern the political involvement of administrators. These reflect the normative expectations among elite and are expressed as formal "rules" although they are, in fact, only incipient norms which I believe are emerging.

RULE 1. An administrator must join the political party.

Every administrator who was asked (41 of those interviewed) stated that he was a member of TANU. All but two felt that membership by civil servants was a good thing. The administrator most opposed responded:

I didn't like having one party; I think there's a need for two. One party to which everyone belongs is not a party. If everyone in a country belongs then it isn't really a party. However, even if there is one party and you have civil servants in it, this is a problem. You're supposed to execute policy. I don't see how they can execute policy and at the same time make policy.

I then asked, "I suppose you haven't joined the party then?" and received the reply: "Oh yes, I joined right away in 1964. My card is right here in this drawer, let me show you." Opposition to civil servants' party membership, therefore, cannot be considered serious, although lower-level administrators have not joined in the 100 percent fashion of the elite interviewed.[17] Moreover, membership is often nominal, for only one of the administrators interviewed was active in local party affairs. These facts, however, do not vitiate the obligation to join the party at least formally.

RULE 2. An administrator must be sympathetic toward national party goals.

This is an official expectation with which a majority of administrators seemed to agree. A number felt that joining the party made their allegiance clear. Only a minority expressed sentiments that seemed to deviate from party ideals or goals and these deviations were primarily on economic issues, not questions of democracy or one-party rule.

RULE 3. An administrator must express his sympathy by: (a) placing development foremost in his priorities; (b) accommodating party officials and attempting to work with them.

Fairly direct evidence for this rule was found in the pattern of expectations concerning a party official's order. Only a minority of administrators would be uncooperative with the official and a majority of legislators expected an administrator to carry out an order. Less direct evidence of administrators' concern with development came from responses to a question about future changes in Tanzania; 96 percent were optimistic about development progress and 58 percent cited progress in agriculture, roads, or construction as important accomplishments. Thirty percent mentioned education and the rest stressed improved social relations in the future. Thus the reorientation from a "law and order" bureaucratic perspective to a development-oriented outlook seemed well under way.

RULE 4. An administrator must defer to political superiors in all policy matters.

17. Interviews outside of Dar es Salaam at regional centers indicated that a high proportion, but far less than 100%, of civil servants have formal party membership. On this point, see Bienen, *Tanzania*.

Elite responses to the first contingency role situation, "official" expectations, and the additional comments of a number of administrators strongly suggested this rule. Precedents and norms determining exactly what constitutes policy, however, were not clear. Moreover, it is possible for administrators to participate in the policy-making process. One example, involving the Local Government Elections Law of 1966, will illustrate this point. This legislation was based on White Paper No. 1 (1966), a document reflecting the results of a dialogue between party officials and administrators. The *One-Party Report* in 1965 had initially urged that the district TANU chairman be made, ex-officio, the head of local government and members of the TANU district executive automatically be appointed district councilors.[18] This recommendation was resisted by ministry officials in regional administration who felt that many TANU chairmen were too busy or too inefficient to act as responsible chairmen of local government. Making the chairmanship largely an honorary post, with an "executive vice-chairman," was a counterproposal put forward by the ministry and supported by both the urban and rural local government associations. Informal meetings, including two seminars at Kivukoni College—the TANU School—in March and April 1966, revealed some important differences between TANU and the ministry. Intensive talks between a group of high-level administrators and an appointed group from the National Executive of TANU (the NEC) were held at Lushoto in mid-April 1966, and compromises were reached. One was that the election for the joint post of chairman of the local government council and TANU district chairman would be held at the TANU district conference in which publicly elected council members would participate;[19] another compromise abandoned the idea that TANU district executive committee members should be ex-officio members of local councils.

This is but a single instance of the various ways in which administrators help make policy. In addition, high-level administrators attend NEC meetings and have been asked to defend their policies there. The interim constitution even provides that two administrators, the attorney-general and the president's principal secretary, be ex-officio NEC members. Though subordinated, administrators are not absent from policy-making.

18. *One-Party State Report*, pp. 24–26.
19. See ibid. and *Proposals of the Tanzanian Government on Local Government Councils,* Government Paper No. 1-1966 (Dar es Salaam: Government Printer, 1966), passim, esp. p. 2.

The institutionalization of these rules for administrative role behavior cannot be considered strong, as the V-scores indicated weak consensus. The tensions between the politicians who have assumed power in Tanzania and the administrators—particularly the Veterans and Technocrats who are more easily identified with the colonial regime—heighten not only role strain, the existence of which was indicated by conflicting expectations among various administrators, but also feelings of anomie or cynicism toward politics and democracy. These feelings were most prevalent among the Veterans and Technocrats, as we have seen earlier. Thus the differences among administrative types help explain some of the variations in their role expectations. Personnel changes among administrators in future years should increase the number of men who share "Modern" characteristics. It seems likely, therefore, that congruent role expectation among administrators will increase and that tensions between politicians and civil servants will decline. At least at the upper levels of the civil service, administrators have the power to bargain with politicians over the specifics of policy. In addition, a number of administrators have been appointed to "political" posts, such as regional commissioner and party executive secretary. This has opened career lines across the party and bureaucratic structure. If this trend and the bargaining power of administrators continue, acceptance of the "official" administrator's role and consensus on the obligations and limitations of this role may be expected to increase. Such expectations for administrative behavior, already widely shared among the elite and consonant with the existing style of politics, are likely to produce greater allegiance among administrators to the political system.

5. The Role of the Legislator

The study of politics in developing countries has tended to focus on the less formal organs of government, such as political parties, the military, the bureaucracy, and even the educational system.[1] National legislatures have often been ignored or rated of little significance in the political process of these states.[2] This practice contrasts markedly with the attention paid to legislatures in Western states. The most obvious explanation is that legislatures in new states usually have little influence. Important decisions and shifts in power are likely to be made or recorded elsewhere in the political system.

The *Bunge* or National Assembly of Tanzania is no exception to this. Nevertheless, an examination of the role of M.P.'s in Tanzania can be illuminating. Nearly all the major political leaders in Tanzania are members of the National Assembly; as *wabunge,* or legislators, they have the formal authority to make all laws. With the concurrence of the president, they exercise sovereignty. Although, as noted in chapter 1, the Assembly is not the major policy-making forum, the fact that some of its members have real power and that it has at least "public" authority makes it an important gauge for politics in Tanzania. I hope to show that the norms that govern role behavior for M.P.'s provide insights not only into the functions of the Bunge but also into the elite political culture of Tanzania and the "closed" pattern of politics which this culture supports.

THE LEGISLATIVE ARENA

Though originally modeled on the British parliamentary system, the National Assembly has never evidenced a similar pattern of legislative function. The most important reason is that no significant opposition organized along party lines has ever existed in the National Assembly. From the first elections in 1958–59, a de facto situation of one-party

1. See for example the six volumes edited by the Social Science Research Council's Committee on Comparative Politics (published by Princeton University Press, 1963–66) and Huntington, *Political Order in Changing Societies.*
2. One exception to this trend is Frey's *The Turkish Political Elite.*

dominance has existed. Initially, that is, before the formal establishment of a one-party state, legislation and other matters were discussed prior to the meetings of Parliament at closed sessions of the TANU Parliamentary Party (TPP). Since all members of the National Assembly were in the TPP, these closed meetings were often the real legislative forum.[3] On occasion, embarrassing questions were raised and critical speeches made during Assembly meetings, perhaps because party discipline was never felt to be at stake. Particularly in the first year, criticism and serious debate occurred regularly, but usually no more than a few legislators ever openly disagreed with the government on any particular issue. As a consequence, President Nyerere and others felt that the National Assembly was not providing the public forum for debate and discussion appropriate to their conception of democracy. In 1965, following the introduction of the one-party state, the TPP was dissolved. Sensitive issues, however, are still discussed privately with legislators. More significantly, the government has not relinquished completely the notion of party discipline. For example, in October 1966, after the Assembly had voted down a proposed loan from the Treasury to the government-supported Tanganyika National Transport Cooperative, President Nyerere cut short an up-country visit and returned to Dar es Salaam in order to resubmit the estimate to the Assembly; yielding to pressure, it reversed itself and approved the loan.[4] Similarly, a supplementary estimate to meet the expenses of the purchase in 1964 of Mercedes-Benz automobiles for regional commissioners and ministries was initially voted down in December 1966. The pattern of discussion and debate in the Assembly has varied over the years, reflecting changes in the mood of the nation, the coherence of the party, and the composition of the Assembly (particularly following the 1965 elections).

The most public and readily discernible behavior of legislators is their performance in the National Assembly. Although their informal discussions, committee meetings (which are private), tours of their districts, meetings with constituents, and collaborations with members of the government are all important aspects of legislators' behavior, Assembly speeches are the only aspect of role behavior readily susceptible to systematic study. Assembly voting is recorded only following a call for a

---

3. One member, Chief Masanja, resigned from TANU to join the ANC in 1962. But this exception has proved unimportant.

4. See *The Nationalist*, September 29–October 7, 1966.

division, and only one division—on a trivial matter—was called in the first five years of independence. Voting behavior, consequently, is not a fruitful field for research.

Therefore, to examine the role of legislators within the Assembly and to document the trends that have occurred in their collective behavior, a content analysis of debates was made. Speeches for five one-year periods beginning with October 1961 (just prior to independence) and ending with the June budget session in 1966 were coded. Each period ends with a budget session, the longest and most important meeting. All speeches in the 1961–62 and 1965–66 periods were coded; approximately 50 percent of the speeches in the intervening three years were coded. In all, 15,421 speeches were analyzed. Each speech was coded according to five characteristics: subject, national or local orientation, position (support, opposition, or neutrality), language, and length.[5] Since many short speeches were quick questions and answers and therefore different in quality from longer, more substantial contributions, speeches were also weighted for length, with short speeches eliminated and long ones counted twice. Patterns among all speeches and speeches weighted for length were calculated. These results document the trends in Assembly debate since independence and provide a measure for the behavior of each M.P.[6]

Trends in Behavior

One striking trend is the introduction of "national" traditions. The quaintly irrelevant powdered wigs, found (1966) in the Kenya and Uganda legislatures, were discarded in Tanzania in 1962. The Speaker, Chief Adam Sapi, adopted a traditional costume which he wore as chief or sultan of the Hehe. Western business suits have generally been abandoned in favor of more functional attiture known as "national dress," which

5. Twenty-eight different subject categories, many related to ministerial divisions such as agriculture or education, were used in coding subjects. Orientation was either national or local. A speech could fall in one of four positions: supportive (of the government's position), critical, neutral (if the speech was balanced or there was no official government position), and question-answer. This last category was used for many of the short questions and answers expressing and responding to demands or problems, usually local, raised by back-benchers. The language was Swahili or English (or in a few instances, mixed). Three length categories were used: short (0 to 1½ minutes), medium (1½ to 7 minutes), and long (more than 7 minutes). The coding procedures and tests for reliability are reported in app. E.

6. A more detailed explanation of the procedures used, along with some additional results, will be found in app. E.

consists of a collarless shirt often worn with matching slacks. More important than these changes in dress has been the introduction of the national language, Swahili. Figure 5.1 charts the conversion of debates from

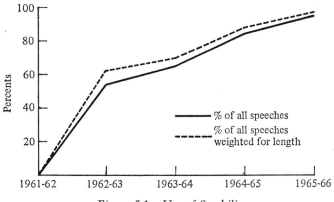

Figure 5.1. Use of Swahili

English, originally the only official language, to Swahili, which became an additional official language in 1962. The use of Swahili allowed many less well-educated legislators to become articulate and express their feelings in an idiom familiar not only to themselves but also to the vast majority of Tanzanians.

A second trend is the decline of speeches dealing with national issues. At the time of independence a vast amount of legislation was placed before the Assembly; major legislation on agriculture, education, local government elections, taxes, citizenship, and the new republican constitution was discussed and passed by the Assembly in the first year of independence. Ninety-six government bills were passed, 44 based on certificates of emergency which allowed the requirements for prior publication to be waived.[7] In the midst of these efforts, little time was left for discussions related to local or regional problems. Few questions were raised about such issues as digging new wells or the improvement of roads. But as the pace of legislation slackened, discussion of local issues increased. Figure 5.2 illustrates the steady decline in speeches devoted to national issues. While the large majority of speeches were still nationally oriented in 1966, there had been a fairly steady decline in the percent of speeches

7. See William Tordoff, "Parliament in Tanzania," *Journal of Commonwealth Political Studies, 3* (July 1965).

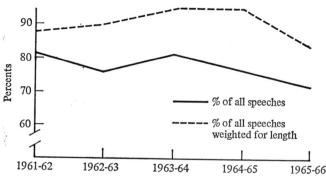

Figure 5.2. Discussion of National Issues

on national issues except for a slight upswing in 1963–64, possibly explained by a renewal of national concerns following the army mutiny in January 1964 and the union with Zanzibar in April 1964.

The way a legislator publicly brings pressure on the government for improvements in his locality is usually to ask questions in the Assembly about the government's intentions concerning a particular problem. A typical question might be: "What are the government's plans to tarmac the road between Dodoma and Morogoro?" or "Will the government build an extension to the overcrowded dispensary in Tukuyu?" These questions and responses constitute a dialogue reflecting persistent and important, though not explosive, demands by constituency representatives attempting to bring the problems of their constituencies to the government's attention and to secure whatever relief or development funds may be available. Competition among legislators for the relatively small amount of government revenue available for the improvement of services and infrastructure has not resulted in open conflicts between representatives of various regions or constituencies, but rivalries of this sort are endemic and occasionally surface. In the June–July 1966 Assembly session, for instance, the minister of education, a member from the Kilimanjaro area, was sharply questioned by several members anxious to have greater educational allocations for their areas. The minister was asked to explain why there were so many schools in the region of his constituency. A member from the minister's region came quickly to his defense, condemned the criticism, and argued that most of the schools in the Kilimanjaro region reflected the efforts of local citizenry or church missions rather than favoritism from the Ministry of Education.[8] Nevertheless, resentments about uneven development are important latent elements in the continual prodding by legislators in the Assembly.

Figure 5.3 illustrates the trend of legislators' demands. It can be seen that these have increased sharply since independence, from 23 percent to

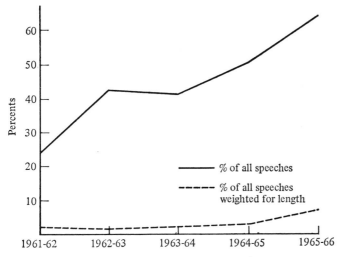

Figure 5.3. Non-Neutral Questions and Answers

nearly 64 percent of total individual speeches. This change reflects clearly the changing nature of the legislative arena. Although, when weighted for length, these non-neutral questions and answers constitute quite a small proportion of Assembly debate, this merely illustrates that the vast majority of these "demand" questions and answers are brief exchanges between legislators and members of the government. Assembly members are often given short, even cryptic, replies. However, since supplementary questions frequently follow a minister's response to the written question, it is not uncommon for a minister and a small number of legislators to engage in a ten- or fifteen-minute series of interchanges, officially in the form of questions and answers, but in fact representing a dialogue and reflecting as much public criticism as can be found in the government. The increases both in local orientation and in these demand-type dialogues

8. See also *Assembly Debates,* February 22–28, 1966, Cols. 115–42 and 169–247.

are important indicators of the role M.P.'s are playing in communicating local problems and dissatisfactions to the government.

Coincident with the rise in demand questions has been a decline in supportive speeches. Speeches whose overall character was to support stated government positions comprised over 30 percent of the total speeches given in 1961–62, but only 12 percent in the 1965–66 Assembly. A more accurate index of the relative proportion of supportive speeches is seen in the weighted index, which removes short speeches (figure 5.4). In this

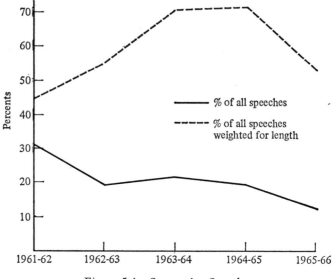

Figure 5.4.   Supportive Speeches

measure there was a general increase in government support from 1961 until 1965, followed by a marked decline after the 1965 elections. This latter pattern in supportive speeches is exactly reversed by the pattern for critical speeches (figure 5.5). Criticism of government policies was frequent, particularly among long speeches, in the early debates of the Assembly. It dropped steadily after independence and by the 1963–64 session it reached a nadir. Assembly debates, although never marked by an active or systematic opposition, were characterized during this period by an absence of criticism that made sessions largely ceremonial and, as one member described them, "rather boring."

It is apparent from the careers of those M.P.'s who were most critical

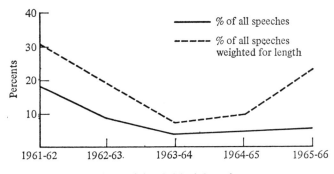

Figure 5.5. Critical Speeches

that no member should become identified with a pattern of opposition. During the first two years of independence only a few members gave critical speeches 50 percent or more of the time. None has since. Those who did included Tumbo and Mkello, labor leaders who were subsequently placed in detention; Masanja, never a serious influence in the Assembly, who defected to the African National Congress (a minuscule opposition party) and has since retired from politics; and Siyovelwa and Mbogo, who, though loyal TANU members, did not stand for reelection. Both were appointed area commissioners, but Mbogo was later removed and imprisoned for theft. Thus none of those who were clearly and consistently critical or who opposed the government in the first five years survived as a popular politician or M.P. Comparatively frequent criticism by an M.P. is often an indication of political ambition. For example, three M.P.'s who were initially quite critical—Mtaki, Wambura, and Mponji— were made junior ministers and regularly entrusted with defending the government.[9] In 1966 all expressed satisfaction with their careers and hoped to continue in their positions.[10] Two Englishmen, Short and LeMaitre, were also frequent critics; both lost their seats in 1962 because they were not citizens.

In the new and expanded Bunge, elected in 1965, discussions became considerably livelier. About every fourth or fifth speaker in the new Assembly who made a lengthy contribution was critical of the government. However, over twice as many speeches were supportive. On balance, the legislative arena is still a forum in which the government's ideas and

9. Mtaki, however, retired from politics in 1967 to enter private business.

10. Another frequent critic, Buhatwa, was also made a junior minister but he lost in the 1965 elections and became an administrator in the Ministry of Housing.

proposals are usually praised or defended and criticism is not systematic, let alone organized. Moreover, among those M.P.'s who were most critical according to the analysis of speeches in the 1965–66 period, by December 1968 nine had lost their Assembly seats for political reasons, either by virtue of having been expelled from the party or because of political detention or exile.[11] Mwakitwange, who in July 1968 accused the government of "tribalism," "nepotism," and slowing the pace of Africanization, was expelled from the party three months later.[12] Anangisye, former secretary of the TANU Youth League, and Masha, who had been national publicity secretary for TANU, were also expelled.

In addition to the enlarged and more critical membership of the Assembly since October 1965, other structural changes have occurred. The committee system has been revised and extended. The number of formal readings through which a bill must pass has been reduced from three to two, and the committee stage has been altered to allow committees a more important voice in the process of legislative approval. The number of standing committees has been increased from two to six, and committees have been empowered to review legislation presented to the Assembly.[13] These changes, however, have not greatly altered legislative practices; no strong committees or committee chairmen have emerged. Three of the members interviewed were committee chairmen, elected by fellow legislators who had been assigned by the Speaker to a particular committee. None was particularly aggressive or saw the committee as his most important legislative task. Two of the chairmen left organization of committee meetings largely to the discretion of staff members of the Assembly. A third chairman was somewhat more assertive in organizing topics of discussion in meetings of his committee. He was reluctant, however, to use

11. See note 82, chap. 1. Kambona was not an Assembly critic, but in private he was often highly critical.

12. See *The Nationalist*, July 11, 1968, and December 10, 1968, p. 1.

13. The six committees are: political affairs, finance and economics, general purposes, social services, public accounts, and standing orders. The last two committees, which have been retained from the original organization, are at present the most powerful. The standing orders committee is responsible for the rules governing the procedures of the Assembly and their interpretation, though the day-to-day responsibility for this rests with the Speaker. The public accounts committee reviews the expenditures of the government and hears reports from the auditor-general. The work of this committee was taken very seriously by the government, and its meetings were the most lengthy. Under its chairman, Dr. Sterling, a national member, activities of the accounts committee were comparatively thorough and exacting.

his role as chairman to develop a pattern of activity inconsistent with practices, or lack of practices, prevalent among other committees. In spite of this caution, his assertiveness most likely contributed to his party expulsion and loss of Assembly membership in 1968. Thus, the committee system of the legislature cannot be considered an important or integral function of the legislative process in Tanzania. While a greater use of committees for examining and discussing legislation and greater specialization of legislators into specific policy areas and subroles is a real possibility, such changes do not seem to be occurring now.

Subject Dimensions

In order to explore the interest of legislators in various subjects, a factor analysis was made of the percentage contributions of individual M.P.'s to each of 28 subject areas. This was completed for National Assembly debates in the 1965–66 period. The results of this factor analysis may be found in appendix E. In table 5.1, seven interpretable dimensions from the analysis are presented. Subjects with high "loadings," above .50, in the analysis are shown along with the percent of variance explained by each factor and the percent that the high-loading subjects contributed to the total debate. This latter figure indicates the amount of Assembly attention devoted to each factor and is the best indicator of the relative importance of each of these dimensions. Names for these dimensions were derived by seeking a common quality among the high-loading variables.

The first factor or dimension of Assembly debates was labeled *Security-Sovereignty*. The high-loading subjects on this factor, such as foreign policy, military, constitutional, party, and national unity issues, indicate a common interest among some portion of Assembly members in this group of issues. The percentage of Assembly debate taken up by these issues declined somewhat after the first year of independence. The legislators' scores on this factor (N = 165) are correlated with their percent of supportive speeches (r = .68). The correlation with critical speeches was .01, although among legislators interviewed, it was .27.[14] Speeches were nationally oriented more often than on any other dimension.[15] In

14. This was the only large difference between correlations in the sample and correlations in the Assembly. Quiet government supporters, "Silent Partners" as we shall call them, contributed heavily to this dimension but were underrepresented in the sample, which accounts for this difference. See page 155 below.

15. For example, the percentage of national speeches was correlated r = .27 with this dimension among those interviewed.

TABLE 5.1. Dimensions of Tanzanian Assembly Debate in 1965–66

		1965–66 (vs. 1961–62) Percent of Assembly Speeches			
	Loading	Total	National	Supportive	Critical
I. Security-Sovereignty					
Law and the courts	.93	1.5 (6.0)	87 (90)	9 (36)	8 (19)
Foreign policy—external	.92	0.7 (1.0)	100 (100)	26 (23)	0 (32)
Refugees	.89	0.1 (0.5)	67 (96)	0 (29)	0 (4)
Foreign policy—Tanzanian	.86	1.5 (2.2)	98 (100)	39 (39)	0 (22)
Military	.85	0.7 (0.9)	100 (83)	76 (40)	0 (28)
Constitution	.84	0.2 (2.0)	100 (100)	27 (46)	9 (26)
Procedural matters	.82	11.3 (11.4)	100 (99)	1 (9)	1 (3)
TANU-ASP	.78	0.5 (0.5)	100 (100)	56 (33)	0 (29)
Labor and unions	.76	2.9 (2.9)	92 (91)	25 (40)	11 (13)
National unity	.71	0.4 (0.9)	100 (100)	60 (29)	0 (37)
% of variance explained = 27.8		% of total speeches = 19.8			
II. Cultural image					
Community development	.92	1.8 (1.2)	85 (76)	8 (44)	0 (19)
Youth and culture	.82	0.8 (1.2)	81 (95)	12 (24)	8 (24)
Praise	.56	0.2 (0.9)	90 (95)	0 (24)	0 (2)
% of variance explained = 6.8		% of total speeches = 2.8			
III. Rural development					
Water and land resources	.85	4.3 (6.3)	56 (63)	15 (27)	5 (19)
Agriculture	.82	7.0 (3.8)	43 (59)	6 (27)	2 (19)
% of variance explained = 5.1		% of total speeches = 11.3			
IV. Administrative performance					
Housing	−.84	2.5 (1.5)	63 (75)	12 (33)	10 (17)
Civil service, Administration	−.78	8.7 (10.0)	73 (92)	17 (30)	9 (26)
Elections	−.54	0.4 (0.8)	100 (94)	50 (33)	12 (33)
% of variance explained = 6.4		% of total speeches = 11.6			
V. Economic management					
Development planning	−.89	2.0 (0.4)	80 (53)	53 (24)	9 (41)
Finances	−.82	8.4 (9.6)	96 (95)	12 (35)	8 (18)
% of variance explained = 5.6		% of total speeches = 10.4			
VI. Infrastructure development					
Industries, Utilities	.81	5.9 (3.4)	34 (52)	3 (26)	5 (22)
Roads, Railroads, Harbors	.71	9.2 (6.2)	36 (45)	7 (28)	5 (21)
% of variance explained = 4.8		% of total speeches = 16.1			
VII. Socialist progress					
Cooperatives, Commerce	−.82	10.2 (3.3)	79 (77)	15 (27)	8 (21)
African socialism	−.72	0.1 (0.3)	100 (100)	50 (13)	0 (27)
% of variance explained = 4.8		% of total speeches = 10.3			

contrast to the 1961–62 session, criticism had sharply declined, while the percent of speeches in support of government positions had increased or remained high on most subjects. Seven out of the ten subjects on which speeches were relatively supportive (25 percent or more) loaded highly on this factor. Military, national unity, and political party activity were supported in over 50 percent of the speeches on these subjects. This apparently reflected a security consciousness among many legislators who were particularly aware of the coups in Ghana and Nigeria which had occurred earlier in 1966. The security and sovereignty of the nation, therefore, were the most prominent subjects discussed in the Assembly and among the most sensitive.

The second dimension of Assembly debate clustered areas pertinent to the image created by individuals or the government and was labeled *Cultural Image*. The three high-loading variables suggest that adult education, improved farming, and household skills (discussed under community development) were common concerns of legislators. These interests related youth and culture, which included government programs to train youth through organizations such as the TANU Youth League and the National Service, with the modernization of traditional cultural artifacts—such as dance and the creation of Swahili literature. Debates were marked by speeches of praise, usually for individual contributions or national projects. This cluster of subjects, however, received relatively little attention in Assembly debates—less than 3 percent. Government officials, in particular, gave few speeches on these subjects.

The third dimension was *Rural Development*, encompassing discussions on water and land resources and agriculture. Both criticism and support in these subject areas had decreased since independence. These subjects had a relatively high local orientation in the earlier session, an orientation which, as evidenced by legislators' speeches, increased. Frequency of speaking correlates with the factor scores on this dimension $(r = .44)$.

The fourth issue dimension was labeled *Administrative Performance*. It combined underlying interest in housing, elections, and administration. Housing is a particularly sensitive topic, since it includes allocation of government housing and office space to civil servants and setting priorities for housing projects throughout the country. Elections are also a government function, planned, directed, and administered under the supervision of a special commission chaired by the Speaker of the National Assembly. Civil service and administration, the third high-loading subject, is a direct government function and received the most speaking attention on this dimension. It included discussions on the localization of the civil service and an important dialogue, initiated by President Nyerere's brother Joseph in February 1966, on the relocation of the government from Dar es Salaam to Dodoma. This dimension of administrative performance was rather controversial. Discussion on high-loading subjects drew both more supportive and more critical speeches than the average. The correlation of critical speeches with this dimension is $r = .47$, which indicates that those who spoke often on this topic also gave a large number of critical speeches in the Assembly.

The fifth dimension, *Economic Management,* accounted for slightly over 10 percent of the total debate in the Assembly, principally on the subjects of development planning and finance. A relatively high proportion of speeches given on this topic were nationally oriented, and it was more often than the average a topic in long and in critical speeches.

Infrastructure Development was the sixth dimension of Assembly debate. Over 16 percent of all speeches were given on subjects loading highly on this dimension. These included discussions of industries, utilities, roads, railways, and harbors. Speeches were notably local-oriented. The percentage of national orientation correlated, $r = -.34$, with legislators' factor scores on this dimension. Members from constituencies without government offices were the most frequent speakers in debate related to this dimension.

The last dimension presented is *Socialist Progress.* This label reflects the common interest in the Assembly on topics of African socialism, cooperatives, and commerce. Implementation of socialism rests heavily on the cooperative movement, of which Tanzania's is the largest in Africa. Producer cooperatives were particularly the target of criticism throughout the 1965–66 sessions and were in part responsible for the establishment of a presidential commission to investigate the cooperative movement. The most frequent criticism among legislators was not the high incidence of corruption found among cooperative officials but rather the low prices that farmers felt the cooperatives were offering. This latter problem proved most intractable for the government since, although it was responsible for local prices, it could act only as a partial buffer between the farmer and the decline in world prices for his produce. Interest in the subject of cooperatives rose sharply, as indicated in table 5.1, from 3.3 percent of Assembly speeches in 1961–62 to 10.2 percent in 1965–66. Although the relative percent of criticism declined, the total criticism directed toward this subject in the Bunge increased from 4 to 15 percent. This reflected a growing concern not only about the functioning of the cooperative movement but about the implementation of socialism. Those who spoke most often on this dimension, as indicated by their factor scores, also tended to have high percentages for lengthier speeches ($r = .41$) and critical speeches ($r = .30$). These correlations suggest that this dimension was one of the most lively and controversial in the Assembly and was of particular concern to the most articulate, or at least verbose, members.

The seven dimensions of Assembly debate accounted for 61 percent of the variance among the 28 coded subject categories, and the high-loading subjects on these seven dimensions accounted for 82 percent of all speeches in the Assembly. Three other factors may be found in table E.6, indicating a unique pattern of discussion on the individual subjects of health, police, and education.

The pattern of speeches in the 1965–66 Assembly revealed that criticism and support were not evenly distributed. For instance, on many of the 28 subjects into which speeches were categorized, not a single critical speech was given. The most heavily criticized legislative topics, in about 10 percent of the speeches, were elections, housing, and labor unions. At the opposite end, military policy received no criticism and was supported by 76 percent of the speeches on the subject; this is in marked contrast to the first year of independence when only 40 percent of the speeches supported military policy and 28 percent were critical. Other areas in which over 50 percent of the speeches given were supportive of the government position were: national unity, party, development planning, elections, African socialism, and foreign policy. On none of these issues, with the exception of elections and development planning, was there a single critical speech, although some were sensitive and controversial areas of opinion among the elite, as the interviews revealed. The lack of criticism in these areas reflects pressures, not organized by any individual or even by the party, but rather generated by latent political norms that dictated that delicate and controversial subjects were either best avoided or commented upon only in a constructive manner. Investigation of legislative role expectations, discussed below, tend to confirm this proposition.

The analysis of Assembly behavior indicates that while M.P.'s have adopted national dress and speech, thereby making the Bunge more effective as an indigenous institution, the role of the M.P. in preparing legislation is minor. Seldom is legislation altered by committee or Assembly action. While criticism of the government increased after the 1965 elections, it tended not to be directed toward critical or sensitive matters. As we have already observed, those M.P.'s who have been noticeably or consistently critical have frequently had their political careers shortened.

LEGISLATIVE TYPES

By analyzing the sample carefully, it was possible to divide legislators into groups based on differences in career length, mode of selection, and the special obligations of those in government posts. These differences, supplemented by several others, were employed to distinguish four legislative types. The types were created by a method of elimination; after a set of common characteristics established one group, the remaining legislators were examined for further possible distinctions.

Fifteen of the 58 M.P.'s interviewed held positions as ministers, junior ministers, or regional commissioners and had already begun their political careers prior to 1958. Because of the long political involvement of this group and their relative success I have labeled them "Politicos." All but one served in the first Parliament of independent Tanzania from 1960 to 1965.

The 43 other legislators interviewed fell largely into three groups— "Locals," "Intellectuals," and "Silent Partners." "Intellectuals" were better educated, more widely read, more interested in politics as a profession and career, and seemed more intellectually involved with questions of national policy. Nine legislators met these criteria.[16] Of the remaining 33 legislators in the sample, 26 were constituency representatives. Twenty-five were categorized as "Locals." [17] Locals represented a constituency, were often from the majority tribe of their area, and most were born in their constituency. Six of the remaining seven legislators, three of whom were

16. The term "Intellectual" is applied with the same general connotation as suggested by Edward Shils in "The Intellectual in the Political Development of New States," *World Politics, 12* (April 1960), 329–68. Legislators with college degrees or post-secondary education and who read widely were selected as Intellectuals. One M.P. with a college degree was excluded from this typology because he did not fit the basic characteristics of either "Intellectuals" or "Locals." He did not represent a constituency, had not given a single speech in the National Assembly, and had no interest in a political career. His work, in fact, often kept him out of the country.

17. The 26th, The Deputy Speaker, is the only nongovernmental member in the sample serving his second term. He was excluded from the typology.

government members with short careers, were labeled "Silent Partners." *All* were appointed rather than elected to the Assembly. Their experience in the Assembly and in TANU (though not necessarily Zanzibar) politics was short, and one may conveniently think of them as quiet (for, as will appear shortly, they seldom spoke) supporters of the government, hence the title "Silent Partners." If more Zanzibaris had been sampled this group would have been larger.[18]

Table 5.2 contains basic background information on these legislative types. Education, amount and kind of newspaper reading, type of membership, career length, and position in the government, all of which varied considerably among the groups, illustrate the distinctions used in defining the four types of legislators. Since Politicos and Intellectuals were better educated and read more widely, they were much alike except for the distinction of government membership. National politics was a career commitment for individuals in both groups. The greatest portion of their life activity was taken up with public matters, particularly meeting the public, talking and dealing with them. In contrast, Locals spent more time in home constituencies, often traveling and speaking with their fellow citizens or tending farms or businesses. Many Locals, while active in politics, were also occupied with some other employment prior to their election for the first time in 1965, and continued to do limited work in their original occupations. Silent Partners had no established constituencies. Outside the Assembly their efforts were largely administrative, either as agents of the government or as party officers. Most Locals were born in their constituencies while many Politicos were born outside their constituencies and were not members of the major or majority tribe. Locals also tended to have won their seats by a narrower margin than either Intellectuals or Politicos.

Attitudes of Legislative Types

The percentage of each legislative type scoring high and low on four attitude dimensions is shown in table 5.3. Intellectuals were nonauthoritarian, particularly in contrast to Locals. They also tended to be low on anomie and high on faith in people. Since democratic practices was correlated with education it was expected that Intellectuals would score

18. The seventh legislator remaining, a national member, did not fit this or any other category.

TABLE 5.2. Backgrounds of Legislative Types
(in percentages)

	Intellectuals (N = 9)	Locals (N = 25)	Silent Partners (N = 6)	Politicos (N = 15)	All M.P.'s Interviewed (N = 58)
Age					
35 or under	44	48	17	13	34
36–40	11	16	0	33	19
41–45	11	24	17	47	28
46 or over	33	12	67	7	19
Religion					
Protestant	44	44	50	47	45
Catholic	44	20	0	27	24
Muslim	11	24	50	27	26
Education					
Less than secondary school	0	64	50	27	41
Secondary school	0	20	33	20	19
Post-secondary	56	16	0	20	21
College or better	44	0	17	33	19
Terms served					
One	100	96	67	7	67
One & part of second	0	4	33	0	5
Two	0	0	0	93	28

Locals/Politicos X^2 = 35.9

Career length					
Began political activity					
1958 or before	44	20	50	100	47
After 1958	56	80	50	0	53

Locals/Politicos X^2 = 20.9

Type of membership					
Elected	67	100	0	60	71
National member	33	0	0	0	9
Nominated	0	0	17	7	3
Zanzibar—appointed	0	0	33	0	3
Zanzibar—Rev. Council	0	0	17	0	2
Regional commissioner	0	0	33	33	12
Member of government					
Yes	0	0	50	100	31
No	100	100	50	0	69
Party position					
NEC	11	4	50*	47	21
Party office or job	22	48	0	53	38
Just member	67	48	0	0	36

Locals/Politicos X^2 = 15.8

Note: These chi-squares are significant at the $p < .01$ level. In most cases the N was too small to meet the standard requirements of an expected frequency of five in each cell for the X^2 test. Rather than collapse cell categories I have kept distinctions which had analytical importance, as was done in chap. 4.

* Two of three members from Zanzibar had high posts in the ASP equivalent to NEC positions; if these three Zanzibaris are included the column reads: 83, 0, 17.

TABLE 5.3. Attitudes of Legislative Types
(in percentages)

	Intellectuals (N = 9)	Locals (N = 25)	Silent Partners (N = 6)	Politicos (N = 15)	Total (N = 58)
Authoritarianism					
High	33	92	50	53	67
Low	67	8	33	47	31

Intellectuals/Locals $X^2 = 9.6$ Locals/Politicos $X^2 = 5.9*$

	Intellectuals	Locals	Silent Partners	Politicos	Total
Anomie					
High	44	80	67	47	64
Low	56	20	17	53	34
Faith in people					
High	67	32	50	67	48
Low	33	68	33	33	50
Democratic practices					
High	44	36	50	47	47
Low	57	64	33	53	53

* These chi-squares are significant at the $p < .05$ level.

noticeably higher on this scale. However, they frequently rejected democratic practices. Distrust of democracy among the best-educated Intellectuals marks them, therefore, as prominent deviants.

Locals tended to be more authoritarian, anomic, and have lower faith in people than other legislators. Their attitudes toward democratic practices, however, differed little from the distribution of high and low scores among the entire elite. Silent Partners did not differ importantly.

Economic Views

The responses of the various legislative types toward questions about economic issues are reported in table 5.4. Intellectuals and Politicos were least satisfied with the rate of change; relatively large numbers in these groups favored either slower or faster change. Silent Partners were fully satisfied with the rate of change, and most Locals were also satisfied. With regard to economic equality, only among the Silent Partners was there a majority who agreed that "Above all else, government must create economic equality among people." Individuals in each group qualified their agreement. Intellectuals expressed the most disagreement with this view.

Moreover, not one of the Intellectuals expressed satisfaction with

TABLE 5.4. Economic Views of Legislative Types
(in percentages)

	Intel-lectuals (N = 9)	Locals (N = 25)	Silent Partners (N = 6)	Politicos (N = 15)	All M.P.'s Interviewed (N = 58)
Economic equality as the most important govt. objective					
Agree	33	44	67	33	41
Qualified agree	22	32	17	40	33
Disagree	44	20	17	27	26
Pace of change					
Too fast	11	20	0	20	16
About right	44	72	100	47	66
Too slow	33	8	0	33	17
African socialism as a concept					
Misleading	89	4	17	20	22
Uncertain	11	36	17	33	28
Good expression	0	32	33	47	33
African socialism defined					
True socialism—Good thing	56	8	0	47	26
African tradition—Good	0	64	33	27	38
True socialism—Bad thing	33	0	0	7	7
African tradition—Bad	11	4	0	7	7

Locals/Politicos $X^2 = 10.2$*

Note: Percentages that do not add to 100 indicate that some respondents did not answer.
* This chi-square is significant at the $p < .05$ level.

African socialism as a concept; eight out of nine disliked it. In contrast, the other three groups indicated ambivalent support for the idea. Forty-seven percent of the Politicos, a third of the Silent Partners, and 32 percent of the Locals felt the term was a useful, helpful, or clear expression.

The evident distaste among Intellectuals for African socialism is reflected in the different emphases with which they defined the term. Five out of nine defined it as true or scientific socialism and viewed this as a positive or desirable goal; three interpreted it similarly but evaluated it negatively. Only one Intellectual understood African socialism as an outgrowth of traditional African practice, and he opposed such a policy.

Locals, in sharp distinction to Intellectuals, tended to hold the view that African tradition was the basis for socialism and they looked favorably on the idea. Only two of the six Silent Partners elaborated their views on African socialism—largely an indication of their unwillingness to assert themselves on ideological matters. They expressed views similar to those held by most Locals. Definitions among Politicos varied widely but were closest to those held by Intellectuals. A majority (eight) defined African socialism as scientific or true socialism and, of these, seven supported this definition or saw it as a good thing. Four others accepted the contrasting view that African socialism is based on tradition and accepted this as a good policy. Only two Politicos expressed unhappiness or dissatisfaction with African socialism.

These economic attitudes among legislators further indicate the similarity between Intellictuals and Politicos. Controversial attitudes and sentiments of dissatisfaction were expressed most often by individuals in these two groups. Similar in several respects, they differ largely in that Politicos are the successful holders of high government posts while Intellectuals, as openly indicated by several, are eager to acquire or share the power of Politicos. Such ambition can have important consequences, since four of the Intellectuals have been expelled from the party and three have been promoted to ministerial positions in the three years following the interviews.

Assembly Behavior of Legislative Types

The performance of the four legislative types in the Assembly provides further clues to the role behavior of members. Different types of members behaved differently, and this suggests they were responding to different expectations—fostered by their own personalities, by different socialization experiences, or by special external constraints such as apply to Politicos who are in the government.

The distribution of legislative types according to the percent of their own Assembly speeches that were nationally oriented, supportive, and critical are reported in table 5.5. Intellectuals were the most nationally oriented, Locals the most locally oriented. Both Silent Partners and Intellectuals were supportive compared to Politicos, who devoted the lowest percentage of speaking time to defending or supporting the government. This relatively low level of support from Politicos is indicative of the

TABLE 5.5. Assembly Behavior of Legislative Types

Percent of Each Legislator's Speeches in 1965–66

	Intel-lectuals ($N = 9$)	Locals ($N = 25$)	Silent Partners ($N = 5$)	Politicos ($N = 15$)	All M.P.'s Interviewed ($N = 56$)
Nationally oriented					
0 to 59.9%	0	36	20	27	25
60% to 79.9%	44	40	20	33	36
80% and above	56	24	60	40	39
Supportive					
0 to 9.9%	0	32	0	53	30
10% to 19.9%	67	32	0	27	32
20% and above	33	36	100	20	38
Critical					
0 to 4.9%	0	12	60	80	36
5% to 9.9%	33	40	40	7	28
10% and above	67	48	0	13	36

Locals/Politicos $X^2 = 18.6$*

Note: M.P.'s were broken into three roughly equal groups according to their speeches.
* This chi-square is significant at the $p < .05$ level.

generalized support which was expected and received from other M.P.'s and which relieved Politicos of the need continually to defend government policy.

While the absolute percent of critical speeches given by M.P.'s was low among all legislators,[19] Intellectuals were the most critical group. Locals were also critical; few Politicos and Silent Partners were ever critical. However, two Politicos, both regional commissioners (a high party and government post) are found in the highest third of those giving critical speeches. This deviation is one of the most striking instances of role ambiguity to be found among legislators. Most regional commissioners, including these two high scorers, were members of the Assembly elected in 1960. As constituency representatives originally, their initial role behavior included making frequent comments on government positions. However, following their appointment as regional commissioners and

19. Members were divided into three roughly equal groups. To do this, it was necessary to collapse critical percentages so that those whose critical speeches constituted 10% or more of their total speeches became the "most critical" group.

hence members of the government, a new set of role expectations requiring them to support and defend government policy was imposed. Even the right of commissioners to question ministers was withdrawn, although later restored.[20] These role ambiguities are reflected in the differing interpretations of their legislative roles given by the seven regional commissioners interviewed. Four saw their principal function as similar to ministers and junior ministers, namely, explaining and defending government policy. Two emphasized their special responsibilities as representatives of the regions for which they were commissioners; one suggested that his job was to "help the M.P.'s from my region explain our needs and problems." Finally, one commissioner confessed that he felt unsure about his role obligations as an Assembly member and simply did not know to what extent he was free to express his own opinions.

These ambiguities explain why the pattern of Assembly criticism among legislators is not more symmetrical. Although Intellectuals and Locals tend to be the most critical and Silent Partners and Politicos the least critical, personal predilections, previous role experience as a legislator, and ambiguity of role definitions—most noticeable among regional commissioners —account for interesting variations from this pattern. Deviants are frequently found in legislative assemblies; what is interesting is how well they fare.[21] Both of the two Politicos who most frequently made critical speeches later lost their Assembly membership, though the shift of one from his role as regional commissioner was to another important post.

ROLE EXPECTATIONS

The role orientations of an M.P. in Tanzania are affected both by official statements and by the subjective views of other M.P.'s. These role expectations form the norms that shape role behavior, and consensus among these expectations strengthens norms. Agreement between the dominant expectations among M.P.'s and the views expressed by government officialdom would indicate low conflict over the "rules of the game." In order to explore the degree of agreement or conflict between official expectations and those subjectively held by M.P.'s, official statements and interview responses have been examined and compared.

20. See Tordoff, "Parliament in Tanzania."
21. Ralph K. Huitt has analyzed the costs of deviancy in the U.S. Senate. See his "The Outsider in the Senate: An Alternative Role," *American Political Science Review*, 55 (September 1961), 566–75.

Official Expectations

The role of a member of Parliament as envisaged by President Nyerere includes three tasks: "(1) To act as a bridge . . . between people and government for transmission of ideas; (2) to deliberate on new legislation; (3) to keep the government actively devoted to the people's interest by intelligent criticism." [22] These views, expressed by Nyerere in a speech to the opening of the National Assembly in October 1965, represent one important change in the official description of an M.P.'s responsibilities outlined by Nyerere in September 1960, prior to independence: the abandonment of the right to "criticize government policy at public or private meetings in his constituency." [23]

Members have been criticized by national leaders for failing to play effectively at least two of the three aspects of their role. Nyerere, in 1962 and again in 1965, called attention to the need for members to participate actively in their constituencies and, where possible, to work physically in nation-building projects—for example, making bricks or working on a road project.[24] Again in 1965, Nyerere reminded new legislators that one of the obvious reasons for the defeat of many incumbents in the 1965 elections was their failure to keep in touch with their constituencies, to find out what their problems were, and to help people to understand what was being done and why.[25] Constituency members are "officially" expected to bring local problems and grievances to the attention of the central government. They are also expected to act as government spokesmen whose job it is to communicate with the people and to carry the government's message throughout the country by traveling in their constituencies and meeting rural citizens who otherwise have only marginal contact with government activity. M.P.'s generally perform their representative function in two ways. First, they submit questions to be answered in Parliament by the appropriate minister. The second method, not used very often, is to approach directly the relevant minister or civil servant.[26]

22. J. K. Nyerere, "Address at the Opening of the National Assembly after the General Election" (Dar es Salaam: Ministry of Information and Tourism, October 12, 1965), no pagination.

23. As cited in Tordoff, "Parliament in Tanzania," from Nyerere's circular letter No. 1 of 1960.

24. *Tanganyika Parliamentary Debates National Assembly Official Report,* December 11, 1961, to February 17, 1962 (Dar es Salaam: Government Printer, 1962), Cols. 124–25.

25. Nyerere, "Address at the Opening of the National Assembly" [p. 5].

26. This latter method may be more effective. One minister commented that few M.P.'s

The other criticism directed toward members by official spokesmen has been their failure to make more than minimal use of their prerogative to criticize in the Assembly. The commission that studied the establishment of a one-party state wrote:

> With a few notable exceptions, debates in the National Assembly have tended to be lifeless and superficial. Legislation of the most complex and far reaching kind is passed rapidly through all the stages without challenge to basic principles or careful examination of detailed provisions.[27]

Nyerere felt it was "fortunate" that a few members disregarded the "party line" from time to time to express their own views, even though they were rebuked for their lapses from party discipline. Questions of detail, timing, and priority should, he felt, be openly discussed and debated in a one-party state.[28]

> Occasionally there will be a division of opinion about the desirability of a particular piece of legislation. In such cases, provided that both sides are honest and are able to advance arguments to support their views, people will be better served by reconsideration of the proposal than by an automatic affirmative vote.[29]

This view, though reflecting Nyerere's own position, goes beyond the view held by other TANU leaders interviewed; or perhaps it simply disguises the question of when opposition is legitimate. The problem of who determines when opposition is legitimate is left unsolved.

Following the elections of 1965 the Assembly has been more active in

---

came to see him with their constituency problems, "but those who have, have received more attention and support than the ones who simply raise questions in Parliament in order to make a show." A principal secretary in another ministry expressed similar views and felt that M.P.'s who met with him were more likely to be effective in understanding a given problem and getting help for their constituency.

27. *One-Party State Report*, p. 20. The report blamed practices inherited from the British, and more appropriate to a two-party system, for the lack of vigor in Assembly debates. In the British party system, private party caucuses and party whips to enforce discipline are accepted procedures essential to maintain the unity upon which the party in power depends for its control of the legislative process. The TPP and the National Executive Committee provided private forums for prior discussions of policy and legislative matters. These prior discussions, the report concluded, inevitably have "inhibited subsequent discussion on the floor of the house."

28. Nyerere, "Democracy and the Party System," p. 6.

29. Nyerere, "Address at the Opening of the National Assembly" [p. 6].

legislative matters. Criticism has increased somewhat and testimony before the four standing committees reviewing legislation has been heard. Private members' motions have been vigorously debated on such topics as education, relocation of the capital, control of salaries in private industry, and the reacceptance of university students expelled after the October 1966 demonstrations. Opposition among legislators has caused a few bills to be altered or even dropped.[30] In general, however, an M.P.'s function in law-making has been more ceremonial than real. His responsibility is to legitimize legislation initiated by the government or the party, drawn up by specialized legal draftsmen, and approved by the cabinet. The only Assembly members who do participate in these prior processes are members of the cabinet or occasional appointees to ad hoc committees. Criticism and debate in the Assembly, in spite of affirmations about their desirability, have not been very important in the legislative process.

Two reasons explain this. First, the vast majority of Assembly members are usually in agreement with the government; and second, for those members who might raise serious criticisms, it is very difficult to distinguish between criticizing a detail of government policy and criticizing the policy itself. The latter is officially not the responsibility of a member speaking in Parliament. Policy criticisms may be raised, but only in an appropriate party—and hence, closed—forum.

Nyerere himself has affirmed that broader questions of policy should be the responsibility of the National Executive of the party, and not subject to legislative debate.[31] Furthermore, every member of the government interviewed mentioned in some manner the subjection of individual M.P.'s

30. In September 1963, the Affiliation Ordinance (amendment) Bill, which would have given legal redress to unwed mothers against the father, met strong opposition and was withdrawn. After weakening amendments were added it was passed in February 1964. In July 1966, Vice-President Kawawa modified legislation on a road toll tax that came under sharp criticism. There was a chance, he admitted, that the legislation could have been defeated. He pointed out that if the government had not revised the legislation and it had not passed, there would not have been any legislation on this point. Another piece of legislation, to establish licensing of casinos, was dropped completely after criticism of it was raised privately in the TPP. These examples, however, are more exceptions than the rule. These references are based on the *National Assembly Debates,* September 10–11, 1963, Cols. 61–160, and February 19, 1964, Cols. 110–112, as cited in Tordoff, "Parliament in Tanzania," and my interview with Second Vice-President Rashidi Kawawa, August 31, 1966. This assertion of Assembly power was also cited by Chief Adam Sapi, the Speaker, in an interview, August 22, 1966. Bill Supplement No. 9 to *Gazette 20* (Dar es Salaam: Government Printer, May 17, 1965), pp. 11–14.

31. Nyerere, "Democracy and the Party System," pp. 6–7.

to party discipline. In response to the question: "Which is the more powerful decision-making body, the National Executive or the National Assembly?," one candid member of government and of the NEC replied:

> It's hard to say. Legally, I suppose, the National Assembly is, but in fact, I think the NEC. These fellows can discuss and air their views here and are free to speak inside the hall; but once they step outside these four walls, they will learn that there are others who have more power. If M.P.'s aren't careful, the party can discipline them and they'll have to recall their decisions since the party has control over them.

This statement, not the strongest among government members, indicates informal boundaries and sharp limitations on the legislator's role as critic. Nyerere has stressed that criticism must be "reasoned," but it is difficult to distinguish reasoned persuasion from passion, and passionate criticism is not acceptable to the party hierarchy. Thus, according to "official" views, the legislator may express criticism if it relates to his constituency, is constructive, and is not in opposition to policies already decided upon by the NEC.

As long as the party remains the only accepted arena for debate on policy matters and as long as National Assembly members lack expertise in legislative matters—unable to wield influence through contacts with civil servants or through quiet committee review of proposed legislation— criticism and controversy will remain largely unarticulated within the legislative forum.[32]

Legislators' Expectations

In order to see how close the legislators' own role expectations were to the "official" ones, the sampled M.P.'s were asked to describe their responsibilities as members of the National Assembly. Their responses emphasized all the role duties contained in official expectations. A few even made specific reference to speeches by Nyerere or Second Vice-President Kawawa about their duties. One M.P., an Intellectual, gave this explanation of his role:

32. Some movement toward changing these conditions has been suggested both by President Nyerere and Second Vice-President Kawawa, who favor strengthening the Assembly members' participation in the legislative process, particularly through the committee system and specialization on the part of members. See Nyerere, "Address at the Opening of the National Assembly." This was also mentioned by Kawawa in an interview.

For an M.P., there are three tasks, as the president stated in his speech last October. First, I must represent the electorate, get their ideas and bring these views to the Parliament and advise the government. Second, I must get something from the government for the people. And third, I can advise the government on my own ideas and criticize constructively.

This interpretation of the president's expectations is not quite complete, since it omits the obligation of an M.P. to explain government policy in his constituency, but it indicates the process whereby official expectations shape expectations of role incumbents. Most respondents mentioned several different duties, most frequently (77 percent) work within the constituency. Most of these (76 percent) cited their duty as explaining or defending government policy to their constituents. Others (66 percent) mentioned meeting with constituents or aiding in their economic development. Bringing constituency needs and demands before the government was the second most frequently mentioned role task. Two other aspects of the legislator's role, as lawmaker and as critic of the government, were mentioned rather infrequently, by only 21 percent and 17 percent respectively. The differing frequency with which these four tasks were mentioned is a fair indicator of the emphasis which the political system places on these duties. Participating in the legislative process or being a gadfly of the government is seldom a part of the legislator's own conception of his role. Much more important is work in the constituency, explaining government policy, encouraging and helping in nation-building activities, and carrying problems and complaints from constituents to the government. The role emerging for an M.P. in Tanzania emphasizes his function as a communicator rather than either a deliberator or a lawmaker.

Those M.P.'s who participate in decision making do so largely in their special positions as members of the government. Ministers, for example, are normally involved in the preparation of legislation. The special responsibilities of members of the government were frequently mentioned in response to the question: "What is the *most important* aspect of your work?" As seen in table 5.6 most Politicos and Silent Partners described their most important activity as either being members of the government and hence involved in planning and directing government activity, or being high officials in the party, responsible for organizing and directing party affairs. Locals tended to stress work with their constituents; 52 percent felt that explaining to their constituents government policy and na-

TABLE 5.6. Role Definition of Legislative Types
(in percentages)

	Intellectuals (N = 9)	Locals (N = 25)	Silent Partners (N = 6)	Politicos (N = 15)	All M.P.'s Interviewed (N = 58)
Most important aspect of role					
Promote constituency	33	24	0	0	16
Legislate	22	4	17	0	7
Criticize	11	4	0	0	3
Explain to constituency	22	52	17	13	33
As member of government	0	8	33	53	21
Party activity	0	0	17	33	10

tional affairs was their most important task, while 24 percent mentioned promoting their constituency interests to the government. Even among Intellectuals, five out of nine (56 percent) mentioned constituency-related activity, but the emphasis was on promoting constituency needs rather than on defending government policies. Intellectuals also emphasized legislative work and criticism.

The pattern of expectations and role emphases reflected in legislative responses is generally compatible with official expectations. The lack of expertise and specialization among legislators and the weakly articulated performance of legislative committees is consonant with the finding that few legislators emphasized legislation or criticism as the main aspect of their role. An M.P. begins participating in the actual legislative process when he attains a position in the government or party. Naturally, those holding such posts usually deem work in these positions the most important. Back-benchers even in the British system have little control over policy and legislation compared with fellow party members who are in the government, so a similarly low involvement among back-benchers in Tanzania is hardly surprising.

Role Consensus

Three open-ended questions about political contingencies were used as a measure of role consensus. Each question explored some aspect of a legislator's relationship to the total political process. Responses to these questions (by both the M.P.'s and high-level administrators interviewed) have been grouped into three categories from weak to strong. Written responses by Tanzanian university students to these questions are also reported as was done in chapter 4.[33]

In an open competitive political system, controversial questions and policies may be subject to widespread debate and criticism. There is a public character to discussion, debate, and political differences, and instances of corruption or internecine feuding are regularly revealed on a public stage in which the principal performers appeal for support. The extent to which politics is open and public is an important variable in Tanzanian politics. Norms prescribing the boundaries within which the legislator may pursue his own or his constituents' interests are investigated by these three role questions. Responses indicate the extent to which a legislator is expected to voice opposition publicly, to denounce instances of corruption, and to feel capable, in a controversy with TANU leaders, to carry the disagreement into broader national arenas.

The first question asked: "If the government introduces a measure before the legislature which you are personally against and which you feel your constituents would not like, what would you do?"[34] The distribution of elite responses is illustrated by the first histogram in figure 5.6. Examples of the three different types of responses selected from interviews are:

> WEAK: He should go to see the minister concerned and talk with him. Possibly he hasn't seen the measure correctly or perhaps people at home have concocted a story to give people fear. In this case he must explain it to them. (A Politico)
>
> MODERATE: I would oppose it, but if the majority are in favor of it I'll throw in my lot with them and then I will tell my constituency that I, with the rest of the Parliament, passed it, and give them reasons why we did so. (A Local)
>
> STRONG: Go to the relevant committee, try to stop it by convincing other M.P.'s. Then raise hell in the Parliament if I have to. Perhaps try to make an amendment. (An Intellectual)

The majority of M.P.'s, while expecting to voice criticism, also mentioned their obligation to support legislation in their constituency once it has

33. See chap. 3, especially note 16, for information about the questionnaire and sample.

34. For legislators who were members of the government, and hence constrained in their M.P. role, these questions were phrased in the third person, and their expectations about the behavior of a back-bencher were solicited. The written versions submitted to administrators were similarly in the third person. See app. B.

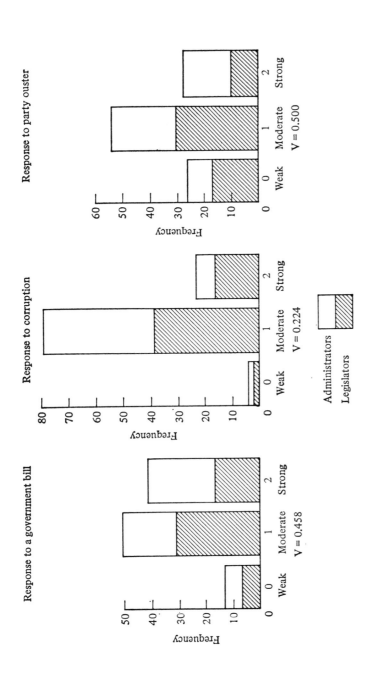

Figure 5.6. Distribution of Role Expectations for Legislators

been passed. Some differences among legislative types on this item are noticeable; Intellectuals tended to mention without qualification that they expected to oppose the legislation.

In contrast to legislators, both administrators and students more often mentioned only the likelihood of criticism in this projective situation. The most frequent responses included dual expectations: criticism, but also an obligation to support the legislation. Although only a few students' expectations included the obligation to support legislation after it was passed, all who did express this idea also approved of it.

The second role question asked what an M.P. would do if he suspected that corruption existed in some ministry. Responses to this question fell into three categories: passivity or hesitancy to act (weak); reporting the suspicion privately to a minister, the president, or the commission of inquiry (moderate); or willingness to raise the issue openly in the Assembly (strong). There was a high degree of consensus on this question, as indicated by the high proportion of M.P.'s who gave the moderate response (see figure 5.6).

The deviant responses indicated insecurity or lack of faith in the system; one Intellectual, for instance, exclaimed: "There is corruption but I just look at it. It is too delicate to approach the president. If I were ever head of state, I'd know what to do, though."

Privately querying the government was the most frequent response among both legislators and administrators. Students fully approved this alternative, though larger percentages expected legislators either to be silent or to raise the issue publicly. But neither of these more deviant responses was approved as highly by students as was the response statistically closest to the mean or norm.

Party membership is a requisite of membership in the Assembly. The third question asked: "If local TANU leaders disagreed with you and informed you they had expelled you from the party, what would you do?" In fact, local party officials do not, according to the TANU constitution, have the authority to expel party members. A bare majority of legislators (52 percent) gave moderate responses by indicating that local officials did not have this power. Nearly a third felt that they would have to accept the party's decision, perhaps even resign—a weak response. A small group (17 percent) gave a strong response, stating they would fight out their differences with local officials or would publicly appeal the decision to higher levels in the national party.

The distribution of responses to these three questions suggests at least partial agreement among elite on these important role aspects. By calculating the variance of responses on these items, a rough indication of the degree of consensus among the elite was obtained. The variances of the three items were: .458, .224, and .500. This yields an average variance of .394, which compares favorably to the average for the administrator's role of .521 or to a situation of role ambiguity in which there would be equal distribution of responses and a variance of .670.[35]

The legislative responses to these three questions, broken down into types, are given in table 5.7. Intellectuals, followed by Locals, consistently gave "stronger" responses than Silent Partners or Politicos. Legislators' and administrators' role expectations were distributed in a fairly similar fashion, while students were more aggressive in their view of the legislator's role. The students' responses anticipated a stronger, more assertive role for M.P.'s than was characteristic of the political elite. This difference in attitude may also have reflected the willingness of Tanzanian students to protest publicly National Service legislation that affected them.[36]

The question on party expulsion revealed that legislators were not clear about the possible consequences. Some felt expulsion would not affect one's status as an M.P.; others correctly foresaw this as one method to remove a deviant M.P. from the Assembly. This confusion is illustrated in two selected responses, neither of which is totally accurate since the NEC has expelled members from the party and if the victim was an M.P. he did lose his seat.

> A branch official can't expel him. Expulsion is only by the Annual Conference and he would still be an Mbunge, although he should resign due to the lack of confidence in him. But the National Conference can't expel him from the Parliament. (A Politico)

> I have their confidence now. But if not, I would appeal to higher-ups who will decide the matter, but I can't be expelled since I am an M.P. (A Local)

35. See app. D.

36. See Raymond F. Hopkins and Neal Sherman, "Students and Politics in Tanzania," in William John Hanna and Seymour M. Lipset, eds., *University Students and Politics in Africa* (New York: Basic Books, forthcoming 1971). Six months after their responses were recorded, in October 1966, 393 students (mostly from University College) were expelled as a result of their protest demonstrations. They were readmitted only after several steps had been taken to ensure that students would conform to the prevalent political norms.

Table 5.7. Role Expectations of Legislative Types (in percentages)

	Intellectuals (N = 9)	Locals (N = 25)	Silent Partners (N = 6)	Politicos (N = 15)	All M.P.'s (N = 58)	Administrators (N = 50)	Total Elite (N = 108)	Students (N = 112)	Students Approving (N = 61)
Response to government bill felt wrong									
Explain to constituency	11	8	33	20	14	12	13	6	100
Oppose only till passed	22	72	67	60	57	38	46	5	100
Oppose	67	20	0	20	29	48	38	89	87
			Legislators/Administrators X² = 3.9			Elite/Students X² = 61.8*			
Response to corruption								(N = 102)	(N = 57)
Nothing, private	11	4	0	0	4	4	4	26	79
Inform government	44	68	67	73	66	80	72	39	100
Denounce in Assembly	44	38	17	20	28	14	21	35	90
			Legislators/Administrators X² = 3.1			Elite/Students X² = 31.2*			
Response to party ouster								(N = 91)	(N = 50)
Accept, resign	22	40	17	33	31	18	25	20	63
Knows local party can't	56	40	83	67	52	46	50	13	100
Appeal, fight	22	20	0	0	17	34	25	67	81
			Legislators/Administrators X² = 4.6			Elite/Students X² = 39.5*			

* These chi-squares are significant at the .05 level.

These responses indicate the extent to which many M.P.'s conceived of an independent status for *Wabunge*—an importance apart from the party. The consequences of party expulsion, which legally would result in dismissal from the Assembly, were not well understood, even by some important political leaders. This confusion serves to underline the ambiguity in role expectations in a new state like Tanzania. The subsequent expulsion of nine members in 1968 from the party, and consequently the Assembly, has no doubt clarified these expectations considerably.

Role Congruence

As described in chapter 4, standard scores for these three items have been averaged as a measure of individual congruence (C) for each legislator. Legislators whose expectations were nearest the mathematical mean of expectations among all elite respondents received high C-scores. Table 5.8 shows the relative congruence among legislative types. It also presents

TABLE 5.8. Role Congruence of Legislative Types
(in percentages)

	Intellectuals (N = 9)	Locals (N = 25)	Silent Partners (N = 6)	Politicos (N = 15)	All M.P.'s (N = 58)	Administrators (N = 50)	Total Elite (N = 108)
Legislative							
High	22	16	33	60	29	38	33
Medium	33	64	50	13	41	24	33
Low	44	20	17	27	29	38	33
			Locals/Politicos $X^2 = 11.1$*				
Average							
High	22	28	33	53	33	34	33
Medium	11	60	50	20	37	36	37
Low	67	12	17	27	30	30	30
			Locals/Politicos $X^2 = 6.1$*				

* These chi-squares are significant at the $p < .05$ level.

their congruence on ten role expectation items, including five items relating to presidential role behavior (discussed in chapter 6) and the two items about administrators' behavior. *Intellectuals are the least congruent in their expectations; Politicos, the most congruent.* Locals are somewhat less congruent in their expectations than the average. Differences among the groups are significant for both legislative congruence and average congruence. As mentioned earlier, of the nine Intellectuals interviewed, four—

all with low congruence—have been removed from the National Assembly by means of expulsion from the party.

The responses of those who are high on both legislative and average role congruence express the expectations which, according to our analysis, are "normative." These "consensual" expectations clearly support a closed pattern of politics and prevent the M.P. from acting in a divisive manner. The response of one Politico with a very high score illustrates this:

> If an M.P. dislikes a particular piece of legislation, he should first see the minister and tell him; try to get it altered. The minister may work through the Cabinet until all are prepared to accept some other version. Finally, and only if necessary, he should raise it in Parliament. If it is passed, however, he'll just have to support it or resign.

Such expectations approximate the official expectations outlined earlier. The similarity suggests that institutionalization of this aspect of the political system has been occurring. Although among students there was 100 percent approval for those expectations closest to the mean among elite, they only infrequently expected the behavior choice which the elite usually expected. For instance, table 5.7 shows that 89 percent of the students would unequivocally oppose a government bill they felt wrong, while only 38 percent of all elite and 29 percent of the legislators gave such a response. This is an important indication of the gap between students and politicians and explains in part the conflicts that led to the mass dismissal of students in October 1966.

Congruence with prevailing norms, as determined by the pattern of elite expectations, was highest among Politicos who had the longest experience and the highest positions. The "consensual" expectations were not only close to "officially" stated expectations but also contained somewhat more restrained role boundaries for the public behavior of M.P.'s than those outlined by the president and second vice-president. It may be that President Nyerere's expectations created opportunities for those legislators willing to be more assertive. This possibility is suggested by the comment of one Intellectual:

> You know, I like to make a lot of noise in the Assembly, and I often disagree. President Nyerere is the only one who understands the need for this. If it weren't for him, they'd never let me get away with it.

For this M.P., as for the few others whose expectations were both deviant and strong, there was an implicit recognition of the informal rules and

restrictions on members' behavior, coupled with a desire to exert themselves in a stronger fashion than expected by most elite in the sample.
This desire, expressed by only a few of those interviewed, is not necessarily
an indication that consensus on the rules or norms for the legislative role
is weak in Tanzania. Indeed, the fact that this legislator was one of those
expelled from the party suggests that these informal role norms have
considerable force.

Predicting Role Congruence and Role Behavior

In order to discover what relationships existed between background and
attitude variables and role expectations and behavior, correlations among
these variables were calculated. Many studies involving role analysis
heavily emphasize the attitudes and backgrounds of role incumbents but
ignore the extent to which these are reliable predictors of behavior.[37] In
order to bridge this analytic lacuna, the Assembly speeches of all legislators
analyzed have been used as one index of their behavior. Comparative
measures on speaking performance, which included the individual M.P.'s
total, supportive, and critical speeches within the Assembly and within his
own set of speeches, provided six measures of behavior. In general, the
results of this correlational analysis (see table 5.9) indicate that role expectations have low predictive value for Assembly behavior. Behavior was
not closely related to attitudinal traits such as authoritarianism or to
important background characteristics such as education. We had anticipated that M.P.'s with high education, long careers, and congruent expectations would speak more frequently and less often in a critical manner. The
role norms, as measured in our data, indicated that M.P.'s who knew the
ropes would be constrained from being highly critical. The correlations
support these hypotheses in most cases, but nearly all are weak and most
are not statistically significant. For example, the relationship between
legislative role congruence and frequency of speeches is positive ($r = .25$),
while congruence is negatively related to the percentage of critical speeches
by an individual legislator ($r = -.33$).

In order better to interpret the correlation results presented in table 5.9,
two further analyses were made. The first was an attempt to understand
why the expected relationships were not stronger. The second was an
attempt to examine possible inferences that might be drawn from my basic

37. See, for example, the otherwise commendable studies by Gross et al. and Wahlke
et al.

TABLE 5.9. Correlations of Backgrounds, Attitudes, Role Measures, and Behavior among Legislators

	Education	Career Length	Authoritarianism	Anomie	Faith in People	Democratic Practices	% of Vote	Member of Government	Born in Constituency	M.P. Role Congruence	Average Congruence
Percent of vote	21	-18	-20	-30	16	03					
Member of government	24	**48**	**-35**	-22	26	-04	03				
Born in constituency	-17	**42**	31	13	-25	-27	13	**-51**			
M.P. congruence	01	05	-04	00	16	03	-27	24	**-40**		
Average congruence	-12	09	-06	-16	06	15	-08	08	**-41**	48	
M.P.'s speeches/All speeches	31	14	-11	-12	25	18	-01	**39**	**-45**	25	16
Supportive/All speeches	25	02	-08	-04	14	-03	-01	21	-14	10	-06
Critical/All speeches	04	-14	24	12	-01	-20	01	**-39**	26	-21	-07
National/M.P.'s speeches	01	24	-13	16	-11	08	-05	-06	-00	-19	**-32**
Supportive/M.P.'s speeches	29	20	16	05	-28	08	10	-07	22	-21	-14
Critical/M.P.'s speeches	-10	10	06	04	-14	03	-03	-24	26	**-33**	00

Note. Boldface correlations are significant at the $p < .05$ level.

assumption, namely that role expectations are an important intervening variable in the political system that affects behavior independently of previous background or attitudes.

The first step was a systematic search through the interviews to find those legislators who were "outliers," that is, whose scores had the opposite relationship from the correlations. Eight or nine M.P.'s who were strikingly deviant were uncovered. When these atypical M.P.'s were analyzed to determine if there was any single common variable that might explain their deviance, no explanation was found. Each was a unique case. For example, Mwari, an Intellectual whose case history is presented below, was relatively low on role congruence but comparatively high on total speeches and low on percent of critical speeches. No other legislator fit Mwari's pattern of deviance, however. It was apparent that the complexities of individual persons as expressed in their expectations and behavior had nullified any strong *linear* relationships between expectations and objective performance.

The second analytic task was to test for spuriousness of relationship between the significant correlation of M.P. role congruence and critical speechmaking. It was predicted that although legislators had different backgrounds and attitudes, the effect of these differences on role performance would be mitigated by the constraining influence of role expectations. The relevant testimony of individual legislators supports this thesis. Several legislators, notably among the Intellectuals, stated that role prescriptions (their views of what others expected) necessarily muted some of the criticism they voiced privately. In order to test what seemed to be a theoretically and anecdotally valid proposition, namely that role expectations intervene between an individual's background and his behavior, alternative models predicting this general relationship were examined utilizing partial correlation and path coefficients.[38]

38. For a discussion of the assumptions and methodology of causal and path analyses see Hubert M. Blalock, Jr., *Causal Inferences in Nonexperimental Research* (Chapel Hill: University of North Carolina Press, 1964), Hayward R. Alker, Jr., *Mathematics and Politics* (New York: Macmillan, 1965), chap. 6, and Dudley Otis Duncan, "On Path Analysis," *American Sociological Review*, 31 (February 1966), 3 ff. Causal analysis is possible if one can make a temporal and proposed causal ordering among variables, and it can be assumed that the effects of external variables not considered may be ignored as not disturbing the causal relationships among the variables being considered. Two assumptions may be made about the temporal sequence and hence causal ordering among background, expectations, and behavior. First, background is assumed to be temporally prior to expectations and behavior. and second, behavior is assumed not to come prior to expecta-

A variety of variables was used in the alternative causal and path models to analyze the relative influence of expectations on behavior. In general, congruence of role expectations gave a better explanation of the relationships in the data than alternative explanations. However, a large portion of the variance in Assembly behavior remained unexplained by the statistical measures derived from the interviews.[39] These analyses, then, although not conclusive, did support the hypothesis that role expectations act as an intervening variable in the behavior of Tanzanian legislators. It is impossible to judge at this point whether role expectations in other systems considered more stable and developed, such as the United Kingdom, are in fact even more closely linked to actual parliamentary behavior and, hence, are a more potent force in shaping behavior than in Tanzania.

CASE HISTORIES

In order to illustrate some of the qualities associated with legislative types and to make clear the diversity and complexity found in the backgrounds and attitudes of legislators, seven of the 58 M.P.'s interviewed have been selected as examples. Two each of the Locals, Intellectuals, and Politicos and one Silent Partner were chosen by examining the scores of all legislators in each type and selecting individuals who were extremely high and low on some measures and who also represented many of the dominant characteristics of their type. For example, of the two Intellectuals presented, one interpreted his legislative role quite strongly and the other rather weakly, but both were low in congruence. As with the administrative types presented, fictitious names have been used along with other devices to preserve anonymity. The relative positions in deciles on nine attitudinal and expectational measures are given in the same fashion as for administrators, and in addition their relative positions (within the sample) are shown with respect to their contributions to Assembly debates in the 1965–66 session.

---

tions. The *ceteris paribus* assumption is a difficult one since, in the actual research, expectations were measured at the same time that the behavioral measure—that is, speeches in the Assembly—was being recorded; but it seems reasonable to assume that expectations were formed earlier, even though some interaction surely occurs.

39. For an elaboration of these analyses see my dissertation, "Political Roles," chap. 5, and my paper, "Constituency Ties and Deviant Expectations Among Tanzanian Legislators," read at the American Political Science Association meetings in Los Angeles, Sept. 7–11, 1970.

Mr. Mwari: An Intellectual

AUTHRN	ANOMIE	FAITH IN PEOPLE	DEM. PRACT.	PRES. ROLE STRENGTH
1st	2nd	2nd	10th	2nd

ADM. CONGRUENCE	MP CONGRUENCE	PRES. CONGRUENCE	AVERAGE CONGRUENCE	
4th	8th	9th	9th	

% TOTAL	% LONG	% NAT'L	% SUPP.	% CRIT.
2nd	5th	2nd	7th	2nd

"He's quite intelligent, but he's not very stable"—thus a colleague who knew Mr. Mwari well summed him up. Mwari followed a winding, erratic career on his way to a seat in the National Assembly. There are numerous disappointments and broken relationships in his past. Two strong influences affect his ideas and outlook: Roman Catholicism and Marxism.

His father was away from home preparing to be a teacher until Mwari was eight. Moreover, his father, a firm disciplinarian, "didn't like him." When Mwari was 13 his mother died and he was sent away to seminary. Here a priest told him about a young French child who had heard the Virgin Mary speak and then died. The story fascinated Mwari, who at the time "felt I never would live to be more than 14." "I did a lot of praying and had a vision of having a large following after my death." But he did not die. Instead, he remained in seminary training for eleven years, becoming one of the brightest pupils. However, the Fathers came to view him not only as talented but also as rude and proud. Rather than train him as a priest, therefore, they decided he should become a church linguist. Toward the end of his studies Mwari became fascinated with politics. A German Father, an ardent nationalist and a Nazi, encouraged this interest, giving him Mein Kampf to read. "I saw how this person [Hitler] could move people by his speeches and I decided to practice public speaking." If Mwari could not die dramatically and have a large following, then perhaps he could be a great political leader like the men whom he admired—Hitler, Churchill, Nehru, and Stalin.

He left the strict discipline of the seminary and joined the army, where he spent two years. Later he accepted a job as a teacher, but after two years resigned in the heat of a quarrel with the principal. He worked for a large British enterprise for a while, then went to study abroad, but he was dismissed for "political reasons" before completing his studies. In the ensuing years he worked as a teacher, broadcaster, salesman, and then played an important role in pre-independence politics as a party organizer. Eventually a second chance for an overseas education came his way and he took it. His many applications to Western universities had failed to bring an offer, so he turned to the East, where he studied Marxism.

> It was here I lost my religion and became more practical. But I don't believe you can do away with God. I was an active Roman Catholic there and chairman of the Catholic students. However, now I see religious people more realistically.

While Marxism was reorienting Mwari's outlook, the Church was causing him displeasure. Several years earlier, while a teacher, he had married a young Catholic girl and now had four children.

> While I was away my wife had two children by someone else, and then my marriage was spoiled by the Church. They wouldn't let my wife come and join me because of a great lack of understanding of communism.

Not long after his return to Tanzania a chance came to reenter politics; the national elections for a new Assembly were to be held. Finding strong support in his home district, he resigned his job and won an impressive victory at the polls in 1965.

Not surprisingly, Mwari's personality and outlook reflect his past experience and training. A strong authoritarian, he has little use for democratic principles. In spite of his triumph at the polls he has little faith in the average voter. As he put it, "I agree with Plato." Democracy is a good thing, but by democracy he means "the power of everybody organized by the government to have its will . . . and to have its standard of living. It's a chance to achieve the daily needs of life without hindrance. It's not just a chance to vote."

He strongly favors government intervention to secure economic quality for everyone, but feels "it is not the government's intention now." He would like to oppose the government on some issues, particularly domestic, but feels it is not safe. He nevertheless is much above average in proportion of critical speeches. If he strongly opposed a government policy he might speak against it, but he would not lobby through individuals. "If you speak privately, there are a lot of people who get paid for informing. I would not vote against it." He understands and accepts this situation for the time being, though he chafes against the role boundaries he perceives for M.P.'s.

Mr. Kazini: A Local

AUTHRN	ANOMIE	FAITH IN PEOPLE	DEM. PRACT.	PRES. ROLE STRENGTH
5th	2nd	6th	10th	4th

ADM. CONGRUENCE	MP CONGRUENCE	PRES. CONGRUENCE	AVERAGE CONGRUENCE	
4th	10th	2nd	6th	

% TOTAL	% LONG	% NAT'L	% SUPP.	% CRIT.
7th	4th	10th	4th	3rd

Born in a rather large village, Mr. Kazini was brought up as a Roman Catholic. Kazini was "sacked off" from school because he "was politically minded and the mission didn't like it." After breaking his relationship with the church, Kazini spent a period away from home acquainting himself with TANU and modern life. When he returned, he had a new mission —to bring progress and development to his relatively retarded region. Within a few years Kazini had involved himself in a number of projects attempting to transform the lives and work patterns of his friends and neighbors. His success in this effort brought him enormous popularity and when he decided to stand for the National Assembly his victory was an easy one.

For Kazini his new job as M.P. has been really only ancillary to his basic commitment to development and change in his home area. Tanzania is a poor country, he insists, and the real job of nation building must be done in the bush. "I hate coming to Dar es Salaam. All these big cars— this isn't the real Tanzania. Living here you would think we were a rich country, but we're not."

Kazini speaks with about average frequency in the Assembly, but more often than not on local issues. Occasionally critical, he is usually supportive of government policy in his longer remarks. But it was not his Assembly performance that he mentioned when discussing his role. His thoughts were directed to what he considered the most important aspect of his work, "rural development."

> I have to interpret our policy of self-reliance and make the people see that they have to work hard for the independence of the country. I need to try to direct the people to think in that way; to educate the people. And I try to keep the people informed of the progress we are making and of the laws passed in the Parliament.

Kazini did not see a narrowly limited M.P. role as did many of his colleagues, nor did he see the president as an extremely powerful figure. His entry into formal politics is recent. His rural orientation and Catholic upbringing appear to be the most plausible explanations for his attitudes, including his high scores on authoritarianism and anomie.

Kazini is not worried about democracy in Tanzania. His concept is a very local one, getting the people involved:

> letting everybody have his say, right from the village. Democracy is not betrayed by a one-party state. It all depends on the leaders. The problem in democracy is if some group decides it wants to have the last word, then democracy is destroyed. If the purpose of democracy is to make people participate, then we have democracy.

Kazini is a social revolutionary, though more an Edward Bellamy than a Karl Marx. His commitment to African socialism, for example, involves economic and social development of the masses. And this is accomplished "by discussion. We achieve two things this way—you educate and you agree on one thing worth while for all the people and the people are, therefore, more willing to work for it. But this must be done on all levels, village to the top."

Mr. Mwabeja: A Politico

AUTHRN	ANOMIE	FAITH IN PEOPLE	DEM. PRACT.	PRES. ROLE STRENGTH
10th	6th	2nd	2nd	6th

ADM. CONGRUENCE	MP CONGRUENCE	PRES. CONGRUENCE	AVERAGE CONGRUENCE	
2nd	1st	3rd	1st	

% TOTAL	% LONG	% NAT'L	% SUPP.	% CRIT.
1st	9th	9th	9th	10th

Mwabeja was the only son of an industrious farmer. He finished high school before beginning work in a job in the modern economy. In Dar es Salaam he joined the TAA and became involved in various political activities. His interest grew because he "wanted to make a contribution to the democratic and social development of the country."

The most important aspect of his work, he felt, was his ministerial responsibility. His job as a minister is "an integral part of decision making and implementation of policy." As an M.P. he is obliged "to know people's wishes and desires and how these can be enacted within the overall needs of the country." Disagreement with the government must be only on "weighty matters." He himself is bound by cabinet responsibility and if he "felt strongly, he would have to resign." An ordinary M.P., even though he opposes a government measure, "may have to go home and try to convince his constituency." The M.P., he believed, even one who is a minister, is bound by the rule of collective decision as taken by the TANU Executive: "If the National Executive endorses, then it's endorsed by the whole country."

Mwabeja had strong views on political matters. He admired Presidents Kennedy and de Gaulle because they were men with moral courage and grand vision. "A leader can't succeed unless he has a view of greatness and a sense of history." He wanted citizens to have constitutional rights and "to understand the constitution which embodies their rights and duties." [40] Democracy, for him, was "the presence of individual freedom."

A hard worker and avid reader, Mwabeja took time from a busy schedule to answer questions and discuss his ideas. He was optimistic about politics and Tanzania's future, stating that the "most fundamental changes will occur in the minds of people" and that this will result in "more understanding among men." His socialist attitudes were also idealistic. Socialism, he felt, "must be practiced in the African context." The label "African" reflects the fact that "just as with the spread of Christianity, socialism picked up local color and culture." But future developments, he stressed, were flexible, because Tanzania "has an open mind" and many political and social changes are possible.

Mr. Nguvu: A Silent Partner

Mr. Nguvu was the most critical and outspoken of all the Silent Partners. He comes from a ruling clan and with the help of his father finished school

---

40. The constitution has no bill of rights in order to circumvent limitations on government power, especially by foreign judiciary. See One-Party State Report, pp. 30–33.

AUTHRN	ANOMIE	FAITH IN PEOPLE	DEM. PRACT.	PRES. ROLE STRENGTH
5th	2nd	2nd	10th	1st

ADM. CONGRUENCE	MP CONGRUENCE	PRES. CONGRUENCE	AVERAGE CONGRUENCE	
6th	6th	10th	10th	

% TOTAL	% LONG	% NAT'L	% SUPP.	% CRIT.
7th	2nd	8th	3rd	6th

through Tabora. After a career in government he moved to politics and a seat in the Assembly. Nguvu is proud of his past. Reminiscing about his life with his parents he said, "We had some style to our life."

As a member of the government, his main job in the Assembly, as he saw it, was to "tell the members what government policy is." Besides that his most important work was "coordination of government policy." He saw the role of an M.P. in rather limited terms, while the president's role he viewed in a most expansive way. His only criticism of the government was that it was "getting hard to get a decision from anybody because power is now so dispersed among different people."

Nguvu accepts democracy and African socialism as the policy of the government, which he therefore naturally supports. But he avoids defining what these ideas mean. African socialism, for example, "is clearly . . . what we want, not copying East or West. We are awaiting a committee which will tell us exactly what this means." Democracy is obviously desirable since "we'd rather not have a dictatorship." His response to a question about equality in democracy was that equality of opportunity and the absence of classes were the basic ingredients of democracy. Freedom of speech was also important, and "we have it in this country. But this doesn't necessarily mean an opposition party in Parliament. People can write what they think in the papers." In response to a question about the rights and duties of a citizen, he responded: "I don't think this matters for our people. It is only a problem for Asians or others. For the ordinary person this is nothing. He is a real citizen, with his own interests, real interests." The only danger he saw in giving everyone the right to vote is that "even intelligent people can be misled . . . and therefore the party must see that there is no misleading of the people."

Nguvu accepted the leadership of the party and the president. Nyerere, he felt, "is leading us along right lines now, teaching us to be self-reliant. I think he is right." For Nguvu the Assembly is clearly not the major decision-making body in the country. It is subordinate to the NEC:

> This is because the NEC is the ruling organ of the party. It meets first to consider what the policies of the government should be. Any ideas which need to be acted on are taken up and discussed at the NEC. Once the NEC decides on something, then the attorney general is called in and asked to draft a law. Parliament can only make slight alterations in this or discuss their ideas about it—but if the NEC has decided upon it, then it must be passed because all M.P.'s are first of all members of TANU.

Mr. Kipiga: An Intellectual

AUTHRN	ANOMIE	FAITH IN PEOPLE	DEM. PRACT.	PRES. ROLE STRENGTH
8th	6th	1st	6th	10th

ADM. CONGRUENCE	MP CONGRUENCE	PRES. CONGRUENCE	AVERAGE CONGRUENCE	
1st	10th	8th	9th	

% TOTAL	% LONG	% NAT'L	% SUPP.	% CRIT.
4th	5th	3rd	2nd	5th

Mr. Kipiga had risen quickly in politics. No doubt his overseas university degree was an important asset in this climb, but even in secondary school he had won a prize for leadership. Like so many of the elite, he attended Tabora and also went abroad for further study. His family had no traditional status. He described his father as "a peasant farmer" (although his father had worked as a cook and a gold miner before Kipiga was born).

Kipiga was active in the party, first through the Youth League, eventually going on to local and national politics. He did not conceal his ambitions. When asked why he wanted to be an M.P. he said, "because I wanted to participate in the shaping of things as a politician." His father had encouraged his ambition. "Taking me aside one day, he pointed to some of our neighbors working in the fields and said, 'look, if you leave school after only a few years you'll be just like them. But if you want to go ahead in school, then you can make something of yourself.' So I de-

cided to go ahead." Not surprisingly, he planned to continue as an M.P.
He explained, "I was preparing for the last election for three years and I
will continue."

Kipiga believed "very strongly" in democracy. "There should be full
and free participation of the people in discussing and carrying out issues
that affect them," he asserted. But "things like freedom of the press, these
don't matter much." What was expected of a citizen was "contributions"
and "being involved." Kipiga was a socialist who did not "believe in
African socialism as a term." Of course, he added, socialism can be
adapted to "specific circumstances of the African scene," but that does
not mean modernizing based on the past. "The masses," he explained, "are
too conscious of inequalities and the government has to create economic
equality whether you like it or not."

Kipiga admired, besides Nyerere, Mao Tse-tung, Nkrumah, Lenin, and
Churchill. Like them, his career and life are dedicated to political leadership. He listed the most commonly mentioned obligations of an M.P.:
"first, to understand what the constituency demands and push that in the
context of the national program, and second, to let the constituency know
the truth about the situation." What he enjoyed most, however, was the
fact that "you can speak your mind and voice opposition." Above all, he
thought it was important to know "what is going on and what role you
play." Kipiga did not seem to feel any role constraint limiting his freedom
as an M.P.

His performance in the Assembly coincided with his description of the
M.P. role. Speaking more frequently than the average member, he had
focused on national issues over a wide range of topics (such as foreign
policy, civil service, finance, and cooperatives), generally taking a definite
position of support or criticism. He went beyond simply speaking on
issues. He organized informally what he himself termed "lobbying" in
support of particular changes. It would be an error, however, to assume
that Kipiga is unaware of any limitations on M.P.'s as policymakers. He
admitted in a matter-of-fact way that the NEC is a more important policy-
making body in the country. But he was interested in exercising all the
influence his role could afford.

Mr. Mlimi commands the attention of his fellow members of the
Assembly by his forceful speaking style. Although he saw the role of an
M.P. in weak terms and the president's role as strong, he was a fairly
vocal critic in the Assembly.

Mr. Mlimi: A Local

AUTHRN	ANOMIE	FAITH IN PEOPLE	DEM. PRACT.	PRES. ROLE STRENGTH
1st	1st	8th	2nd	2nd

ADM. CONGRUENCE	MP CONGRUENCE	PRES. CONGRUENCE	AVERAGE CONGRUENCE	
4th	8th	6th	7th	

% TOTAL	% LONG	% NAT'L	% SUPP.	% CRIT.
3rd	6th	4th	4th	3rd

There is a certain emotionalism or enthusiasm about Mlimi which has not always served him well. He has twice been disappointed in his political career. During the period before independence, Mlimi lost an upper-level party position: "Because I was a hot member, I was kicked out." He continued to work for the party and eventually felt he was in line for a good party position. When his bid was turned down he quit the party and got a minor government job in his home area. Now he has returned to politics, capturing his Assembly seat with a three-to-two margin over his opponent. Mlimi knew the rules of the game for M.P.'s with regard to criticism. For example, he suggested the following formula if he wished to oppose a bill.

> First I would explain to the government the idea behind the opposition, and be the agent of people's ideas. And if it is passed, then I would explain it to the people and honor the bill.

On balance, however, his views were comparatively incongruent.

Mlimi comes from a royal lineage, but his father left a traditional occupation to take a construction job. His childhood was therefore a mixture of traditional and modern influences. Living in town and attending school for six years prepared him for his work as a clerk. However, life at home with his father, mother, and the other five wives taught him to value his traditional family, whose genealogy and exploits he extolled at some length. His interest in politics seemed natural to him. "My father was a politician. He often went to the government to ask about problems for people. And I'm a politician from when I was in school." The most important part of his job as an M.P. was, he thought, "to see people and tour many parts of the constituency. I have to lead our people to know what to develop in the country and to get people to be like me—to have a good house and clothes."

Mlimi thought the good citizen should "be loyal to his leaders and the government and participate in nation-building projects, giving money for these projects" but he is "not able to expect any rights." As an M.P., Mlimi saw his job as largely that of a government servant, helping the people in his area and taking their common complaints to the central government. His role was circumscribed by party authority. For instance, to be liked and respected as an M.P., Mlimi felt one must "follow the party constitution and the government, and not oppose the party or the government." In spite of the control the party has, Mlimi felt Tanzania was definitely a democracy. "I'm sure we have it here. After all, the party allows everybody to speak to the party and say what they want to say." Unlike some who gave similar responses, Mlimi showed no cynicism about this judgment. Likewise, to the question about an M.P. who felt corruption was occurring in the government, Mlimi responded that the M.P. would be impotent—"he couldn't do anything." Mlimi's weak view of the M.P.'s role was consistent with his attitude toward the NEC, which he says "has full powers. After all, NEC members select who can be an Mbunge."

Mr. Kinifu: A Politico

AUTHRN	ANOMIE	FAITH IN PEOPLE	DEM. PRACT.	PRES. ROLE STRENGTH
5th	2nd	8th	7th	1st

ADM. CONGRUENCE	MP CONGRUENCE	PRES. CONGRUENCE	AVERAGE CONGRUENCE	
8th	9th	7th	10th	

% TOTAL	% LONG	% NAT'L	% SUPP.	% CRIT.
9th	1st	6th	1st	10th

Mr. Kinifu is a tough, old-line politician who has been active in TANU since shortly after its formation. Like a few of his colleagues he has spent time in jail for his political activities. As a member of the government he acknowledged special obligations and duties. Among these was to "make sure what is said by an M.P. is really what people think—we know exactly what people think often better than other M.P.'s." Kinifu was loyal to Nyerere whom he admired greatly, but his loyalty to the party seemed even greater. The most important aspect of his work was the party, "the source of all other things." Among his duties, therefore, he listed seeing that "people understand the party and its policies, and that they *like them*." Although he held a post in the government it was the party to which he looked for directions and instructions.

Kinifu had a tough climb to his present position. His father was an entrepreneur in the small fishing village in which they lived. Kinifu recalled that his father worked hard, for which he was apparently unpopular with his neighbors. His mother, the first of five wives, had five children, but all except Kinifu died from malaria as youngsters. After five years of formal schooling he got a job as a houseboy for an English family. When this proved demeaning, he quit and then held a succession of jobs working in a hotel, on a sisal estate, as clerk in a town government, as a maintenance worker at an airport, and as a bus conductor. He even settled down for a short period among another tribe, raising cattle. Eventually he found each of these careers unsatisfying and, returning to his home area, became active in political causes and the TAA. A champion of local grievances, his career in TANU led him to continually higher posts. After many years of wandering from one loyalty to another he had made the party his life, and it was TANU and not a separate conception of country or government with which he primarily identified. In the Assembly, Kinifu was supportive in his few long speeches—more so than most government members.

Kinifu was somewhat authoritarian in his outlook and dubious of democratic principles. In response to the question "What does the term democracy mean to you?" he stated:

> This is a new word learned in school, but it was here [in Tanzania] very much before schools. There was no need for a new application of it for people, because democracy organized from the people. A chief was elected for what he did. In the past children were watched, and a leader was picked who had the best characteristics. Nowadays people don't understand when a man goes on a platform and says I can do this or that. When a man loses his people are happy. . . . For example, people don't see the need for the President [to be elected]. If someone took him away forcibly and replaced him people would accept it. . . . Of course, the election was a good idea since it pleased a few who wanted it because they learned it somewhere else.

Kinifu was distrustful of the educated. "These are the people who ask and receive and still want more." He saw three kinds of people in Tanzania: the *Wazee* (elders or, better translated for his meaning, the traditionally oriented); the young, uneducated workers; and the educated. He saw politics as a struggle between the Wazee, who "all believe in unity even though not all are in TANU," and the educated, who, though they were most "like us" (the party leaders), "are in fact taught only how to develop into a bourgeoisie."

> These educated youth are selfish and fighting for titles. They have different ideologies and ideas and are the cause of trouble among themselves. The workers are neutral and don't know which group to follow. They are pulled first by the educated class and then are pulled back by the Wazee. Some are pulled each way but this group can always pull down the educated. If the Wazee and the neutrals can lead, then the educated in TANU will have to go along. The fully educated fear this because they don't carry the belief, like the Wazee do, in old time behavior—in the human fraternity.

It seemed clear to me that Kinifu himself felt the tensions of the "neutral" and was pulled both toward and away from "modern" ideas. For instance, strong identification with the party may explain some of the confusion and discrepancies in his attitudes and feelings about elections and democracy. At one point he implied, as cited above, that elections were merely catering to the educated, but elsewhere in answering a question about voter competence he declared: "For me, stick with TANU principles; you can't discriminate on color, education, or religion. To turn back and not give freedoms is a bad thing . . . the last elections showed that only the fully educated fear giving the free franchise." Elections are good, according to TANU principles, hence the educated whom he dislikes must not believe in them. Perhaps these feelings are also reflected in his relatively high anomie and low faith in people.

Emerging Legislative Norms

What does this information about Tanzanian M.P.'s tell us? Various legislative groups, significantly different in their attitudes, their role expectations, and their Assembly behavior, have been identified. Infrequent criticism, however, was found to be a product not only of membership in a particular group but also of general expectations about the role requirements of an Mbunge. These expectations form norms or rules that serve to sustain a closed system of politics for Tanzania.

Rules for Legislators

The role expectations of legislators, combined with statements of official expectations and other material, permit a listing of a few of the rules governing legislative behavior, which were a part of the elite political culture.

> RULE 1: A legislator may express criticism or opposition to a government policy only on practical grounds, not on principle.

This rule stresses the maintenance of unity and ideological solidarity. It represents a point made by Nyerere in several of his speeches and was affirmed by a number of the legislators, most notably the Politicos, during their interviews.

> RULE 2: An M.P. may not publicly oppose a policy decision made in the party's National Executive Committee (NEC).

This rule, though closely related to the first, is an important addition. Distinguishing between practical opposition and opposition that has an ideological bent and is flatly contradictory to government policy is not an easy task. For example, in June 1966, the government officially stood behind legislation designed to provide a favorable climate for investment. But the question of nationalization was a fit subject for debate and was suggested by several members. In contrast, one member argued that nationalization of private business would violate the constitution and the principles of the Tanzanian government, which were to "encourage the establishment of private industries."[41] The NEC, in January 1967, adopted the Arusha Declaration, which called upon the government to take further steps in the "implementation of the policy of socialism," including control of the major means of production, such as utilities, transport, textiles, and "any other big industry upon which a large section of the population depend for their living."[42] Two weeks after the NEC's adoption of the Arusha Declaration, when Parliament was asked to vote on five bills that would effect the recommended nationalization, these bills received the unanimous support of members "who, one after another, took the

---

41. *The Standard,* June 24, 1966.
42. *The Nationalist,* February 6, 1967.

floor to deliver militant speeches commending the Party, the government and the correct leadership of President Nyerere." [43] Rule 2, moreover, is not only visible in practice but several M.P.'s explicitly articulated this obligation. "If the NEC has passed it, then the members must support it," stated one Politico.

This second rule has an important effect upon the style of Tanzanian politics. Critics of government policy, or those dissatisfied with the pace of implementation of vaguely declared goals, such as socialism, are enabled to announce publicly their support for more rapid progress, or changes in or abandonment of present policies. For example, Michael Kamaliza, then minister for labor and secretary-general of the government-regulated national trade union, NUTA, in addressing the fifth general council on December 27, 1966, made a strong plea for the government to move forward in the study of socialism and criticized high salaries in private industry and the government's policy of encouraging private investment.[44] His speech was a full month before the Arusha Declaration, which moved the country in this direction. Once policy has been decided in the NEC, however, and specific statements are endorsed, then criticism or opposition such as Kamaliza and others declared publicly would be considered a violation of this rule. Disagreement among elite members may be publicly aired and argued only prior to NEC decisions. The closed, though by all accounts stormy, NEC meetings may resolve an issue, and this at once signals the end of controversy or discussion and the initiation of praise and rededication to the party's policy decisions.

A corollary also follows from this rule, namely, that the M.P.'s role as legislator is subordinate to his role as party member. "TANU is supreme —even above the government," Second Vice-President Kawawa told Parliament.

> The President of our Republic who is also the President of TANU, has in no uncertain terms made it clear that TANU is more supreme than the government and that the government as such is the people's instrument for administration.[45]

43. Ibid., February 15, 1967.
44. Ibid., December 28, 1966. Kamaliza has since lost his post and in 1970 was arrested and tried for treason.
45. Ibid., June 12, 1966.

This statement was in response to a question by a Local (also a member of the NEC) who had inquired about what was being done to popularize the supremacy of the party in view of the fact that government employees were sometimes accorded more respect than party officials.

That supremacy of the party has been at least partially established can be illustrated in two ways. First, although M.P.'s are an important link between citizenry and government, the party is seen as an even more important and powerful link. In a survey among the Dar es Salaam electorate in 1966, people were asked: "If you have a problem in your district which requires government action, to whom should you go first —your representative in the National Assembly or your local TANU official?" Fifty-two percent stated they would go to their local TANU official first, while only 35 percent chose their Assembly representative. City residents were also asked: "If you have a specific complaint against a particular government official or government action, to whom would you complain?" Fifty-six percent named their local TANU official compared with 28 percent who would contact their M.P. A second illustration of the party's potency compared with that of the Assembly was the response to another question in the Dar es Salaam survey: "Which do you think has more influence in the way our government is run: the National Assembly or the National Executive Committee of TANU?" Thirty-four percent said the National Assembly; 40 percent the NEC, and 11 percent felt they were about equal. The same question, when asked of 29 M.P.'s during their interviews, revealed that every member of the government (eleven) considered the NEC the more important organ. Among those not in the government, however, 67 percent (12 of 18) felt the National Assembly was more powerful. Four of the six who felt the NEC was the more powerful were Intellectuals. The reluctance to acknowledge the paramountcy of the NEC was found predominantly among Locals whose participation in debates on general policy is relatively low.[46] While such attitudes

46. A revealing incident occurred on one occasion when I raised this question subsequent to an interview (since the question was added part way through the interviewing process) in the presence of another Tanzanian. When the M.P. (a Local) declared that the Bunge was more powerful than the NEC, the other Tanzanian burst forth with, "No, no! That's the wrong answer." He later took me aside and explained, "Some of these M.P.'s just don't understand the way things are." The deviance of Locals underscores the often unexpressed desire among Locals to increase the power and importance of the Assembly and, as a consequence, their own power and importance.

among M.P.'s present some challenge to party stability, and party stability
is the bulwark of Tanzanian stability, they are not a serious threat.

> RULE 3: An M.P. may oppose government policy in party discussion
> or within the Assembly before the Assembly votes, but if the
> policy is passed he must support it among his constituents.

This rule emerged directly from the role expectation question concerning opposition to a government policy. It closely resembles the classic
formulation by Lenin of "democratic centralism." The rule encompasses
the many bills whose details have been drawn up by the government and
not the NEC. Discussion of this sort of legislation, as well as numerous
embarrassing questions, may be raised in the Assembly; following the
election of September 1965, criticism of this nature increased.[47] But once
the measure has passed, the M.P. must support it. He may not publicly
voice his criticism to his constituents. The possible consequences for
M.P.'s violating this formal dictum were outlined by Vice-President
Kawawa in Parliament itself. He discussed legislation that would make
it unlawful for a person to foment discontent or ill will for "unlawful
purposes" and pointed out that such criticisms as those contrary to government plans would "be going against TANU and the Afro-Shirazi Party.
. . . All Members here are members of TANU and Afro-Shirazi Party, and
there is a special procedure of dealing with any problem in a Party way." [48]
Unnecessary and uninformed criticism has also been condemned in the
party press and by party leaders, particularly Kawawa.[49]

Withholding one's own views if they conflict with a decided policy is
a type of secrecy. Thus, a necessary adjunct to rules 2 and 3 is that information about political cleavages ought not to be publicly discussed.
This secrecy is an important norm not only for legislators but for all
members of the elite.

A revealing instance of how this rule works is the case of Oscar Kambona, former minister and party secretary-general. Although Kambona

---

47. Debate and criticism in the Assembly meetings that took place after the period
covered by the content analysis, at least from September–October 1966 until July 1968,
seem to have continued these trends. Policy initiative and criticism, judging by newspaper
accounts, apparently increased.

48. *The Nationalist,* June 29, 1966.

49. See, for instance, *Sunday News,* July 10, 1965, p. 5, and a *Nationalist* editorial,
July 14, 1966, p. 4. Former Secretary-General Kambona also condemned "petty criticism"
in an address to the National Assembly on July 14, 1965.

fled Tanzania in July 1967, and apparently engaged in actions of a questionable nature, it was not for several weeks—until he had violated the important norm of privacy by publicly attacking TANU and government officials—that President Nyerere and the party press took open action against him. The sin which apparently finally triggered official counterattacks was Kambona's open discussion of political cleavages.

Unfortunately there is an almost irrational quality to these prescriptions for a closed politics. Leaders are warned that it is sinful to reveal party or state secrets; articles in *The Nationalist* stress the presence of Western spies eager to pry secrets from gullible leaders and civil servants and to foment divisions.[50] In contradiction to this there are equally frequent statements by leaders that people should have nothing to fear and that criticism is welcomed. A consequence of these apparently contradictory norms is what amounts to, at least collectively, a schizophrenia about revealing information related to policy disputes. For example, committee meetings of the National Assembly are held in camera. Some members interpret this to mean that they are forbidden to mention or discuss what occurs in these meetings. Others talk freely about committee activity, including the procedures, participation, and substantive issues discussed. On a few occasions members have even raised details of committee work in Assembly debates. The need for secrecy that arises from rules 2 and 3 is a problem in Tanzania and a source of anxiety for at least some elite respondents because it is not clear what constitutes private party or state matters.

RULE 4: An M.P., not a member of the government, must consider constituency work his most important obligation.

The expectations of Locals, interviews with members of government, and public statements by the president, vice-president, and others all give evidence of this informal rule.[51] Many members from constituencies take this dictum seriously. When Parliament is not in session, a typical M.P. spends two to three weeks each month traveling in his constituency. One M.P. estimated that he met or addressed 10,000 constituents each month. The M.P. often has a secretary, sometimes shared with another M.P. or

50. See, for example, statements of the Mwanza Area Commissioner, *The Nationalist,* April 28, 1966, and frequent columns of "Pressman's Commentary" in *The Nationalist.*

51. For example, Vice-President Kawawa, addressing the Parliament December 17, 1965, urged M.P.'s to "tell people what we do," and to explain to constituents what action the government had decided upon. *Assembly Debates,* December 17, 1965, Cols. 268–80.

the district party office. Either the M.P. or his secretary is available each day to hear complaints from constituents. The most frequent are about low agricultural prices or involve accusations of mistreatment or misunderstanding on the part of government officialdom. The M.P.'s interviewed commonly stressed a tendency for troubled constituents to approach them rather than government officials. The average daily number of complaints ranged from five to twenty. Hence, the role of the M.P. in his constituency is an important extension of his general function as a legitimizer of the political system. As one legislator remarked, "People most often come to me because they think of me as their man in the government."

These four rules dictate that the M.P. who is not a member of government is above all else a communication link, a popularizer and legitimizer for the party and the government. He is not a lawmaker. In a few rare instances, notably among Intellectuals, he may become a lobbyist.[52] For instance, some M.P.'s articulate the interests of various publics, such as workers and farmers, when they have some claim to be spokesmen for the sentiments of these groups. Representing special interests or raising problems in the Assembly seem to provide a catharsis for both M.P.'s and their constituents. By vehemently announcing their unhappiness over falling farm prices, for example, they reduce the political impact of this problem, which is largely insoluble. In an even more general sense, an M.P. may affect policy making by his independent and uncoordinated criticism (as opposed to organized criticism). When such individual efforts multiply, as has occurred on a very few occasions, it has proven effective. For instance, numerous criticisms of affluence and arrogance were leveled toward regional commissioners and other party leaders in mid-1966 Assembly sessions. These pressures were quite important in effecting changes such as the "voluntary" salary reduction of ministers and higher civil servants, the withdrawal of government Mercedes-Benzes from personal use or assignment, and the stiff new rules limiting accumulation of wealth among leaders that were included in the Arusha Declaration of 1967.

This examination of the role of the M.P. reveals two things about Tanzanian politics. First, role expectations among the elite contain rules that support a pattern of closed politics. Major policy cleavages or serious leader-

52. This term was actually used by one Intellectual describing his efforts to pressure the government on insurance regulation.

ship splits, such as the one between Nyerere and Kambona, are contained normally within the private arena or the party structure, indeed, within the upper echelons of the party structure. The continually stressed theme of unity both helps contain cleavages and is preserved by their containment. This fundamental principle of unity is stressed by all leaders, including Nyerere, and is supported by a set of rules channeling political cleavages into the party structure to be absorbed and eventually resolved by the party executive. The role of the Assembly in this framework has been principally to legitimize government and party decisions within the constitutional framework that gives Parliament supremacy over legislation.

The second conclusion suggested is that in spite of "rules of the game" that foster closed politics, the National Assembly is not anachronistic or a mere showcase for propaganda purposes as the comparable body may have been in Ghana under Nkrumah, for example. M.P.'s play an important role as links between the government and the countryside, and their criticisms in the Assembly have affected some policies. The ability of the Tanzanian government to remain responsive depends in part on their activity.

If M.P.'s were to exercise greater influence, comparable to the collective authority of the NEC, for instance, what effect might this have? By most criteria it would make Tanzania more democratic, since it would strengthen the elected representatives of the people. However, it would also have, I believe, other effects that would probably be detrimental to democracy in the long run.

Frederick Frey has noted that "lawyers tend to be the largest single occupational group in parliament after parliament all over the world." [53] Yet, the Tanzanian Parliament contained only two lawyers, one of whom was the attorney-general, appointed by the president. The requisite level of legislative sophistication and skill is simply not generally found among Tanzanian M.P.'s in a degree sufficient to warrant their increased participation in lawmaking. The expression of provincialism, idiosyncratic to legislators, is frequently in evidence in Tanzania and is a singularly inappropriate goal. Increasing legislative power in Tanzania would, I believe, result in heightening regional and ethnic differences, encouraging pork-barrel bargaining and deals, and increasing the possibilities for corruption. None of these outcomes is conducive to economic growth or

53. Frey, *Turkish Political Elite*, p. 395.

national integration. Moreover, such a trend, although appearing to be a move toward promoting democratic practices, would eventually alienate intellectuals, technocrats, and others, and spur the demise, not the growth, of representative procedures in the national governing system. Given the background and skills found in the National Assembly and the rules for role behavior already developed, many M.P.'s perform an important function in the political system already as the people's surrogates, meeting with the governing elite, serving as a cathartic and legitimizing force in Tanzanian politics, and ameliorating the otherwise closed politics of the party.

6. The Role of the President

In a nation with a long history and with traditions firmly embedded in the memories of its elite and populace, the role of the president or political leader is bounded by many important and firmly held expectations. In the United States, for example, the presidential role is independent of the temporary occupant. The authority and popularity of an individual are enhanced by the presidential role far more than the role is honored by the occupant.[1] Obviously, within the bounds of the role, individuals may interpret their role in weak or strong terms and others may judge how well the role is played. But institutionalization of a political role implies that the role acquires a set of expectations and demands that help shape the attitudes, interests, and behavior of the occupant. If the presidency of a nation is institutionalized, for instance, one expects it to be an independent force, shaping the role incumbent's behavior and providing him with a new set of perspectives and norms.[2]

In a young country, however, where indigenous traditions undergirding the national political institutions are weak or do not exist, the prior attitudes and behavior of political role occupants are likely to be important in determining both the norms for their roles and the extent to which institutionalization occurs. To a crucial extent the role may be what the first incumbent believes it to be. Where role occupants, over time, accept the legal restraints and normative expectations attached to a given position, institutionalization is likely to occur. In Latin America, for instance, the failure of presidents to abide by the rules of their constitutions has been one contributing factor in the institutional failure of democratic practices. The formal rules in many Latin countries may not have been appropriate to the exigencies of political life, but rather than being reshaped, the formal rules have often been publicly affirmed and privately broken, resulting in anomie and weak institutionalization.[3]

1. For instance, the popularity of political leaders, notably Eisenhower, Kennedy, and Johnson, as measured in opinion polls, rose after they became president.

2. See Richard Neustadt's description of the American presidency in *Presidential Power* (New York: Wiley, 1960) and the argument made by Lasswell and Rogow that the presidency may improve personal rectitude in *Power, Corruption and Rectitude.*

3. See John Gerassi, *The Great Fear in Latin America* (New York: Macmillan, 1963) for a vivid characterization of the disintegrative forces in Latin America.

Tanzania lacks its own national traditions, although it does retain some residue of the British heritage. The role of president, while constitutionally defined, is largely a product of the actual behavior of the first and only occupant of this office, Julius Nyerere. In much the same vein that Nkrumah's charisma legitimized political institutions in Ghana,[4] the popular affection for Nyerere has helped legitimize and institutionalize the political patterns and practices emerging in Tanzania. In order to understand the character of the presidential role emerging in Tanzania, therefore, two types of information are important: an understanding of Nyerere's life, ideas, and past actions and the role expectations for the presidency held by the elite. As the role model outlined in chapter 2 suggests, the interactions of these variables are principal factors shaping the role of the president.

President Nyerere

Rise to Power

Julius Nyerere was born in 1922, one of the 26 children of Chief Nyerere Burito, a Zanaki. In the 1957 census the Zanaki tribe ranked 69th in population size in Tanzania. Historically the Zanaki did not have a strongly hierarchical system of authority, but rather a generational system in which spokesmen for each generation were elected. Under German rule, their political system was altered as the Germans appointed certain spokesmen (*Mwami*) as chiefs. Following the death of his elder brother, Nyerere's father was appointed chief in 1912, a position he held until his death in 1942.

Nyerere's early childhood differed little from that of other children in a traditional environment. The customs and practices among the Zanaki are similar to those in a majority of the other tribes in Tanzania. Zanaki children are educated by older females of the extended family. Courtesy and deference for age are important norms and younger boys are subservient to their elder siblings. The great deference accorded age is reflected in the importance of elders, called *Bakaruka,* who were customarily consulted by the Mwami before he would act. The requirement of their support was an effective sanction on the powers of a Mwami. Although Nyerere was the son of a chief the economic benefits of this social status were minimal. The grass hut in which he lived with his

4. See David Apter, *Ghana in Transition* (New York: Atheneum, 1963), pp. 303–08.

mother, two brothers, and three sisters leaked when it rained and there was not always adequate food for their single daily meal. These early life experiences are important in understanding some of Nyerere's attitudes and actions in later life. Deference and respect for elders, expectations of docility and obedience from youth, and an abiding concern for the poverty-level living conditions of the vast majority of Tanzanians are important characteristics of Nyerere's leadership.

At the age of eleven he was sent to a native authority school in Musoma. During his three years at this school Nyerere developed an interest in Roman Catholicism and attended catechism classes at Nyegina Mission. In 1937 Nyerere was admitted to the Tabora government school, where he compiled an excellent scholastic record, was twice made a house prefect, and became acquainted with a number of the men who later became officials in the party and government. Here an early crystallization of nationalist sentiment emerged that eventually led him into a political career. For example, he debated with his fellow students whether an African could not perform many of the roles reserved for Europeans in the colonial situation. Also, his ties with Catholicism were strengthened during this period. He attended catechism classes at the Tabora Mission, and after his graduation at the age of twenty-one he was baptized and took the name Julius.

In the same year, Nyerere had begun a three-year course at Makerere College. Here, as at Tabora, he associated with an elite group of Tan-zanians, many of whom he later worked with in building TANU and in restructuring the colonially inherited government apparatus. He helped found the Tanganyikan African Welfare Association which, he has said, was "frankly political." [5] This organization was eventually abandoned and Nyerere, along with several college associates who were similarly politically inclined, resolved to work through the established Tanganyika African Association (TAA) in pursuing nationalist goals. After completing his studies at Makerere, Nyerere accepted a position at St. Mary's second-ary school in Tabora, where he taught history and biology. For three years he taught and was active in the local TAA branch, becoming a familiar figure and most popular teacher among the students both at St. Mary's and at the government secondary school, where he frequently lectured and debated. A number of the elite interviewed, both admin-istrators and legislators, were either former students of Nyerere's or had

5. Listowel, *Making of Tanganyika*, p. 184.

become acquainted with him during these periods of his career. He was most frequently described by them as reserved, modest, and intense. These traits, along with his recognized intellectual abilities as a lecturer and debater, survive as memorable impressions among many of the elite respondents.

In October 1949, with a scholarship from the Church, Nyerere enrolled at Edinburgh University and studied history, politics, economics, and sociology. In 1952 he received an M.A. and returned to Tanzania to spend the next three years teaching at St. Francis Pugu School near Dar es Salaam. Nyerere has described his overseas experience as an important formative stage in his life and thought.

> I . . . spent much time arguing with fellow students about every-thing under the sun, except Marxism which is above the sun. I did a great deal of thinking about politics in Africa. . . . I evolved the whole of my political philosophy while I was there. I wrote [a master's thesis] on race and politics in East Africa . . . in which I expressed for myself what I have since been trying to put into practice.[6]

A year and a half after his return, Nyerere, as president of the Dar es Salaam TAA, transformed this organization into the Tanganyika African National Union. He became the founder and has been the first and only president of the party. His stability in office rests largely on his intellectual talents, his ability to write and to think clearly. While sharing the nationalist and socialist sentiments of many of his early African colleagues in TANU, he also has had a capacity for responsiveness to the problems and feelings of both the uneducated and unorganized Africans in the towns and countryside and the urbanized elite, including British colonial officials. In part, this responsiveness explains why the struggle for independence and the rise of TANU as a potent political force in Tanganyika were accomplished with very little violence.

Statements of colonial officers testify to what amounted to an uncanny ability on his part to legitimize nationalist demands by placing them within the framework of values accepted by the British, by pursuing a policy of accommodation rather than total belligerence, and by securing alliances with Asians and Europeans willing to follow his leadership. His public speeches, notably those to the United Nations, have been described

6. Ibid., p. 201.

by many commentators as more articulate and more reasoned than those of spokesmen attempting to defend British policy in Tanganyika.[7] When he was accused of making libelous and racist statements at a public rally he offered the chief secretary a tape recording of his talk; the accusation was dropped and an apology made. When the Criminal Investigation Division (CID) was instructed to maintain a surveillance of TANU activities in one district, TANU learned of the order and invited the local CID superintendent to attend their meetings. When the colonial government offered Nyerere the status of a seat on the Legislative Council he accepted, but after a few months, frustrated by the lack of effect which his verbal eloquence in the chamber produced, he resigned. In doing so he attacked not the colonial system but its unresponsiveness to opposition that was voiced in legitimate form. In 1958, when he was convicted on libel charges, he chose the alternative of paying a fine rather than going to prison, reasoning that the latter course would raise political passions among Africans but not speed the progress of independence.

In the 1958–59 and again in the 1960 elections, prior to independence, seats were reserved for Asian and African candidates. TANU itself admitted only African members, so to assure complete victory it had to find suitable Asian and European candidates to support. Several loyal friends of Nyerere were already available. Ahmad Jamal, for instance, now a minister, had been a friend and associate since 1954 when they were brought together through common ties with the Fabian Society. Derek Bryceson, a European farmer and the president of the Conservative Club when he was at Cambridge, was also ready and willing to merge his political career with the rise of TANU.[8] These and other friendships that crossed racial lines suggest that firm convictions underlie Nyerere's avowed principle of nonracialism. Indeed, an analysis of the colleagues with whom he is reportedly closest, and who under his tutelage have been given posts of responsibility, suggests that those Tanzanians, regardless of race, who share his concerns for human welfare, socialism, and democracy and who exemplify these concerns in their actions have continued the longest in his favor and have consistently held responsible political posts. These in-

---

7. See Chidzero, *Tanganyika;* Taylor, *Political Development,* pp. 124, 163; and Listowel, pp. 239–311.

8. Bryceson, now minister of agriculture and cooperatives, maintains a home adjacent to that of Nyerere.

cidents illustrate the strategy established by Nyerere in the pre-independence period: he worked from within rather than outside the established institutional framework; he was responsive to the pressures and sentiments of both ardent nationalists and colonial officials, utilizing wit and intellect to win acceptance on both sides for policies of accommodation which resulted, by all accounts, in a peaceful transfer of power sooner than either had initially anticipated.

A month after independence, in January 1962, Nyerere announced his resignation as prime minister and devoted his attention to the organization of the party, the creation of a new republican form of government, and the longer-range problems and goals for the new state. Since his inauguration in December 1962 as the first president, Nyerere has remained as head of state, head of government, head of the party, and is now commonly referred to as *Baba ya Taifa,* Father of the Nation.

Style of Leadership

Another of Nyerere's titles which has become official is *Mwalimu,* "teacher." The image of Nyerere as *Mwalimu* summarizes many of the qualities that characterize him as a leader. In the student-teacher relationship the teacher is expected to explain and interpret the world to the novice. Honesty, wisdom, and the ability to communicate are the skills expected of the teacher, while the student is expected to be able to learn, to recite, and to challenge. In the classroom there is freedom to debate and discuss ideas; intellectual ability is rewarded. But the final arbiter in matters of dispute is the teacher. The ideal teacher is benevolent, the ideal students are orderly and eager. While it would be inane to interpret all of Nyerere's behavior as leader of the party and the nation as reflecting a continuation of the role behavior he learned earlier in his life as a teacher, the image of the teacher and the role expectations associated with this position constitute an extremely useful approach to an understanding and interpretation of the style of leadership he has developed.

How does Nyerere make decisions? Obviously no leader makes every decision in the same way. Some decisions may require lengthy deliberation and consultation while others, often trivial and of a managerial nature, can be made swiftly and alone. Nevertheless, a review of Nyerere's role in party and national decision making reveals a pattern of strong and independent leadership. Party and government are organized in such a way that Nyerere heads what resembles an "executive centered coalition" [9] in which he is the key figure. A few examples will illustrate this.

In 1956, when Steven Mhando exceeded his authorized travel plan, at Nyerere's initiative he was speedily removed as secretary-general of TANU.[10] In 1958, when Sheikh Sulemani Takadir complained about the small number of Muslim candidates selected by TANU, Nyerere, through the central committee, quickly stripped him of his power and position as head of the elders for the party. In this same year two other decisions of critical importance were arrived at by Nyerere, largely independently. In one instance he was faced with the alternative of a prison sentence or a fine stemming from his conviction on libel charges. He chose to pay the fine, and only afterward justified his action to his followers. One of the most revealing instances of Nyerere's leadership occurred at the annual conference held in Tabora in January 1958. The question of whether the party should participate in elections planned for that year was to be decided. Since the elections called for a racial parity of seats, ten Africans, ten Asians, and ten Europeans, and in addition was to be based on a limited franchise, it manifestly contradicted stated aims of the party. At the beginning of the conference the majority of the delegates favored boycotting the elections. Nyerere was in favor of participation and had announced this earlier before the U.N. Trusteeship Council. The issue of participation was debated heatedly. When the issue was finally voted, Nyerere's position was upheld by the delegates. His reasoning and arguments had not only convinced many delegates but defused the passion of the controversy so that only a minor splintering of the ranks occurred.[11]

Another occasion on which Nyerere committed TANU prior to party approval was in 1961, when he offered to delay Tanganyika's independence if it could be coordinated with the independence of Uganda and Kenya and thereby promote the possibility of a political federation in East Africa. Because the situation in Kenya was still unsettled, colonial authorities did not act on Nyerere's offer. It was not necessary, therefore, for Nyerere to secure the support of the NEC, and this might indeed have been difficult

9. This term is used by Robert Dahl in *Who Governs?*

10. Mhando in 1968 became minister of state for foreign affairs. His return to a high post exemplifies another characteristic of Nyerere's leadership—the willingness to forgive insubordination or disloyalty *after* a period of penance.

11. Zuberi Mtemvu, at one time organizing secretary-general of TANU, resigned allegedly over the principle of participation in the elections and established his own Tanganyika African National Congress. In 1962, Nyerere defeated Mtemvu for the presidency of the newly formed republic by an overwhelming margin.

since the majority of NEC members were reluctant, to say the least, to approve such a delay.[12] Again, in January 1962, when Nyerere announced his resignation as prime minister, he reached this decision independently. He then spent several days explaining to TANU leaders the reasons for his action and convincing them of its correctness.

Not all of Nyerere's decisions since he became president of Tanzania fit the pattern of the decisional episodes just sketched, but many do. He developed a pattern of deciding for himself, or in discussion with a varying but small set of colleagues, policies which were then announced or proclaimed rather than debated or submitted for approval. This seems to hold true not only for broader or general policies but also for more narrow and particular decisions. A number of the high officials interviewed said that the president simply informed them of their appointments. One even confessed that he had first learned of his appointment over the radio on an evening news broadcast. Of course some decisions cannot be made as quickly and decisively as these. For instance, the implementation of the one-party system in Tanzania evolved over several years. Nyerere's own ideas on the subject crystallized in 1962, but three years of conversations, bargaining, and investigation of alternative modes of organization preceded the formalization of the one-party system in the interim constitution of 1965. When Nyerere feels determined on an issue, however, he does not hesitate to act. His years as leader of a broad-gauged national movement have not taught him hesitancy or equivocation. The breaking of diplomatic relations with Great Britain on December 15, 1965, perhaps best illustrates Nyerere's style. The break was one of a number of contingencies discussed and approved at the Organization of African Unity (OAU) meeting in the spring of 1965 in Accra. Following the declaration of independence by Rhodesia in November 1965, an emergency meeting of the OAU was held in Addis Ababa. Vice-President Kawawa was briefed on the decisions made at Accra and given carte blanche authority to support any OAU policy within this framework. With great fervor the OAU voted nearly unanimously to break relations with Great Britain in one month if it had not taken effective steps against the "illegal regime" of Ian Smith. When news of the OAU's decision reached Tanzania, Nyerere was in Arusha. He returned speedily to the capital, called a news conference, and announced that Tanzania intended to support this resolution. In the subsequent month a great deal of maneuvering and equivocating

12. See Martin Lowenkopf (unpublished M.A. thesis, University of London, 1961).

occurred in other African states. Pressure from the U.K. and from other African countries (whose OAU representatives were later rebuked for their actions) was brought against Tanzania, but Nyerere steadfastly maintained his position and became, with Ghana, the only former British-controlled country to break relations with Rhodesia.[13]

Nyerere's leadership style, as illustrated by these actions, is characterized by three qualities: strength, independence, and legality. This third aspect, his dedication to a rule of law, deserves further elaboration. The Tanzanian president has vast powers; Nyerere has even suggested that under the present constitution he already has sufficient power to be a dictator. His disposition, however, is not to flaunt this power, and it is difficult to judge just how extensive his decision-making autonomy actually is. A state house aide, discussing Nyerere, was asked: "Is there anything Nyerere couldn't do, that is, you just wouldn't imagine or expect him ever to do?" The aide responded quickly: "Yes, he would never break the law." There is reasonable evidence to suggest that this statement is more than official sentiment for public consumption. In the 1964 army mutiny, Nyerere was particularly embittered that Tanzanian soldiers were prepared to take "illegal" actions in efforts to resolve their grievances. When these same mutineers received what seemed to Nyerere light sentences (three years of imprisonment), he upheld the court's action and sovereignty while publicly admitting his disappointment.

For Nyerere, law is not a tool for the political struggle but a basic set of rules within which all conflicts and grievances must be worked out. The alternative is chaos and social disintegration. In his speech explaining Tanzania's decision to break diplomatic relations with the United Kingdom, he stated:

> In an ordered society, when a man is wronged by an illegal act he does not, and should not, take the law into his own hands. He applies to the law, and those responsible for enforcing the law, for redress. And he expects that action will be taken to relieve him of the wrongs which he is suffering because of an illegal action. It is by such procedures that peace and justice are maintained within states. It is by

13. After the military coup in 1966, Ghana restored relations. The UAR also formally broke relations, but her ties to the U.K. were weaker and, except for the ambassador, the British mission in Cairo was not asked to leave. Tanzania restored relations in 1968 after it became evident that no further support for Rhodesian (Zimbabwe) Africans would result from a further diplomatic hiatus with Great Britain.

similar procedures that international peace and justice can be maintained between states.[14]

It was because Great Britain had the duty to enforce and maintain the
law with respect to Southern Rhodesia and appeared unwilling to accept
this responsibility that Nyerere took such a firm stand in breaking relations. Thus, in spite of his broad powers, Nyerere's personal commitment
to law is a constraining moral force upon him. It is an important self-
limitation which he brings to the role of the presidency and which, under
his influence, may become institutionalized.

ELITE EXPECTATIONS

Presidential Role Expectations and Consensus

The 109 elite in the sample were queried about their expectations with
respect to five contingency questions related to the presidency. Each question dealt with some aspect of the president's role. As with responses to
similar question dealing with the roles of administrator and M.P., responses have been collapsed into three general categories reflecting varying
degrees of strength and independence of action. The first question asked,
"If the president wished to change local leadership, what would he do?"
The president, acting through his Ministry of Local Government, has the
power to dismiss local councilors, an action which he took in 1963 against
the Bukoba council when it proved unreceptive to TANU guidance. Most
responses, therefore, dealt with what consultations, if any, the president
would make before taking action against local leaders. The distribution of
responses among legislators and administrators on the first question is
similar (as A in figure 6.1 illustrates). A majority expected the president
to undertake some consultations before he acted. But a sizable portion,
37 percent, expected the president simply to act. Students, in contrast to
the elite, were more prone to expect the president to consult the public
either locally or nationally before acting. This tendency among students
to expect public participation in political controversies, reflected also in
responses to the fifth question, may have stemmed from implicit desires
on their part to be more involved and consulted.

The second question probed the relationship of the president with
M.P.'s, focusing particularly on his expected reaction to criticism. Among

14. Julius K. Nyerere, "Address to the National Assembly, 14 December 1965" (Dar es
Salaam: Ministry of Information and Tourism, 1965), p. 1.

legislators and students, a sizable number expected the president to respond directly to a critical M.P. by criticizing him, threatening him, or, as
suggested by several, even placing him in detention.[15] Other responses,
such as ignoring or accepting the criticism or responding to the criticism
(rather than the critic!) were also expected by fairly large proportions of
the respondents. The diversity of opinion on this question (see B in figure
6.1) suggests an uncertainty and flexibility of norms governing the relationship between the president and members of the National Assembly.
On this point it is particularly interesting to note the student responses.
A plurality expected action directed toward the M.P., but among these
only 43 percent approved of this behavior contrasted to 88 percent who
approved of the president responding only to the criticism. The gap between students' ideas of what is expected and what is desirable (as indicated by the percentage indicating approval) is greatest on this question.

The president's action in response to tribal unrest was also explored.
The question was: "Opposition to the government breaks out among a
rural tribal group. What action would the president order to be taken?"
The use of persuasion and understanding was the predominant expectation among the elite (scored weak ["0"] in figure 6.1). Only 25 percent
anticipated the use of force or emergency powers. Among students, however, 61 percent believed that the president was likely to invoke force, although they approved more highly of the president's using persuasion
rather than force in such a situation. The differences between student and
elite expectations probably reflect even more basic differences in orientation. Students generally were more prone to expect the president to act
strongly than were members of the elite. And the elite, perhaps owing
to their experience in dealing with various matters involving tribal loyal-
ties, were more sensitive to the dangers of exacerbating conflict between
national government regulation and tribally linked sentiments and activities. Such orientations among elite respondents may explain their
general agreement on the desirability of persuasion as the reaction to
tribal dissidence.

According to the constitution, the high court of Tanzania has the
authority to interpret the constitution.[16] It is not inconceivable, therefore,
that an action might come before it that raised the question whether

15. In fact, one of the M.P.'s interviewed was placed in detention for remarks apparently made in a most inappropriate forum, an ad hoc gathering at the army base on
the outskirts of the capital in July 1967.

16. *Interim Constitution of Tanzania, 1965*, para. 64.

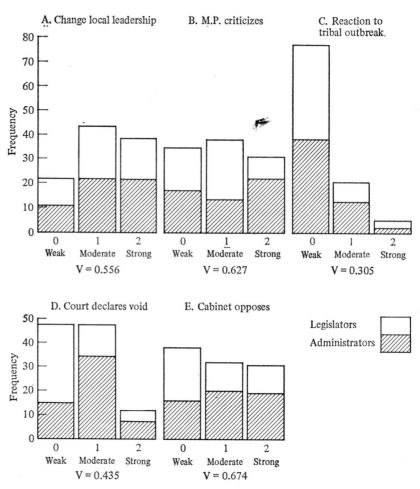

Figure 6.1. Distribution of Role Expectations for the President

the president acted within his constitutional powers, though a number of the elite expressed doubt that such an issue would arise. Indeed, the One-Party Commission specifically recommended divorcing the court from political involvement.[17] In order to test expectations regarding the president's role vis-à-vis the court, the following question was asked: "A court rules the president has exceeded his authority in a particular matter and declares his action void. What would the president do?" Three types

17. *One-Party State Report,* p. 33.

TABLE 6.1. Presidential Role Expectations of Elite
(in percentages)

	Adminis-trators (N = 50)	Legislators (N = 57)	Total Elite (N = 107)	Students (N = 100)	Students Approving (N = 56)
Wishes to change local leadership					
Consult public	22	19	20	58	79
Consult advisors	44	39	41	22	93
Will act	34	39	36	20	78
Elite/Students X² = 32.4*		Legislators/Administrators X² = 0.2			
M.P. criticizes				(N = 103)	(N = 57)
Accept or ignore	34	32	33	31	68
Respond to criticism	50	25	36	30	88
Respond to M.P.	16	40	29	39	43
Elite/Students X² = 2.2		Legislators/Administrators X² = 10.2*			
President reacts to tribal outbreak				(N = 104)	(N = 56)
Use persuasion	78	68	73	39	95
Use force	16	23	20	46	78
Use emergency powers	6	4	5	14	75
Elite/Students X² = 27.1*		Legislators/Administrators X² = 1.2			
Court declares action void				(N = 106)	(N = 55)
Accept	64	26	44	53	74
Ask parliament	26	60	44	21	71
Override court	8	12	10	26	53
Elite/Students X² = 17.3*		Legislators/Administrators X² = 15.9*			
Cabinet opposes views				(N = 108)	(N = 61)
Discuss, use persuasion	44	28	36	45	79
Go to Parliament	24	35	30	4	100
Act dramatically, alone	22	33	28	51	71
Elite/Students X² = 30.3*		Legislators/Administrators X² = 4.1			

* These chi-squares are significant at the $p < .05$ level.

of responses are reported in table 6.1 and illustrated by D in figure 6.1. One alternative, expected by a majority of administrators and students, is that the president would simply accept the court's action. Such expectations, I believe, reflected an acknowledgment of Nyerere's commitment to rule by law. Several respondents recited specific examples in which Nyerere stressed the necessity of accepting legal decisions even if one did not wholeheartedly agree with their content. Legislators, in contrast to

the administrators and students, were more apt to expect the president
to circumvent the court's ruling. The majority (60 percent) suggested
the president would act within legal, constitutional bounds, asking Parliament to change the law or constitution so that he might act legally. Only
10 percent of the elite and 26 percent of the students thought the president
would take action directly against the court, overriding the decision or
even dismissing the judges, thereby violating the independence of the
judiciary as established in the constitution. The underlying conviction that
many respondents expressed in answering this question was that the
president certainly would act lawfully. Several answers even implied
that respondents felt the president viewed the court system and legal
procedure as more sacrosanct than they did.

The last question was in the area of the president's relationship to his
cabinet. Since the cabinet may be expected to contain, particularly in a
one-party state like Tanzania, most of the important political figures in
the country, cleavages in cabinet opinion would represent an important
factionalizing of politics and present a real threat to the unity of the
country. Support by cabinet ministers is certainly an important source
of authority and strength for presidential action. The question posed to
probe this sensitive area was: "The president finds a majority of his ministers opposing his views. What would he do?" Answers ranged widely
from an expectation that the president would yield to the cabinet majority
and change his views to the quite contrary expectation that the president
would dismiss his cabinet or would even place dissenting members in
detention. In Uganda, for example, then Prime Minister Obote had just
done this, arresting and detaining five cabinet ministers who opposed him.
The most common expectation among the -elite was that the president would discuss the matter with cabinet members and use persuasion until some common agreement was reached. The left column of
figure 6.5 indicates the slight predominance of this response. It was difficult for many to conceive of a controversy being carried to a wider arena.
Other elite respondents, however, were prepared to acknowledge the
possibility of what the question implied, namely a difference in presidential and cabinet opinion that was not resolvable by discussion. They
mentioned two general alternatives: first, that the president would ask
Parliament to resolve the disagreement; second, that the president would
act on his own initiative, perhaps in a dramatic fashion, to resolve the

issue either by dismissing dissenting cabinet members or by taking it to the nation in a new general election.

The responses suggested the degree of arena expansion that important political conflict might generate. Certainly a large number of students and elite did not expect such controversy to go beyond the more or less private discussions of cabinet members. But some did anticipate that disputes could enter wider arenas and suggested that the Parliament might be a forum for resolving political disputes between the president and a majority of his cabinet. Some elite respondents would not have been surprised even to find the president appealing directly to the public on such an issue. Students were rather likely to expect this third possibility, perhaps because they saw the president acting strongly in general and/or because they preferred situations in which the public, including themselves, was able to participate or voice an opinion. Since the president has broad powers of detention, even those respondents expecting the most assertive behavior by the president—such as arresting his dissenting cabinet members—were not expressing expectations that the president would act illegally or beyond the scope of his power.

Presidential Role Strength

Elite responses to the five presidential role questions were categorized into a three-point continuum from weak to strong expected behavior. The responses of each elite member were summed to form a scale of presidential role strength (RS). Table 6.2 shows the percent of administrators and

TABLE 6.2. Presidential Role Strength among Elite
(in percentages)

	Administrators (N = 50)	Legislators (N = 55)	Total (N = 105)*
High	28	47	38
Medium	28	35	31
Low	44	18	30

* Chi-square (X^2) is 17.6, significant at the $p < .01$ level.

legislators who were high, medium, and low on this scale. Legislators expected much stronger behavior on the part of the president than did administrators. Those legislators who expected the presidential role to be potent tended also to feel a relative impotency in their own role as indicated by the correlation of .31 among legislators between presidential role strength and weak responses with regard to their own role.[18] To the extent that the president has great power in the system, legislators seemed to feel that their own powers and alternatives for action are limited. Several legislators indicated that an M.P. who attacked the president might find himself in detention.

Administrators, perhaps because of greater awareness of boundaries and rules imposed by the bureaucracy, expected less strong behavior on the part of the president. Power in the presidential role did not seem to be related to views about power in the administrative role, or to administrators' expectations of strength in the legislative role either. They exhibited an independence of judgment with respect to the strength of their own role and that of the president. What is it then for administrators that provides boundaries for the presidential role, leading them to view it in weaker terms than legislators? An examination of background and attitudinal variables among administrators suggests that commitment to democratic practices, which is clearly correlated with presidential role strength with $r = -.55$, is the best explanation. These findings indicate that norms of a general nature, in particular attitudes about democratic practices and commitment to legalized procedures, constitute the attitudinal reference that anchors and informs expectations among administrators. In responding to the contingency questions about expectations, administrators drew upon these attitudes in forming their expectations.

Legislators, on the other hand, had a tendency to view politics and power arrangements as a zero-sum game. If the president has greater power, legislators will have less. Power for them was a limited quantity. Occupants of roles with less power were therefore more susceptible to influence from the incumbent of the more powerful role. Unlike administrators, legislators seldom viewed power relationships among roles as established or bounded by an underlying set of rules or practices that would be equally effective in placing limits on all political roles. For legislators, presidential role strength seemed rather strongly related to anomie ($r = .49$) and to length of party membership ($r = .41$),[19] but only

18. Significant at $p < .05$. The correlation is based on summing legislators' responses to the three legislative questions to achieve single scores for each legislator.
19. The correlation of party membership with anomie is $r = .12$.

slightly, if at all, to belief in democratic practices ($r = -.15$) or authoritarianism ($r = .23$). Longer experience in the party, which could indicate greater familiarity with Nyerere's role as political leader and possibly more generalized political awareness, may explain the correlation of party membership with presidential role strength. A long-time member would have a more intimate knowledge of Nyerere's decision-making style, which could in turn lead him to expectations of strong behavior by the president. The correlation of anomie and role strength might indicate either that normlessness produced a tendency to want, and hence to expect, strong presidential leadership, or that a person who expected strong and perhaps unpredictable behavior from a political leader might feel more anomie. Either interpretation—and interaction among these variables makes both interpretations likely—supports the view that legislators' attitudinal networks were more anchored in immediate feelings about political relationships and their own power, and relatively less anchored in a set of underlying or established political norms or cultural attitudes.

Presidential Role Congruence

Averaging standard scores on presidential role expectation items yielded a scale of role congruence in the manner explained previously. This procedure establishes a mean or norm for each question and the distances of individual responses from this mean are the measures of congruence. Elite responses closest to the mean on each question were also most in agreement with student subjective evaluations, with one exception. In the fourth question, 74 percent of the students approved of the first response (expected by 44 percent of the elite), while only 71 percent approved of the second response (which is closer to the mean and also expected by 44 percent of the elite). In general, the normally expected response, in the sense that the response is closest to the mean according to our analysis, was also the response to which the greatest percent of students indicated approval. Trichotomizing elite respondents on measures of presidential and average congruence (see table 6.3) reveals that administrators and legislators are distributed in nearly equal proportions in each segment of the scales. Administrative and legislative *types* are less evenly distributed on presidential consensus, but differences are not great enough to be statistically significant.

Responses of a "Modern" administrator and a "Politico" legislator who

TABLE 6.3. Role Congruence among Elite
(in percentages)

	Administrators (N = 50)	Legislators (N = 58)	Total (N = 108)
Presidential			
High	30	31	31
Medium	36	31	33
Low	34	38	36
Average			
High	34	33	33
Medium	36	36	36
Low	30	31	31

had the highest scores on presidential role congruence are presented below
to illustrate congruent "normative" expectations.

ITEM 1 *Change Local Leadership*
The president would consult with local council and TANU officials
along with the area commissioner.

The president would work through the Ministry of Local Government.

ITEM 2 *M. P. Criticizes*
The president certainly wouldn't attack the M.P. or have him detained; he would probably listen to the criticism and then have his
ministers explain or defend his position.

If the criticism were constructive, he'd listen and perhaps respond
to the M.P.

ITEM 3 *Tribal Opposition Breaks Out*
The people in this case are probably ignorant. The president would
discuss the matter with them and try to find out what the problem is.

ITEM 4 *Court Overrules President*
The president respects the law, but I'm not sure this arises—the
president can't be overruled.

The president would accept it initially but would probably go to
the legislature to have his powers legally enlarged.

ITEM 5   *Cabinet Opposes Views*
   If the president couldn't reconcile his views with the cabinet, he'd
turn to the Parliament for support.

The character of these responses does not indicate expectations of a weak
president but does indicate that the president's role is bounded by some
legal restraints.
   The expectations of the elite, particularly those that are most congruent,
were in general consonant with the style of leadership and the attitudes
toward authority that Nyerere has demonstrated during his years as
president of TANU and president of Tanzania. Interactions between his
behavior and elite attitudes seem to be producing a hardening or institutionalization of the presidential role, at least as reflected in some of the
role norms of congruent elite members that may be inferred from responses.

Predicting Role Congruence

   In order to discover whether any background or attitude traits could
account for elite role expectations, measures of role strength and role congruence among elite were correlated with several background variables.
Table 6.4 contains some of the resulting correlations. An initial examina-

TABLE 6.4. Correlations of Role Measures with Elite Characteristics

	Pres. Role Strength	*Pres. Congruence*	*Aver. Congruence*
Career length	.05	−.06	−.14
Education	−.23	.13	−.06
Traditional status	.24	−.19	−.06
Authoritarianism	.17	−.07	−.02
Faith in people	−.08	.06	.10
Democratic practices	−.33	.22	.18
Presidential congruence	−.26	1.00	.40
Average congruence	−.18	.40	1.00

Note: Based on 108 subjects, the boldface correlations are significant with $p < .05$.

tion of this table of correlations suggests that no single variable is closely
associated with either presidential congruence or with the average degree
of congruence for all items. It would be premature to suggest, however,
that such background variables do not account for or cause differences in

role congruence. It may well be that complex interactions among elite characteristics that result in canceling effects have masked otherwise stronger relationships or that some relationships are curvilinear in nature.[20] Problems in specifying covariance relationships, coupled with the possibilities of measurement error, make it extremely difficult to interpret with much confidence the rather low correlations between role congruence and elite characteristics.[21]

There are a few relationships that deserve discussion. Presidential role congruence appears related to belief in democratic practices. This indicates that those members of the elite with greater acceptance of democratic procedures were in the mainstream in their attitudes and expectations involving presidential behavior. Among all elite respondents, expectations of a weaker or less assertive presidential role were more likely to be found among those with higher education and greater commitment to democratic practices, while those with higher traditional status were more likely to expect strong behavior from a president. Finally, those who interpreted the presidential role in strong terms, which might include such assertive behavior as detaining M.P.'s or cabinet members who disagreed with him, tended to have incongruent expectations; that is, the distribution of responses is such that those who held these views are the deviant rather than the typical cases. To the extent that these correlations represent an emerging although weak pattern of backgrounds, attitudes, and expectations, it is possible to predict that greater education and strength of commitment to democratic practices, particularly if reinforced by "congruent" behavior by the president, are likely to further the institutionalization of normative boundaries for the presidential role and increase the distance between those who expect powerful and extralegal actions from a president in ambiguous circumstances and those with more common sets of expectations which reject or at least do not expect such behavior.

20. For instance, the relation of education to role congruence might fit this pattern. Education is significantly correlated ($p < .05$) with expectations of role strength regarding the president, but not with presidential or average consensus.

21. In general, the possibility for type II, or Beta, error inhibits interpretations of table 6.4 which conclude that no relationships exist among the variables with nonsignificant correlations.

THE INSTITUTIONALIZATION
OF THE PRESIDENCY

Rules for the President

The pattern of elite expectations uncovered in this study, coupled with the actions and speeches of President Nyerere, provide a basis for proposing a few rules or norms that appear to be emerging in relation to the role of the president. These act within the Tanzanian political system as a set of norms and guidelines for presidential behavior.

RULE 1. The president may not violate the law.

This rule reflects the expectations of elite that the president would not act arbitrarily against the judiciary or members of the Parliament. It is also consonant with the modal expectation that persuasion is the principal tactic to be expected from a president in resolving conflicts, whether arising from tribal cleavages in the country or from issue-oriented cleavages in his cabinet. Nyerere's own ideas and actions have reinforced this rule. He has stressed the rule of law in a number of speeches and has emphasized the importance of legal considerations as a constraint on his behavior. His acceptance of the weak punishment of army mutineers in 1965 is an example already cited. More recently, legality was emphasized as an inhibiting factor in his refusal to remove Oscar Kambona from the National Assembly, an action urged by a delegation of elders following Kambona's sudden departure from the country.[22]

RULE 2. The president must be responsible to the people, not Parliament or the administration. In case of disputes or ambiguities, the people to whom the president is responsible are embodied in the party.

Evidence for this rule comes not only from particular expectations, such as responses indicating that the president would seek popular support when turning out local leaders or dismissing dissenting members of his cabinet,

22. Kambona's split with Nyerere occurred after Kambona apparently fled the country with a large sum of money in July 1967. He subsequently made political attacks on Nyerere and several other politicians and bureaucrats. Nyerere pointed out to elders demanding his ouster as an M.P. that Kambona could legally be removed only when either the Parliament was dissolved or Kambona missed three sessions unexcused. Nyerere did not discuss another possibility, a legal conviction against Kambona that would disqualify him from membership. See *The Nationalist,* August 24–28, 1967.

but also from responses that described attributes desirable in a leader and associated with Nyerere. The most frequently mentioned attribute was responsiveness to the people, an evident humility and tact in dealing with the masses.[23] Nyerere's style of making decisions independently, sometimes in the face of strong subsequent disagreement with members of his cabinet, has already been described. Following such "strong" decisions, it has been the practice to hold large public rallies at which Nyerere publicly has explained his actions and urged leaders to explain the government's policy throughout the country. These rallies have been typically organized by TANU, and the crowds have regularly carried signs indicating support and solidarity for Nyerere. Parades through the capital normally precede or follow Nyerere's address. Such demonstrations of public support and solidarity behind Nyerere have followed his decisions to break relations with the U.K. and to dismiss protesting university students and his announcement of the Arusha Declaration. By establishing such links between presidential action, which itself is not free from controversy among politicians, and strong displays of public support and solidarity for the president, the general expectation that the president is responsible and sensitive to the people has been reinforced. He has been seen as a man of the people, not necessarily tied to intermediate organizations such as Parliament or the cabinet.

RULE 3. The president must be free to act unhindered by legal constraints.

This rule seems on the surface to contradict rule 1 and promotes ambiguity in political role expectations for the president. As we have noted, the president has been given sweeping powers outside the jurisdiction of normal legal restraints. In order to minimize potential conflicts with the judiciary, for instance, a bill of rights has deliberately *not* been included in the 1965 constitution. The *One-Party State Report* declares:

> In this transitional period the maintenance of the rule of law to which we attach the greatest importance requires particular care that occasions for conflict between the judges and the executive and the legislature should be reduced to a minimum.[24]

The president's power as commander-in-chief of the armed forces, as sole head of the executive branch unchecked by the cabinet, and his special

23. See table 3.22.
24. *One-Party State Report*, p. 31

powers under the detention act to imprison without outside review all reflect this rule.

The interviews revealed considerable affection for and trust in Nyerere among most of the elite. These feelings have greatly increased the flow of power into Nyerere's hands. The trust sometimes extended to dependency on Nyerere's interpretation of events and ideas; one respondent remarked with respect to African socialism, "I'm not really sure about this notion, but whatever Nyerere does about it will be right." There was a widespread feeling that in difficult situations Nyerere's decision would be the right decision; most respondents approved of the previous strong decisions Nyerere had made. He has become a man whom people trust in power, who is credited with the ability to make the right decision, and whose opinion is looked upon as a source of wisdom.

Opinion formation among the elite, therefore, the group that would be expected to have alternative sources of information and independent judgments on political matters, is closely linked to statements and cues supplied by Nyerere. It seems doubtful that any presidential successor to Nyerere would enjoy this degree of trust and position of opinion leadership. Since it does exist at present, it tends to support the generalized norm or rule that the president, since he is Nyerere, must be free to act and to exercise his wise judgment unencumbered with legal restraints. Reconciliation of rule 1 and rule 3 has been accomplished in practice by providing the president with the virtual legal power of a dictator. This is not to say that a number of legal restraints on the role of the president do not exist. There are, however, two qualifications to these legal and constitutional restraints: first, the powers that the president has at present, particularly the detention act, provide sufficient leverage to remove most and perhaps all legal barriers to action without the violation of any formal law. In addition, and this is particularly true of legislators, there is a willingness among many to expand the president's legal powers. Thus, the admittedly great power of the president is limited at present more by Nyerere's own self-restraint than by the expectations of the Tanzanian political elite.

The Presidency and the Political System

The role of the president in Tanzania serves in many ways as a linchpin holding the system of closed politics in place. The presidential role as developed by Nyerere is a strong one that incorporates broad powers and responsibilities. These responsibilities include enforcing the principle of unity and the set of rules and norms that structure the system of closed politics and ensure a high degree of unity. The great powers delegated to the president are generally not seen as a threat to the actions and legitimate behavior of other role occupants. In part this is due to the president's observed proclivity to impose self-restraints on his exercise of power. Moreover, several conditions have tended to retard development of expectations that might limit presidential role behavior. Many of the elite sense a vulnerability to both foreign manipulation and internal dissent which, they feel, could undermine or divide national efforts. In addition, the demands of rapid economic modernization are believed to require strong and forceful leadership.

These attitudes, coupled with a strong personal trust in and affection for Nyerere, have reinforced a set of expectations and rules that act to institutionalize ambiguities and deliberately retain tensions. These rules are not fully reflected in congruence of individual answers, and hence are not well institutionalized compared with rules for the role of legislator, because they are by their very character more ambiguous. This conclusion is based in part on the variance of responses that indicated some role ambiguity and role conflict among elite expectations. They also indicated, if the rules presented were an accurate reflection of the norms that were becoming institutionalized in Tanzania, that there was a built-in quality to this ambiguity and a protection of presidential autonomy by such expectations. Moreover, to the extent that Nyerere's emphasis on the rule of law is internalized by a wide spectrum of the elite and serves to shape their expectations, it seems likely that in time effective role boundaries may develop.

During the formative period in Tanzania, Nyerere's style of leadership and personal ideas and goals have been an important influence in shaping not only the role of president but also the entire political system. However, the autonomy enjoyed by the president may be waning. Already some expectations concerning the role of president are expressed by elite members in a manner independent of the incumbent. For instance, several respondents discussed the presidential role in terms of what they would do if they were president. At what point expectations about the presidential role are sufficiently institutionalized to exercise strong and effective constraints on any incumbent is difficult to judge. Certainly the length of Nyerere's tenure and the degree to which a successor remains within the expectations generated by Nyerere's conduct will be important determinants of the institutionalization process.

At present an informal set of norms or rules for several roles has been widely learned and accepted by elite and subelite. The actions of the president will continue to fulfill a crucial function, providing mechanical, rather than automatic (as one might expect in a fully developed or institutionalized system), reinforcements to stabilize and maintain rules for political action. With increased institutionalization, a decentralization of responsibility for rule enforcement will be both possible and likely. As this occurs, support for rule 3, which presently assures the president of great powers and a wide range of authority, is likely to decline and will be accompanied by a hardening of boundaries that circumscribe presidential role behavior. Such changes do not seem immediately on the horizon, but if a change is to occur in the system of politics by means other than through military or external intervention, gradual decentralization of rule enforcement together with increased institutionalization of the normative attitudes and expectations now emerging seems likely. These changes, still in the future, would mark the initial stage of a decline in the system of closed politics.

7. Political Roles, Stability, and Democracy in Tanzania

Stability and democracy are, in my view, two of the most central goals of political development.[1] Definitions of these two concepts, while readily available, are not commonly accepted; I shall therefore depend on stipulative definitions. Stability refers to the condition of a political system whereby change is orderly and established procedures channel political actions in such a fashion as to maintain political authority even though personnel and policies are changed. Democracy consists of two elements, a set of procedures enabling nonleaders to exercise control over leaders and a set of rules defining political liberties.[2]

Unfortunately these two goals are not entirely compatible. Seymour Martin Lipset makes this point in discussing the establishment of new polities.

> The issues involved in the emergence of legitimate national authority and a sense of national unity, and those which pertain to the establishment of democratic procedures are clearly separate problems. . . . To create a stable, representative, decision-making process that provides a legitimate place for opposition, that recognizes the rights of those without power to advocate "error" and the overthrow of those in office, is . . . particularly problematic in new states which must be con-

1. See note 1, chap. 2, and my article, "Aggregate Data and the Study of Political Development," in *Journal of Politics,* 31 (February 1969), 71–94, which shows how these goals are often included in other political scientists' definitions of development. Economic equality and the elimination of class privilege and corruption are also important goals, but these include social and economic considerations as well and can be pursued more effectively when political development occurs.

2. For a discussion of democracy see Robert A. Dahl, *Preface to Democratic Theory* (Chicago: University of Chicago Press, 1956) and Deane Neubauer, "On the Theory of Polyarchy: An Empirical Study of Democracy in Ten Countries" (unpublished Ph.D. dissertation, Yale University, 1965). The definition of stability is similar to the definition suggested by James S. Coleman in "African Political Systems," in Walter Goldschmidt, ed., *The United States and Africa* (rev. ed. New York: Praeger, 1963), p. 39, and to my definition of institutionalization in chapter 2, except that it adds the condition that authority, not merely a pattern of behavior, is maintained.

cerned also with the sheer problem of the survival of national authority itself.[3]

In a new state like Tanzania, however, these two goals, though separate,
are interrelated. It may be true that democratic procedures are risky in a
nation in which national identity is not firmly established. In the formative
years of the American political system, before democratic succession to
office had been institutionalized, there is evidence that criticism was considered "damaging to the nation." [4] On the other hand, violations of
formally established democratic procedures may not further the development of political authority and stability in a nation, particularly if important segments of the elite strongly hold democratic norms. Thus, where
political patterns are not yet institutionalized, a state should emphasize
neither goal to the exclusion of the other but establish political practices
that balance the conflicting desiderata of each goal. If this analysis is
correct, what then are the prospects for stability and democracy in Tanzania? [5]

The Institutionalization of Political Roles

A brief review of the distribution of responses to questions about role
expectations (see figures 4.1, 5.6, and 6.1) indicates that the amount of
agreement among expectations on various contingency questions differs
widely. If it is assumed that differences in the amount of agreement are
not simply produced by the questions, but rather reflect differences in the
degree of ambiguity or conflict versus the degree of consensus surrounding
each role, it is possible to assess the relative level of consensus among
Tanzanian elite respondents with respect to each of the three roles—
administrator, legislator, and president. The relative level of consensus for
each role reflects, in some sense, the degree to which that role is institutionalized. Institutionalization varies directly (but not only) with the
degree of consensus among the elite and implies greater pressure imposed
upon a role incumbent to conform to normative expectations. The statistical variance for each question was calculated and the average variance

---

3. Seymour M. Lipset, *The First New Nation* (New York: Basic Books, 1963), p. 36.
4. Ibid., pp. 43–44.
5. My substantive conclusions should be accepted only with an awareness that numerous
possibilities for error and bias occurred in the study. The methodological conclusions,
derived from problems encountered both during the research and in the subsequent data
analysis, are discussed in the appendixes.

among questions for each of the three roles is presented below. The rationale and procedures for this calculation are elaborated in appendix D. Greater agreement or consensus on a role is indicated by a smaller variance.

AVERAGE ITEM VARIANCE BY ROLE

Administrator	Legislator	President
.521	.394	.519

For instance, if expectations were completely ambiguous—that is, if we posit a null model and thus equally distribute expectations—the variance would be .670, and if conflicting expectations were found—that is, a clearly bimodal distribution existed—the variance would be .800 or above.[6] Since the average variance for the three roles examined is well below these figures, we can say that a degree of consensus has emerged in Tanzania.

The role of legislator is more institutionalized than that of either president or administrator. Expectations about the behavior of M.P.'s were less ambiguous and more consensual. The boundaries beyond which an Mbunge is not expected to proceed in playing his role were sharply defined by the elite respondents. Expectations with respect to the administrator's role were more ambiguous and conflicting, presumably—as noted in chapter 4—because of the new role definitions assigned to administrators following the assumption of power by TANU. Some of the elite have retained older pre-independence notions about the administrator's range of legitimate authority and decision-making initiative which, however accurate in reflecting the great power exercised by the administrators in the colonial system of government, is no longer accurate or considered desirable by the politicians who have assumed the power. The lack of institutionalization of the administrator's role relative to that of the legislator, however, is likely to change. As noted in chapter 4, the greatest deviance in role expectations among administrators was found among those with long careers stretching back into the colonial era. Since the replacement and retirement of these older bureaucrats occurs steadily, it seems likely that this conflict in expectations will be reduced, and institutionalization of political rules for administrators will proceed.

6. There are statistical tests to measure differences between variances, but all such tests assume two or more independent groups, not two items from the same group. Hence the comparative properties with respect to "significance" of differences for this measure are difficult to assess.

The relatively low consensus on the role of the president is a reflection, I believe, of role ambiguity, as discussed in chapter 6. More so than many other "modern" political positions, the role of president is especially new to Tanzania. Although it has drawn upon traditional notions of authority, particularly attitudes toward chiefs, and combines—at least for elites—ideas of authority derived from the roles of both governor-general and prime minister, it also reflects some learned expectations produced by Nyerere's activities as head of a national movement. There is, therefore, no clear set of ideas about presidential behavior. In contrast to the administrator's role, introduction of the role of the president a year after independence did not involve narrowing or reformulating the scope of power of an older political role. Rather it required creating a new one out of bits and pieces pulled from different traditions, cultures, and institutions. The consequent weakness of expectations deeply imbedded in an interlocking network of attitudes toward politics and the political regime has provided President Nyerere with a wide scope of alternatives in his role.

The Role-Learning Process

The unsurprising proposition emerges that novel behavior or change in behavioral patterns by a role incumbent may lead to changes in role expectations on the part of observers. A classical notion in role theory has been that a change in one's position will lead to a change in one's role expectations. Samuel Stouffer found evidence of this in his study of the American soldier during World War II, and Seymour Lieberman made a longitudinal study that corroborates the proposition that changing a person's role is likely to change his attitudes and expectations.[7] This proposition suggests that a social system may remain fairly static due to the constraining effect of social structure. In a political system where the norms and attitudes governing behavior (that is the social structure) are incipient and not deeply anchored in personality or memory, the actions of a few individuals and the consequent overt and attitudinal reactions of others are more likely to shape role expectations and determine the degree of "hardening" in the social structure. Individual actions will be more important and structural constraints weaker.

7. Samuel A. Stouffer et al., *The American Soldier: Adjustment During Army Life, 1* (Princeton: Princeton University Press, 1949), and Seymour Lieberman, "The Effects of Changes in Roles on the Attitudes of Role Occupants," *Human Relations, 9* (1956), 385–403.

In chapter 2 it was suggested that the learning of role expectations is a circular process and that the behavior of individual role occupants at one point in time has noticeable effects on role expectations at a later point in time. The interviews have supported this proposition; a number of elite respondents explicitly cited the expectations of others in discussing their own role orientations.

This process may be illustrated by a description of the political situation of the presidency in Tanzania. At some initial point in time, President Nyerere enjoyed wide affection, in large part because his actions were identified with the achievement of independence and increased power and dignity for his countrymen. When he acted, therefore, in his role as president, there was a tendency to transfer the positive feelings toward Nyerere to his actions, thus legitimizing them. His actions were then perceived and incorporated into the expectational networks of Tanzanians, elaborating and perhaps restructuring their networks. Over time, Nyerere's actions have tended to create a body of expectations among the Tanzanian elite with regard to what he is likely to do and also what it is legitimate for a president to do. *If* Nyerere's actions remain consistent and *if* positive affections toward him remain high, expectations about the role of president will become more interwoven with other attitudes and will become more consensual and deeply anchored.[8]

Utilizing this general theory of balance, and accepting the two contingencies above as valid on the basis of recent Tanzanian history, the continuing institutionalization of the role of the president within the rules suggested by the role expectations of the Tanzanian elite surveyed may be predicted. Similarly, recent developments with respect to administrators and legislators indicate that the norms described have been operating in Tanzania and that these roles are also becoming institutionalized.

Role Congruence and the Costs of Deviancy

On the basis of the congruent role expectations, supported by additional information concerning individual attitudes and recent political actions, a set of rules for political behavior was inferred. The wording of these rules in absolute terms may give an exaggerated precision to the behavioral

8. For elaboration of the theories that inform this discussion see Robert P. Abelson et al., eds., *Theories of Cognitive Consistency: A Source Book* (Chicago: Rand McNally, 1968). An application of attitude theories to interpersonal relations and norm learning based on stochastic processes was made by Uriel G. Foa, "Behavior, Norms, and Social Rewards in a Dyad," *Behavioral Science, 3* (October 1958), 323–24.

norms which they reflect. The degree of consensus supporting different norms or rules varies. Nevertheless, they do describe in a specific manner some of the ways in which political activity in Tanzania limits conflict and insures unity. I have not attempted to measure the intensity with which these rules are held or to assess the circumstances under which violations or exceptions might be allowable. Nevertheless, the initial specification of the rules is a beginning; it suggests the way informal norms and rules reinforce a style of closed politics in Tanzania.

Deviations from acceptance of these rules for each role player were assessed by the extent of individual congruence. This measure assumes that the further an individual's role expectations are from the mean expectation of others, and the greater the role consensus, the less congruent are his expectations. Individuals with the lowest scores on role congruence were those whose expectations were the most deviant and hence most in conflict with the norms which, it is proposed, are emerging from the political process in Tanzania. Among civil servants deviant or nonconsensual expectations were related to longer experience in the colonial administration. Among legislators, deviant expectations were found most often among those with local constituency ties and were found also to be related to deviant behavior as evidenced by a high percentage of critical speeches. If the political rules and the style of politics in Tanzania are becoming increasingly institutionalized, it seems reasonable to assume that individuals who are highly deviant in expectations about their roles are likely in some sense to be "punished" by the system, while those who are highly congruent in their expectations will probably be "rewarded."

After completing my research in Tanzania and subsequent analysis of the data, I investigated career changes that had occurred among members of the sample between the interview period (1966) and December 1968, a two-year span.[9] For many there had been no change; for a few, changes had been lateral, with no noticeable movement to a more or a less powerful position; and information on a few was unobtainable. Table 7.1 presents the results of these investigations. Of those elite respondents with scores in the upper half on congruent expectations, 20 percent had moved to higher positions in the political or administrative structure while only 5 percent had been demoted. Among those with relatively noncongruent

9. I wish to thank Professor Carl G. Rosberg, who kindly supplied information concerning the occupational status as of December 1968 for nearly all the elite members I had interviewed. Only six administrators were not traceable.

TABLE 7.1. Changes in Elite Position, 1966–1968

POSITION

Role congruency	Higher	About Same	Lower or None	Total
High	11	41	3	55
Low	2	33	13	48
Total	13	74	16	103

Note: Chi-square = 12.4, which is significant at $p < .01$. Information on only 103 of the 109 respondents was available.

expectations, 4 percent had advanced and 27 percent had moved to less important positions. Although this finding rests on only gross changes, it still seems significant. It indicates that whatever the qualities are that produce success or failure in the political system as presently organized in Tanzania, role expectations (as measured by this study) are related to, and possibly are even a cause of, the behavior which the system has so clearly sanctioned.

Among the elite in the samples who held better positions and who had high scores on role congruence were the new heads of the civil service, two newly appointed ambassadors, the party's new executive secretary, and a new minister and junior minister. Among elite respondents with low role congruence scores who had been demoted were a regional commissioner dismissed from his post, several legislators, and two party officials, one of whom was not only removed from office but also placed in detention. This evidence suggests that the newly created political system is already acting to recognize and punish deviants and to reward conformers. In addition, it suggests that the deviance of an individual's role expectations is a good predictor of future success within a political system.

Expectations alone, however, hardly determine success or failure, even in the most institutionalized of political systems. In Tanzania, the majority of the elite sample did not change status over the two-year period, regardless of whether they were high or low in role congruency. Although deviant expectations only imperfectly relate to improper role performance, such behavior, as perceived and assessed by others, is likely to affect the role recruitment process of the system. It is worth noting that of the 29 clear changes in position status within our sample, 24 were in the direction that crude knowledge about role expectations would have suggested.

Moreover, two of the five cases incorrectly "predicted" were borderline. This strong association is evidence to support the proposition that the political system in Tanzania has developed institutional procedures to reinforce the rules, expectations, and role behavior which—from the interactions of individual political actors—have emerged as the normative pattern and political style of the system.

SYSTEM STABILITY

What may be said about the likelihood of stability in Tanzanian politics? Stability here refers to orderly change in which personnel, policies, and even, perhaps, procedures are altered without violating authoritative expectations or basic rules of the political formula. One method of analyzing the degree of stability in a political system is to ask how much deviant behavior among individuals at what level in the political hierarchy could produce changes that violated the norms of the political system as it presently operates. Certainly the potential for political instability, particularly through military intervention, has become manifest throughout Africa as over a dozen successful military coups have occurred since 1963.[10] Moreover, unsuccessful military interventions—all of which were resisted with the assistance of foreign troops—have occurred in Gabon, Congo (Brazzaville), Uganda, Kenya, and Tanzania. Many factors contribute to this proclivity toward military rule in Africa. The most important include the weakness of political institutions and organizations, the lack of social norms opposed to military rule, and value conflicts between military and political leaders. The strength of these factors is reflected in the nature and distribution of politically relevant values, attitudes, and knowledge among the members of the political system.

In assessing the stability of Tanzania, therefore, the resources of actual and potential participants throughout the political system and the probability of their deviation to a degree that would permanently alter one of the parameters of the system must be considered. Deviant action, dysfunctional to the system, is unlikely to the extent that members, and especially the elite, accept and are satisfied with the rules for political action and expect that deviant behavior on their part is likely not only to

10. Military force accompanying nonlegal changes has occurred in Algeria (1965), Central African Republic (1966), Congo (1965), Dahomey (1965, 1967), Ghana (1966), Nigeria (1966), Sierra Leone (1967), Togo (1963), Upper Volta (1966), Mali (1968), and Somalia (1969).

be unsuccessful in changing the system but may result in serious deprivations. Since the innermost thoughts and ambitions of public men are
seldom open for contemporary review, a conservative approach would be
to assume that, if presented with what appeared to be an opportunity,
members of the elite would willingly violate rules of orderly process in
order to achieve either their own highly valued national goals or their
own personal ambitions. With this assumption, the fundamental question
is whether political rules are sufficiently widely shared and valued in
Tanzania that the possibility of achieving power by violating or overthrowing these rules appear, to a given individual or group, unlikely.

My findings do not offer certain answers to this question, but they do
provide a basis for reasonable conjecture. It appears that, from the tangle
of expectations which existed at independence, a consensus on rules for
closed politics is emerging, that over time it is likely to be strengthened,
and that deviant behavior has been and is likely to be followed by fairly
serious penalties. It seems probable that Nyerere, with his broad popularity,
will remain in power in the foreseeable future; instability in the presidency
seems unlikely as long as Nyerere retains that office. With respect to other
political roles, such as legislator and administrator, it seems reasonable to
expect stability. M.P.'s have tended to emphasize, as prescribed by the
system output aspects of their role, working in constituencies to support
and explain government policy. Administrators apparently are adjusting
to the decreased political power accorded their role without noticeably
widespread discontent. Disturbances caused by discontinuities and growing disparities within the social and economic arenas in Tanzania also
seem unlikely. The government has pursued policies to reduce inequalities
in living standards and advancement opportunities between the urban and
rural areas, between the more advanced and less advanced regions, and
between the public and private sectors. The rate of urbanization has been
deliberately slowed and the character of the school system has been
scheduled for drastic change.[11] These efforts, if successful, all suggest
increased harmonization of social processes and greater balance between
aspirations and opportunities, political demands and political capacities.
Moreover, the government, or at least Nyerere, is sensitive to the value of
timing and balance in introducing change. Addressing a news conference
in March 1967, he stated:

11. For an elaboration of these plans, see *Tanzania, Second Five-Year Plan*, Vol. 1,
General Analysis.

In the case of the main part of Tanzania, we achieved our independence peacefully, and therefore the fulfilment of many of our socialist programmes have to come gradually. But when does this come? I am convinced that we have done it at the right time. Not merely the nationalization, although it gets more publicity than the other ingredients of the Arusha Declaration, the emphasis on self-reliance and the conditions of leadership [were also well timed].

We could have nationalized in 1965 or 1964, it does not matter very much. But it does matter in that [using] nationalization to cover up self-reliance and the conditions of leadership has helped us a little bit because nationalization is very popular. . . . It is very difficult after nationalization to oppose self-reliance or to oppose the conditions of leadership. I think both combinations of timing were right, but that is a question of judgment. We can never be sure we have timed it correctly. I think we did.[12]

If the rate of social mobilization does not accelerate to bring expanded demands on the government, and if economic and social inequalities do not increase, instability resulting from a general imbalance of political demands and capabilities is not likely in the near future.[13]

The points at which the political system seems most vulnerable, aside from externally induced crises, are deviations in the presidency and deviations by the military. The reorganization of the army following the mutiny in 1964, the emphasis on political education of the military at all levels, the establishment of party cells throughout the army, and regularized contact between higher-ranking officers and civil servants, the second vice-president and the president, are all reasons to discount the probability that military men might have or develop deviant expectations about their roles or come to believe that their accession to power is possible or desirable. Indeed, an apparent effort by a politician in 1967 to arouse some soldiers to rebellion resulted only in the speedy arrest of the leader.[14]

It is in the presidency, then, that the greatest potential for instability lies. If Nyerere were to alter his style of behavior, act independently of the

12. Julius K. Nyerere, press conference, March 4, 1967, reported in *The Nationalist*, March 6, 1967, p. 4.
13. For a study of the development of social mobilization in Tanganyika with an indication of the fairly low level at which it stands, see Hugh Stephens, *The Political Transformation of Tanzania* (New York: Praeger, 1968).
14. Eli Anangisye, July 21, 1967, as reported in the *New York Times*, July 24, 1967.

law, or fail to use the powers of his office to reinforce the currently emerging system norms, important changes could occur.

What form might such changes take? To strengthen his role further
Nyerere could weaken the party, consulting it less and using it as an
instrument of control rather than of interest aggregation. This could
undermine and weaken the whole system and, in the long run, limit
Nyerere's range of action. Given Nyerere's views, such behavior seems
unlikely. However, unexpected events could remove him from the presidency, and another man would almost certainly not hold the affection and
legitimacy that Nyerere commands. To the extent that this weakened the
office, the occupant would be less capable of directing and reinforcing the
rules of the political system. The costs of punishing departures from
widely accepted norms would tend to increase. Greater severity or laxness
by a subsequent president could alter the calculations of many potentially
deviant participants; some might try to make politics in Tanzania more
competitive or, alternatively, more oligarchical. To do so they would
probably have to acquire power in defiance of established legal patterns
and informal rules. The system, therefore, is heavily dependent upon
continuation of the current presidential performance. If the office retains
its authority and dominance in decision making, fissiparous tendencies will
remain checked, congruence among major political roles will be reinforced,
and the system will likely remain stable.

Democracy in Tanzania

Most elite respondents considered democracy the desirable form of government for Tanzania. They indicated trust in the average man to choose
good leaders. Many were sensitive to criticisms of the one-party state and,
during the interviews, volunteered unsolicited defenses of it. In the press,
Nyerere and other TANU leaders have regularly emphasized the popular and
democratic character of the Tanzanian political system. With general popularity, free elections, a parliamentary system, and broad attitudinal support for democratic symbols and practices, there seems a prima facie case
for democracy in Tanzania.

Nevertheless, I think that by most measures Tanzania is not democratic
at present. Obviously this judgment rests on criteria for democracy that
differ in some respects from those considered by the elite in Tanzania. But
even employing some of their criteria—for instance, the free expression of
ideas—Tanzanian democracy does not measure up completely. In fact, it is

questionable whether achieving a high level of "democracy" is really an important goal for Tanzania, at least at present.

Democracy may be thought of as a set of qualities that a political system exhibits in varying degrees. A country is not simply democratic or not democratic, but rather ranks somewhere along a series of dimensions. Some procedures indicative of democracy include: (1) the ability of a populace at regular intervals to change their leadership; (2) an equal weighting of their votes; (3) ability of the electorate to insert its own alternatives on the ballot; (4) an opportunity for rival policies or candidates to come forward without severe penalties to appeal to the electorate; (5) subordination of government decisions in some fashion to prior electoral decisions, that is, control of nonelected officials by elected officials. These are what might be called the characteristics of "polyarchy." They are derived from the ideas of popular participation in government and political equality. In addition, there are certain other characteristics that must be associated with democracy. These are political liberties, such as: (6) freedom of speech; (7) right of a fair trial for all "crimes"; (8) a free press and a certain minimal level of communication capability; and (9) the right to organize for political purposes such as lobbying and propaganda.[15]

On many of these criteria Tanzania would rank low. First, with regard to polyarchy characteristics, the legal procedures operating to control elections do not satisfy the conditions suggested above. The party's National Executive, for instance, may control nomination of candidates. It is true that if only one or two candidates petition to stand in a local constituency, the Executive cannot intervene; but the NEC could easily encourage two candidates it approved to petition and then select them regardless of the initial preferences indicated by voting at the district annual conference. The present constitution allows for only one candidate for president. There is no provision for write-in candidates. Constituencies, shaped to a large extent on old district boundaries, often contain unequal electorates. Registration in the largest constituency in 1965 was 60,818 and in the smallest was 4,930. But such inequalities do not appear to be important impediments to democracy, particularly since they do not represent gerrymandering. Moreover, electoral districts for the mainland were increased from 107 to 120 in 1968, remedying some inequalities. There are no elected representatives from Zanzibar to the Assembly.

15. See Neubauer, "Polyarchy," for an elaboration and discussion of these characteristics.

One aspect of the electoral system is a positive democratic feature. This is the control of the campaigns of candidates so as to minimize the effect of differences in economic resources available to them. This procedure goes far to restrict translation of economic differences into power differences.

More basic than these considerations, however, is the fact that the closed system of politics places serious constraints on public consideration of alternative national policies and on the public articulation of group grievances or dissent. Recruitment for the most important leadership posts occurs within the party and many of these posts are nonelective. Only Nyerere, with his notable electoral success, establishes a distinct line of control of elected leaders over nonelected leaders. It would be inaccurate to say that opposition candidates or policies are forcibly suppressed in Tanzania; their potential is, at best, scattered and weak. However, it is apparent that procedures for channeling alternative policies and candidates into a public arena where they may vie for popular support do not exist.

Nor are characteristics of political liberty well established. The party and state exercise controls that inhibit political dissent. Criticism, particularly if related to national political issues, is expected to be channeled through the party and not aired in public. The press, a portion of which is a direct organ of the party, is encouraged not to carry stories that could promote political divisions. The *Daily Nation*, a Kenya-based paper, has been criticized on several occasions in the National Assembly and by the local press for reporting and "distorting" potentially divisive political events. In 1968, legislation allowing strong government control of the press was passed. For those who discourage participation in nation-building projects, or whose attitudes and behavior pose an even more direct threat to the system, the rather severe sanctions of prison or detention have been threatened and, in a few cases, invoked.

In spite of these characteristics, Tanzania is certainly not a monolithic one-party state or a radical mobilization system in which political control is used as a tool to transform social and economic practices.[16] Democracy and democratic institutions are highly valued by most members of the elite, and the rights of criticism and freedom of thought are widely accepted. Nyerere, in his speeches and writings, indoctrinates democratic beliefs, particularly general notions of popular support for government

16. This term is suggested by David Apter to describe systems such as that of Tanzania. See his *Politics of Modernization*.

and the value of open discussion. Indeed, the inculcation of generalized support for democracy is perhaps the strongest indication that democratic characteristics may develop in Tanzania. The fact that the polyarchy and political liberty conditions suggested are not fully, and in some cases not even partially, satisfied in Tanzania does not imply that the level of democracy achieved is unjustifiably low, especially when compared with other economically less developed countries. It may be that nonfulfillment of these conditions in a political system whose modern political organizations are weakly institutionalized and whose populace is largely illiterate and traditional in its orientation should not be criticized. Indeed, the constraints on political activity—generally not severe—that the closed system enforces may be justified if they prevent fragmentation and preserve stability, which is also a valued outcome of development and one related to the establishment of democracy in the long run.

Why has this closed, somewhat undemocratic system of politics evolved? Certainly the transition to a one-party system followed quickly the accession of the nationalist movement to political power. One irony of the republican constitution adopted only a year after independence was that the first important matter discussed under its aegis was its own revision. The answer is not that the closed system is simply a mechanism devised by politically avaricious nationalists who, having acquired high office, wish to preserve their positions. The attitudes and sentiments elicited during the interviews and the rapid turnover and demise of political leaders do not support such a thesis. A more tenable explanation for the style of politics emerging in Tanzania is that the one-party system with its emphasis on solidarity and unity is a reaction to feelings of insecurity. The weakness and vulnerability of political institutions in Tanzania were recognized and mentioned by many of the architects of the political system. These feelings were certainly heightened by the military mutiny in January 1964. Nyerere, in his speech at University College in August 1964, emphasized Tanzania's fragility in defending the need for detention without trial.[17] The potential for instability was also expressed during the interviews; respondents mentioned themes such as the illiteracy of the population, the ease with which they might be swayed by "false prophets," the weakness of the police and armed forces and of their subordination to civil rule, and the general vulnerability of the system to tribal residualism or external penetration and influence. These characteristics were often

17. "President Nyerere Opens Dar es Salaam University College Campus," pp. 16–17.

cited as justification for the establishment of a democratic system that was "different but just as good" [18] as those in Western countries. Occasionally, desiderata of economic development were also cited as reasons for the emphasis on unity and solidarity in the political system. As one intellectual remarked, "In 20 or 30 years, when we're more developed, two parties may emerge."

A common opinion among elite respondents was that the latent strength of centrifugal and divisive forces in Tanzania was sufficient to justify a system that could nullify and smother their effects. Frequently added was the argument that the smothering of public controversy is in the African tradition and does not limit real expression, which is possible "through the proper channels." To some extent this view reduced attitude incongruities among elite who had absorbed Western norms of democracy and free expression.

Is this assessment by the elite of fragility in the political order correct? Without some means to compare the strength of these tendencies in Tanzania with that in other countries, no answer can be definitive. It is clear, however, that the government has refrained from testing its strength on certain issues. The withdrawal of the prosecution of Chief Fundikira, the caution with which integration with Zanzibar proceeds, and the hesitancy to penetrate and alter economically regressive or fissiparous tribal patterns of activity through the use of force are perhaps indicative of weakness in the government and party. Bienen argues that, indeed, conditions in Tanzania vitiate the capacity of political institutions for transforming the economy or regulating life in rural areas.[19] However, avoiding tests of strength and the political reactions that could result might also, at least in part, indicate prudence. For instance, if a full and open debate on the Arusha Declaration had been held it would certainly have been a lively one, with the potential of creating divisions among the national elite and even local leadership, had they been invited to participate. One can imagine sharp national cleavages emerging as the full implications of the policies of self-reliance and conditions of leadership were realized and challenged. But such divisions are incompatible with beliefs in a classless state; ideological disputes, therefore, have been condemned as foreign and unreal. Thus decisions were simply announced, not debated. The arenas in which the Arusha policies were officially approved consisted of a series

18. A phrase used by one Modern.
19. Bienen, *Tanzania,* passim.

of accolades and ritualistic ceremonies. The effective decisions had already been reached and political divisions avoided.[20]

What are the latent divisions or cleavages against which the closed system of politics guards? A few have already been discussed. There is nearly an even split between Christians and Muslims (aside from a large number of adherents to traditional animistic religion). Tribal and ethnic differences are also important, with the advantaged Chagga, Haya, and Nyakusa tribes overrepresented in important posts of the modern sector. Europeans and Asians, who continue to occupy many middle- and upper-class economic roles, are objects of political distrust. Reference to these differences in a political context is stringently proscribed by political norms. Nyerere's personal ideology of a solidaristic and socialistic community labels such differences illegitimate and threats to the public interest. A clear extension of this outlook is the denial of ideological or fundamental cleavages.[21] However, differences in ideology do exist as responses to economic questions indicated; but these cleavages, especially, are masked by the closed system of politics.

There are at least two high-level elite groups between whom the political struggle, such as it is, has been carried on. Delineation of these two groups rests largely upon an analysis of elite interviews and observations of elite behavior in 1965 and 1966, although there is an apparent continuation of political divisions along these lines. Neither group was formally organized and the criteria for membership were not clear, even in an informal sense. What distinguished the two groups and bound each together in an unorganized and informal fashion was their sharing of certain attitudes and concerns. The groups differed in their attitudes toward Tanzanian progress, toward the outside world, and toward each other.

The first group will be labeled "ardent socialists." Individuals associated with this group had strong ideological commitments. They felt that the term African socialism, for example, was a smokescreen inhibiting implementation of true socialism. They tended to reify concepts like "imperialism" and "capitalism." Identifications with the West, particularly the

20. The surprise announcement of nationalization may also be justified on grounds of economic strategy. A prior public debate might have caused detrimental reaction among the bankers and businessmen who were caught by surprise and were unable to respond.

21. For a discussion of Nyerere's ideology see Harvey Glickman, "The Dilemmas of Political Theory in an African Context: The Ideology of Julius Nyerere" *Boston University Papers on Africa, Transition in African Politics,* ed. Jeffrey Butler and A. A. Castagno (New York: Praeger, 1967), pp. 195–223.

United States, were negative while communist countries, particularly China, were viewed more positively. Most of the xenophobia toward the West was generalized and friendships with Westerners were relatively frequent among this group. Some of the attitudes toward the West seemed to be reinforced by the vicarious pleasure derived from symbolically reasserting the power acquired by Africans initially at independence. There was a doctrinaire rather than adaptive quality to conversations on socialism among some members. This group was the most critical of domestic policy, at least the official policy of 1966. Criticism and disaffection in this group were expressed infrequently and in a low key manner. One of the characteristics that justifies labeling this unorganized collection of individuals as a group rather than simply a category is that they viewed one another as friends and others as enemies. Communication and interaction among "ardent socialists" was relatively high, based partially on similar intellectual interests and mutual trust. Enemies were to some extent the product of the ardent socialist's own analysis since they consisted mainly of individuals whose attitudes were more pragmatic and whose ascension to power would be a threat to his own ambitions and aspirations.

The second group, here labeled "nationalist neutrals," displayed even fewer characteristics of cohesion than the first. The boundaries determining adherence were difficult to establish and the attitudes and outlooks of those assigned to this group varied more widely than among the "ardent socialists." In terms of national policy goals and evaluations of internal domestic policies, members of this group tended to concentrate their efforts on narrower, more particularistic situations and to prefer less radical economic policies. Their commitment to Tanzania as a nation and the advancement of Africans was as great as that of the first group but was less ritualistically expressed. Their attitudes toward foreign nations tended more toward neutrality, but reflected familiarity and sympathy with Western styles and traditions.[22] The cleavages between these groups, if released into the political system, could exacerbate latent cleavages of an economic, tribal, or religious nature. More than any other factor the closed system of politics has prevented this, but the containment of these conflicts has been achieved by a reduction in democracy.

22. The key figures in each "group" were Oscar Kambona and Rashidi Kawawa respectively, but neither was a regular spokesman or organizer of the two groups. Kambona, along with Hanga, Phombeah, and others, lost considerable influence after 1967. However, the issues that separated them from other leaders still seem to be alive.

CONCLUSION: THE ELITE CULTURE OF CONTAINMENT

A closed style of politics has emerged in Tanzania and is becoming institutionalized in the political system. The arena in which major decision making occurs is a small and private one. The role expectations of the elite, many of whom have access to the private arena of politics, are generally in harmony and tend to support this political style. The system has developed a capacity to control individual behavior and to enforce the rules for role behavior that presently structure the political process. If these are indications of the strength of institutionalization in the political system, what are the possible weaknesses?

Three major weaknesses have been discussed. First, there is the crucial position of the president, whose role performance is vital to reinforcing and legitimizing the rules and behavior of the political system. Second, there is the potential effect of attitudes unconducive to democratic processes. Low correlations between commitment to democratic procedures and other attitude measures such as authoritarianism, faith in people, and role congruence indicate that these attitudes may not be as interrelated or firmly anchored as in Western democratic states. Thus, latent authoritarianism and weakly held preferences for democratic procedures, exacerbated by ideological differences, might prove destabilizing. A third weakness is discontinuity and possibly incongruence in the attitudes and expectations of the nonelite relative to those of the elite. The elite political culture and the structure it shapes among the elite in Tanzania may not be congruent with the "parochial" political culture that characterizes the attitudes and sentiments of most Tanzanians, who live in rural and quite traditional ways.[23] While there is little supporting evidence, this structural and cultural duality, combined with low effectiveness of the central government, increases the probability that disruptive political acts may occur. To the extent that incongruity between modern structure and traditional culture does exist, this is another destabilizing element in the Tanzanian system. But these weaknesses, acting independently, will probably not undermine the present character of the system.

The elite political culture that has emerged is, in fact, partially a re-

23. Sidney Verba suggests that cultures of the traditional type are still dominant in less developed states such as Tanzania. The result is a "parochial" political culture mixed with a "participant" culture among modernized portions of the population. See Almond and Verba, pp. 18 ff.

sponse to the pressure of these political weaknesses. The demands of economic development, the hostilities and pressures caused by change, the uncomfortable patterns of living, and the attitudinal disagreements among occupants of modern political roles have often been cited as major factors in the decline of democratic practices and the increasing frequency of military interventions in newly independent states, especially in Africa. These factors make more difficult the institutionalization of a stable pattern of politics, particularly one that is democratic. From such pressures evolve patterns of political activity that limit expression of political demands, often through oppressive means. An alternative reaction, absorbing demands or pressures through strong and responsive political institutions, appears less frequently in developing nations.[24] According to Huntington, this latter alternative is the major characteristic of development.[25] In fact, one of the crucial questions for a study of political development to ask is how is a system likely to respond to pressures, demands, or crises which it may confront.[26]

I would suggest that three patterns of attitudes and sentiments, that is, political cultures, may evolve among the political elite in a developing nation. These three—bargaining, coercion, and containment—are subculture variations within the total national political culture of most underdeveloped states, which Verba has termed a "parochial-participant culture." This term refers to the coexistence of a small modernized elite, sharing in varying degrees Western political values, and a largely illiterate and traditional populace little affected as yet by modernization. Within this general culture, however, the three variants suggested above are possible. While many Tanzanian elite respondents preferred a system with widespread citizen competence and participation, most recognized that such a pattern of politics was illusory in the near future. Thus they stressed participation by the populace in nation-building projects, while deemphasizing their roles as voters or critics. In this sort of political culture, where the mass of the population lives traditional lives in an essentially residual

24. See Joseph LaPalombara, ed., *Bureaucracy and Political Development* (Princeton: Princeton University Press, 1963), p. 29, on this point.

25. Huntington, *Political Order*.

26. The Social Science Research Council's Committee on Comparative Politics has isolated five crises that characterize problems faced by developing polities. These are the crises of identity, legitimacy, penetration, participation, and distribution. This analysis is described briefly in Pye, *Aspects of Political Development*, pp. 62–67.

sector,[27] elite members' views about each other and the similarity of their priorities and concerns are particularly important.

In an elite political culture characterized by coercion and conflict, differences among elite will probably be translated into hostile attitudes and patterns of nonlegal retribution and maneuvering for power; Samuel Huntington has characterized this pattern of politics among elite as "praetorian."[28] The Soviet Union, particularly during the 1930s, Ghana under Nkrumah, Indonesia, particularly after the unsuccessful coup in 1965, South Korea, and South Vietnam constitute instances of fragmentation, coercion, and conflict among modernized elites. Students, the military, and workers have regularly resorted to violence in order to press demands or bring about change.

A second elite culture is characterized by a pattern of bargaining associated with polyarchy.[29] The United States, Great Britain, and West Germany illustrate this pattern among modernized nations, while India and Israel are examples among less advanced nations. In these cultures, groups may legitimately struggle to influence policy, and elections resolve open political differences by offering some alternatives.

A third cultural pattern is containment. The set of attitudes and expectations that comprise this elite culture is particularly evident in Tanzania and also was probably present in Turkey in the period between World Wars I and II. A containment culture represents a compromise between an open style of politics supported by a culture of bargaining and a conflict style based on coercion and reinforced by attitudes of personal insecurity. If indeed the crises of development and modernization tend to overload a government's capacity to respond effectively—that is, to remain in harmony with its environment and at the same time maintain some level of security and liberty for the members of the system—the institutionalization of an elite political culture of containment may be a solution.

The suppression of political opposition in Tanzania in recent years raises a question whether the culture of containment is in fact moving toward one of coercion. Since 1967 a number of major political leaders have gone into exile, been jailed or executed. Oscar Kambona, along with

27. This term has been used for the underlying population of African states by Aristide Zolberg, *Creating Political Order* (Chicago: Rand McNally, 1965).

28. See Huntington, pp. 192–263.

29. See Robert A. Dahl and Charles E. Lindblom, *Politics, Economics, and Welfare* (New York: Harper, 1953), esp. pp. 324–65.

some close associates, fled to England, where he remains a rallying point for political opposition. Hanga, former vice-president of Zanzibar, along with twelve others, was sent under arrest to Zanzibar, where, along with two other prisoners, he was executed. In 1970 a "treason trial" implicating several formerly important leaders was conducted. Since little information has been published about the considerations that led to these actions, whether suppression of opposition has exceeded the need for stability that justifies containment, thus moving Tanzania toward a pattern of coercion, is partly speculative. However, it seems unlikely. The broad though weak support for democratic practices in the elite political culture is unlikely to have been altered significantly by these events. Moreover, the parallel between Turkey and Tanzania, if accepted, suggests that limited violence need not vitiate a closed, but non-Praetorian style of politics. It should be recalled that in the 1920s Ataturk was responsible for the death of a number of his political opponents, far in excess of those affected so far in Tanzania.

Closed politics, which seeks to contain political dissent, remains a more accurate description of Tanzanian political life than the politics of coercion. A strong presidency, as created in Tanzania, increases the ability of the system to "manage" its environment. By responding promptly to crises and increased system load, it may prevent a lag in reaction and allow the system to gain its objectives more rapidly. This is likely, however, only so long as important and decisive actions undertaken by strong leadership and supported by this elite culture are also aimed in the needed direction, that is, are based on accurate predictions of future conditions.

Such an elite culture, without entirely sacrificing democratic procedures or limiting elite participation, may be more capable of absorbing and resolving political conflict by structuring and constricting the arena for decision making. Emphasizing material development at the expense of traditional practices and their protection by democratic procedures can reduce support for and effectiveness of the government. An elite political culture conducive to containment and some pattern of closed politics may be able to avoid the conflicts and violence that could result from such reduced effectiveness, a violence that is common to many of the less modernized states and contradictory to democratic expectations. If Tanzania can maintain stability and some degree of democracy, it will be within such an elite culture of containment and through the institutionalization of both closed politics and at least minimal norms of popular sovereignty.

Appendixes

Appendix A

THE METHODOLOGY OF ROLE ANALYSIS

Comparing the utility of some of the procedures I employed in analyzing political roles with alternative approaches to the measurement of role expectations has been helpful in assessing problems and weaknesses I encountered in both the research and the subsequent analysis. It will be seen that methodological problems exist that affect some of the substantive findings, requiring that these be offered as suggestive rather than conclusive results. However, since the procedures followed in this study, both in the field and in the subsequent data analysis, are described in the text and in this appendix, every individual may judge the importance and reliability of the findings for himself.

Difficulties in measuring both roles and role expectations bedeviled each stage of the research. I used systematic interviewing to break into the cognitive and affective network of each respondent at one point in time and to measure in a comparative fashion expectations about a small number of specified roles. Concern over eliciting pseudo-attitudes and imposing falsely structured alternatives led to the decision to use projective and open-ended techniques. However, the more open-ended the question, the less comparable were the responses and hence the more difficult it was to quantify them. The initial decision to guard against artificiality led me eventually to recategorize responses artificially along three-point continua in order to interpret the results. The open-ended approach also vitiated measurement of the intensity with which an expectation was held, since noncomparable indications of intensity occurred during the interviews. An alternative procedure for measuring role consensus, employed in a role analysis study by Neal Gross and his colleagues,[1] is to suggest a particular role behavior and ask the respondent to indicate whether such action is obligatory, irrelevant, or anathema for the role occupant. Since this procedure involves closed choices it was rejected. Another question that might be asked is whether an expectation is central or peripheral to the role. For instance, some Muslims might feel strongly about drinking but not transfer this attitude to behavioral prescriptions relevant to political role occupants. Measurement techniques such as these, I now feel, would have yielded more satisfactory data than did the open-ended question approach.

1. Gross et al., *Exploration in Role Analysis*. See chap. 2 for a discussion of this procedure.

A further dilemma in measuring role expectations is whether one wishes to measure what a person predicts or what he desires. In this research, respondents were asked what they thought *would* happen. Information about what they believed *should* happen would have been valuable, but limitations of time and considerations of interviewee sensitivity prevented this. With such information, discrepancies between what was considered likely and what was considered desirable in actions of political leaders might have proved useful indicators of legitimacy, perhaps even of stability. Indications of discrepancies of this type were elicited from students and were reported in aggregate fashion with respect to individual questions (see tables 4.5, 5.10, and 6.1). Another dimension of role expectations not measured was that of sanctions for violations of role norms. Individuals are likely to differ in their notions about how often and how severely a role incumbent may violate expectations for his role behavior before sanctions are justified. There may also be disagreement over the nature of appropriate sanctions. Information of this sort is important to establish the latitude of accepted behavior for a role occupant with respect to certain problems. Again, this study has no direct measures of this order. Role boundaries, therefore, to the extent they have been discussed at all, have been inferred from central tendencies and other information. A final consideration in creating a measurement instrument for role expectations is the number of items required for a satisfactory measure. A large number of items on each role is desirable. Moreover, where it is important to assess differences between roles, equivalences among questions for each role are needed. As was noted in the text, the number of items per role is few in this study and equivalences nearly nonexistent.

In defense of these clear methodological weaknesses, three points may be made. First, recognition of the complexity of variables distinguishable in any analysis of role expectations does not mean that a study that focuses upon role expectations must contain instruments sensitive to all these variables. Indeed, no study, even one with a relatively high control over subjects, has elicited information relative to all the considerations and difficulties suggested above.[2] Second, the more a researcher is concerned with contemporary social or political processes, the less likely it is that his study will be sensitive to all the dimensions of role expectations just suggested. It is more likely that one or two aspects of expectations will be selected for examination. The fewer the roles and the fewer the role expectation variables included in a study utilizing interviews, the greater the number of items possible per role and the greater reliability the study is likely to have. Therefore, increased complexity in terms of roles and variables involves a loss in reliability if the total number

---

2. Of course, some studies have obtained information for several variables of role expectations. See the variety of studies reported in Biddle and Thomas, *Role Theory*.

of items remains constant. Furthermore, greater precision and greater complexity both place constraints on the possibilities for social and political implications of the study.[3] The third consideration is the nature of the situation in which expectations are elicited. In this study, political elite were the subjects, and they were examined by a foreigner. Few rewards and practically no deprivations were available to me as the researcher. Respondents were willing to cooperate largely to the extent that they felt the research might be useful to their country or that they found the interview enjoyable. In addition, interviews had to be limited in duration, politically nonsensitive, and personally nonthreatening. This established serious limitations on the design of the questionnaire. These three points perhaps justify, though do not excuse, the methodological problems and weaknesses of the study.

What changes in research procedures might have been desirable? In retrospect, it seems possible that the role expectation items could have been less open-ended and utilized more forced-choice techniques. The total number of items probably could not have been expanded, but greater initial preparation of forced choices along a continuum of obligation would have been wise. Pre-tests of the interview schedule did not include this possibility. This "confession" will perhaps be relevant to future researchers undertaking similar projects and provide a catharsis for other researchers whose methodological clumsiness is often a source of undisclosed frustration.

3. Control of the situation, as in laboratory research, however, holds more promise for developing precise notions about social behavior. The frequently made point is that much important political and social action does not occur in controlled situations and can only be assessed by less rigorous measures.

Appendix B

Interviews with 109 civil servants and National Assembly members were conducted between mid-April and July 1966. The purpose of the interview was explained briefly to each respondent either by letter or phone. Mr. E. Kapinga, a second-year law student at the University College, Dar es Salaam, assisted in the interviewing. He helped translate portions of the questionnaire into Swahili,[1] and conducted 42 of the interviews, 25 with civil servants and 17 with M.P.'s. A number of these were in Swahili. He also assisted or conducted jointly with the author two of the interviews with civil servants and three with M.P.'s. The remainder of the interviews, 24 with civil servants and 38 with M.P.'s, were conducted solely by the author.

The Sample

The universe of 157 administrators was established by listing those civil servants appearing in the March 1965 government directory who held positions as principal secretary, assistant principal secretary, senior assistant secretary, or administrative secretary (one for each of the seventeen regions of mainland Tanzania). Commissioners, directors, ambassadors, and counselors, the latter two posts being foreign service positions, were also included. Purely technical posts, although often receiving similar or higher salary considerations, were not included. The resulting names represent a compendium of the upper-level administrative positions and their incumbents as of early 1966.[2] Seventy-two names were randomly selected from the original 157 for interviewing. It was realized that a number of foreign service officers would probably be chosen who would not be available for interviewing. But I felt they should be included since they were part of the upper-level administrative structure of Tanzania, even though they were not in the country at the time

1. I wish to thank Mr. John Msenga of MARCO Surveys, whose comments on translation procedures as well as other problems encountered in this study were most helpful.

2. Foreign service personnel were included because their positions were graded as equivalent to principal secretary and principal assistant secretary and because those holding foreign service positions could be and often were transferred to administrative positions in the government and vice versa. A few individuals who were either studying abroad or seconded to the East African Common Services Organization in Nairobi may have been excluded from this list.

of the survey.[3] Fifty-one interviews were completed out of the 72, and one partial interview was done. Of the remaining, there were one outright refusal, two clear evasions, two who proved to be so busy that mutually agreeable times were never found, three who were initially busy and call backs never proved possible, one individual who was never found, three who were posted up country—one of whom was unavailable even when the author traveled several hundred miles in an attempt to interview him—and eight who were out of the country on foreign service missions.

Between February and June 1965 there were 185 members in the National Assembly. A random sample of 67 was selected for interviewing. Of the 67, 54 were interviewed completely. In addition, three interviews were partially completed but are not included in this study. No M.P. directly refused to be interviewed. However, two, for various reasons, failed to keep appointments. Of the remaining eight, six postponed appointments indefinitely. They either agreed to be interviewed at a later date (unspecified), or suggested they wanted to think about it and asked to be contacted again. Two M.P.'s were never located. These two failed to make any but the briefest appearance at the June-July meeting of the National Assembly. Four additional M.P.'s not in the original sample were also interviewed; three were interviewed in their home constituencies as part of an effort to examine the role of the M.P. in his own constituency. Of the interviews reported in detail in the text, all but one were conducted by the author.

Conducting the Interview

The interview situations varied widely. The vast majority of the interviews with civil servants were conducted in their offices, but M.P.'s were interviewed in their homes, in bars, in hotel rooms, in rooms within Karimjee Hall (where the National Assembly meets), and on the lawn outside. The average length of the interview was two hours, with a range from an hour and twenty minutes to four hours. The order and phrasing of questions varied only slightly from interview to interview. Occasionally a respondent would talk freely and extensively after an open-ended question, supplying a good bit of information that would have been elicited by subsequent questions. Consequently, additional questions, for instance on life history, were often not necessary. On a few occasions, either through neglect or in order to speed up an interview which had a time deadline, questions were omitted. Nevertheless, the interview reproduced below is an accurate and fairly typical form.

3. See H. H. Hyman, G. N. Levine, and C. R. Wright, "Studying Expert Informants by Survey Methods: A Cross-National Inquiry," *Public Opinion Quarterly, 31* (Spring 1967), 18–19.

The respondent was usually told that his answers would be kept in confidence, but in some cases, as in the example below, this promise was not made. It is my belief that, in general, promises of anonymity had little or no effect on the openness or guardedness with which respondents answered.

I have reproduced this interview, rather than just the questions used in interviewing, in order to give the reader an understanding of the procedures that underlie this study. During each interview notes were taken. Often only key words or phrases were recorded. These notes were then used in taping a more complete record of interview soon after it was completed. This method seemed to yield an accurate summary of the facts brought out in the interview, as well as a number of verbatim or nearly verbatim quotations.

The Interview

Part I of the interview consisted of largely open-ended questions. Part II was more structured and formal, requiring responses to prepared material. In the sample interview presented below, all statements by the interviewer are italicized. Two procedures were used to organize the questions. Procedure 1 was used with M.P.'s and included, in part I, question 19 as it appears in the interview below, and in part II, questions 4b, 5b, 9b, and 12b. In procedure 2, used with administrators, questions 4b, 5b, 9b, and 12b of part II replaced questions 19a-e in part I and 4a, 5a, 9a, 12a, and 13 were used in part II.

PART I

Thank you for finding time to help me in this project. As I mentioned earlier, I am trying to get a better idea of the National Assembly and how it works by talking with some of the M.P.'s, like yourself. I'm trying to learn a little about people's backgrounds, their ideas about what the role of the National Assembly is, and what they think the future holds for them and the country. [Pause. Often, at this point, the respondent would ask questions about my background, the authorization for the study, the form that publication or writing up of this material would take, and what I hoped to find out. This discussion seldom lasted longer than a few minutes.] *If you don't mind, why don't we begin with your early life?*

1. I wonder if you could tell me a little about when you were born and where you were raised.

Monduli, Masai Headquarters, 1933. Small township 6 miles from town. *How about your family? Would you say they were average, above average, or below average in terms of wealth?*

Average.

2. How about your childhood? Would you say it was particularly happy or sad?

Happy—yes. Nomadic—but we did not move, had green grass and water. I looked after the goats, and when I was older, cattle.

3. Do you remember anything about your grandparents?

No—died before I was born. Grandfather—very rich, and father as eldest had largest share.

4. How about your father? What sort of person is he?

Raising cattle, no school. In the eyes of the public, a good and kind man.

Would you say he was easygoing or harsh?

He was a tough man, particularly with us kids when we were young.

Did he decide everything in the family or did he consult others, your mother for instance?

Father.

5. How about your mother? How would you describe her?

Very kind, very soft-spoken. Comes from a very wealthy family.

Was she the only wife?

Yes.

6. How about any brothers and sisters? Could you tell me a little about each?

Two elder brothers—both herdsmen (also mixed farming and cultivating); myself; two younger brothers—lower primary school; no sisters.

7. Now how about school? Where did you start school?

1949, village elders came around and said one child from the family had to go to the Masai district school. I was selected. I was considered the one most needing an education. Altogether 45 were picked from among those with the most children. Masai district council had made a law— so many each year—and I was the one that year.

What about your playmates or classmates from early school days? Do you ever see or hear from them now?

Yes, well there's K. R., he went to Haverford U.—then to Ministry of Labour. Also J. K., same village, now teacher at Kiluryu Agricultural College, Mwanza.

What sort of teachers did you have?

Paid by the council. Most were Masai, all were African.

What was the routine like? Were there other things to do besides studies?

Lots besides normal academic. Looked after 300 head of cattle of the council, dipping, milking—and grew fodder crops for animals.

8. After primary school, what did you do?

Moshi, Holy Ghost Secondary School, 1956–58. This was the first mission in Masai-land. I had become a Catholic in school from other students. I left before Std. X exam—I was sick. I was ill for all of 1960, weak and in bad health. Operation on stomach, lived at home and hospital. 1961, recovered.

How about any activities, sports, or special honors in school?

Sports—none. Great interest in sciences; very good results in the exam. Except for the fact of the sickness, I would have continued because I was first in Std. IX and X exams.

Do you remember any situation where you disagreed with a teacher?

Yes.

What happened?

I organized a strike because two boys were expelled for reasons we did not think were sufficient. Later they were reinstated.

9. *What did you do after you finished school?*

I worked with the Masai federal council, 1961–65, as a committee clerk. Left—promotion. 1962 became secretary to the council. Went to Mzumbe in Morogoro for the course in local government, public administration. And also in '62, July, for a U.S.-sponsored study, I went through the western part of the country studying cattle for four months. 1963 I went on a study tour of Israel, then Ministry of Local Government gave me a fellowship to go to Germany, where I studied local government and finance for three months. I resigned as secretary of the council in August 1965 to stand for elections.

[10. *What other work did you do before you entered Parliament* (with administrators, *civil service*)?]

11. *Now I wonder if you could tell me a little about your present life; for instance, are you married?*

Yes—1962. She lives with my parents—from home village. She has never traveled abroad or been away from home.

How about children?

We have two boys.

What about your free time? How do you usually spend it and with whom do you spend it?

Most of my time with studies, local government courses; I've been reading in this area. I hope to sit for the adult entrance examination at Makerere. However, becoming an M.P. has made me change my plans. Also I've been active in TANU; helped build TANU headquarters in Monduli. I've been active since 1958.

When you have a chance to read, what sort of things do you like to look at?

Economics, anatomy.

Do you like to read papers or listen to the radio?

Yes.

What papers do you read and how often?

Daily—*Nationalist, Daily Nation, Standard* (monthly subscription), and any other I get.

What sort of programs do you listen to on the radio?

News only—Tanzania, VOK, Ethiopia, BBC, VOA, Peking.

12. Comparing your family now to your parents, would you say you are happier?

I am happy. I want to be in public affairs.

Would you say you are better off financially?

No, about the same. I'm the only one remaining with my parents.

How about your children? Do you think you give them more or less or about the same attention as your parents did you?

Less. Father and Mother look after my children.

13. Now perhaps we can turn to your present work. I wonder if you can tell me why it is you became an M.P.

For my district. It is one of the backward districts in the Republic. We have no people who have been determined to change ideas of the people from the old ways and to make them more responsive to change. My work in the council led me to believe it would be right for me to involve myself in politics so that everyone might become responsive to modern life.

Do you think anyone may have influenced you in your interest in politics, for instance, your parents or a teacher?

My parents aren't happy. They were against my decision. At 16, I was chosen by Masai youth as a traditional leader. My parents worry about this life, my going into public life. They felt I was overburdening myself —a person on whom the whole district depends. They felt I wouldn't be able to look after our own cattle and my own children. But in 1964 I was urged by the people; they kept urging me because we had no representative in the previous Parliament. Then we just had to stand and I lost a good career in local government.

14. How would you describe your job as an M.P.? What are the most important things you have to do?

Well, we have 20,000 square miles in my district, so first I bring the difficulties and problems of my people and make them understood by the government so they can help us overcome these. Second, I take government policies back to the people and help them to understand them.

15. Let me ask you a few questions about your philosophy toward work; for instance, (A) would you say you dislike work which requires a great deal of attention to details?

No. It's impossible because I have no help except for a clerk in the office when I'm away.

(B) *How about working on a fixed schedule? Do you find this difficult?*
Yes.

(C) *Do you always finish tasks you start, even if they are not very important?*
Yes.

(D) *Do you dislike changing your plans in the midst of an undertaking?*
Yes, I never do.

(E) *In general, do you think of yourself as methodical in everything you do, such as organizing a meeting or speaking to others?*
Yes.

16. *In general, who can give you instructions about your work or to whom are you responsible?*

No one can give orders—I'm responsible to the people. If people want, and I think it's right, then I can do it.

Some people feel a superior should say just what is to be done and exactly how to do it if people are going to do a good job. Would you agree with this?

No. All people have different ways of doing things. I don't like to compel people to follow my orders.

17. *Thinking of the different things that you're responsible for in your work, what would you say is the most important aspect of your job?*

When we discuss with people their own problems.

What would you say is the most difficult aspect of your work?

Carrying out all the wishes and plans of development in my constituency.

And what is the most enjoyable aspect of your work?

Seeing a good achievement, if you can.

18. *Suppose the president were to ask you to perform a particularly difficult task, say mediate a dispute or represent the nation abroad. How would you feel about this?*

I'd think it over very carefully.

Would you do it?

Yes, why not?

What skills do you think you have which might be helpful?

Anything in the area of local government.

How about skills or abilities in which you might be weak? Can you think of any?

I wanted adult education in economics and history. I intended to do more good if I had acquired knowledge. I still feel this way.

19. (A) *Suppose the government introduces a bill before the Assembly that you personally oppose, and that you think most of your constituents wouldn't like. What would you do?*

Tell directly to the government that this is opposed to the wishes of my people—explain in Parliament and request the government not to pass—

then I'd vote against it. Of course, once the Bunge has voted, I should have to accept it, then an M.P. can only raise the matter later, some other time in Parliament.

(B) *Suppose an M.P. wants to be recognized and liked by the president, ministers, and other important people. What would he do?*

I don't know—do favors, go and see them I guess, but that's not my intention. I am here only to represent the wishes of my people.

(C) *Suppose local leaders or* TANU *get into a disagreement with an M.P. and inform him that they have expelled him from the party. What would he do?*

The district committee has no power to expel from the party, this is the central committee's responsibility. The first thing I'd do is learn the reasons why, and then submit to the appropriate party committee.

(D) *Suppose you believe corruption is occurring in a ministry. What would you do?*

First I'd bring the matter to the notice of senior government officers in the ministry; second, if serious, I'd report it to the police; third, if there has not been any action, then I'd bring it to the National Assembly.

(E) *Suppose an M.P. is defeated, as happened in the last election. What sort of job do you think he should expect? And what about politics?*

He shouldn't expect anything. If he fails to maintain the confidence of the people, then he should expect nothing from the government or the people. He can stay in politics depending on the circumstances of his area and his personal interest. If he is of use, why not; and if not, live like anyone else.

20. *One of the things we're interested in is your ideas of leadership. I wonder if you could tell me if there are any leaders, either in this country, in Africa, or anywhere in the world, whom you particularly like or admire?*

There are two leaders in Africa: Mwalimu [Nyerere], here, and Nkrumah; then there's the late President Kennedy.

What qualities or characteristics of these leaders do you admire the most?

Nyerere—a man whom everybody should follow; both theoretical and a man of action in his policies and in his own deeds. Personally, I like him the most. Kennedy—I met him in the States in 1962. He respected all men irrespective of color. Also I saw him in Germany in 1963, in Berlin. He had a spirit of nonracialism, and he loved and worked for underdeveloped countries. Nkrumah—I respect him for his work in areas outside of Africa to get people to understand Africa. Not for his policies of force, but for the African freedom which he was so successful in bringing.

21. *Everyone I have spoken with has been concerned with problems of nation building. If we could turn to this topic for a minute, one of the problems that*

has been discussed is the need for good citizens. I wonder what you would consider to be the most important responsibilities and rights for a good citizen.

First, make his own local government understand him; and second, be loyal and follow government policies. Rights—full protection and understanding of him by the government. The government should listen to what he says, and he has the right to bring constructive criticism to the government.

Some of the people I have talked with have suggested that giving the people the ability to vote a political leader out of office can be dangerous because the average voter is not competent to choose leaders who will serve the long-run interest of Tanzania. Would you agree?

No.

22. Another problem in development is the need to change many things. What changes do you think will occur in Tanzania in, say, the next 10 years?

Our country can be divided into three groups. First, there's the highly advanced, educated group; then there is second, a middle class; and finally, third, those that are still backward. My intention, and I expect the government agrees with this, is that government must be prepared to help those who are still backward, and help them in developing—not leave them as the colonial government did, without hospitals and schools, but to provide these and raise them to a high standard. This task is basic and a necessity, and I think the government accepts it, but it is difficult to catch up because those ahead will continue to go ahead. In 10 years, the basic necessities the government expects will be brought about, we should have mechanical cultivation, houses, schools, clean water. I intend to settle people in my own area so as to give them these sound facilities.

What about politics in 10 years?

It will be the same. It's fairly good now, it allows expression and more understanding by the people. Of course, new leaders will emerge and other problems of nation building.

What about in 25 years?

Well, the most backward areas will be up to where the more advanced areas are at the moment. The better part of the population will—a great part of the population will be literate and more changes will have been effected. As for politics, present arrangements may fit us more now than in the future, and therefore changes are likely.

Some people have said they felt the overriding task of government should be to create economic equality among people. Would you agree with this?

Well, I believe the natural resources of the government should be controlled by the government, and not private individuals, so that private individuals get advantage. Socialism is socialism, but it cannot affect the elementary social differences. For instance, one person will be rich and another poor, according to the work they do.

How about the pace of change these days? Do you think things are changing about the right speed, too slow, or too fast?

I think it's about the right speed, but things will move faster than we or the government can cope with. For example, in education, our own national income will not allow us to meet the requirements now. The government has been asked for better houses. The demands will grow faster than we can meet them.

Some people have suggested that things are changing so fast these days that no one can tell what will happen or who will cause things to happen. Would you agree with this?

It is difficult to say. It may be true, but people should double their efforts and not worry about this.

23. Now turning to yourself in all this, what do you see yourself doing in the future? For instance, what do you think you'll be doing, say, 10 years from now?

I'll still be an M.P.

Do you think this is likely to happen?

I think my chances are good. I should imagine I might still be an M.P.

24. Nowadays, one hears a lot of talk about African socialism, democracy, and so on. I wonder how you feel about these ideas.

African socialism—very difficult. There are differences in ideas. Some people have gone further than I would. Some people say that all people should be equal, not simply that socialism is government ownership. But to me the extended family, as Mwalimu has said, where a man can depend on his relatives, is African socialism. All people equal here? No, because the more property you have the more people you can support and help the community. Those who have should always give to others. Life is assured in the community in this way. African socialism is exactly what we had here; we can live and depend upon others to help us provided we work and are not idlers. This is what I understand by African socialism.

How about democracy?

In a democracy, man has freedom to express his own views; then democracy is fulfilled and it is very good and necessary.

Do you think democracy is the best form of government for Tanzania?

Very much so.

Is equal treatment for everyone a part of this?
   Yes.
Is it practiced?
   We've been doing satisfactorily. The constitution is an example. All
   people are under the law, even the president himself, and everyone is
   guaranteed the right to express ideas in speaking and in writing. In
   advanced countries the government needs more control over natural
   resources; otherwise, under capitalism, a few will be able to control
   everything. But in the tribe land is owned communally, and you can use
   it freely until you go away, then another person can come and own.
   Now the government here has modeled its policies on this idea, except
   in the urban areas where you can have a right to a plot of land to develop. No one can barter or trade on the land, and I support this very
   much.

25. *About two years ago the government changed its policy with regard to
civil servants joining* TANU, *allowing any civil servant who wished to join
the party to do so. What do you think about this?*
   It was a good change. You cannot have a class of people not able to
   express their ideas about their own government. The government was
   wise. Many of the civil servants attended TANU meetings, and now some
   hold official positions.

26. *Which would you say was more powerful or more important for making
decisions in the country, the National Assembly or the National Executive
Committee of* TANU?
   Parliament is more important because it is elected by the people where
   the NEC is not. We are the body that makes the laws and really represents all the people.

Part II

*Before we finish, there's just one last thing I'd like you to help me with if
you will. I have conducted a study among Tanzanian university students
here in East Africa. They were asked a number of questions about what
people in different situations in the country might do. On some of the questions I got a wide range of answers. I wonder if I showed you some of the
questions and the responses that I received if you would tell me what you
think to be the best or most correct answer or answers. For example, here's
the first card. You see above is the question and then beneath are all the
different responses which the students gave.*

[Questions, typed on 5 x 8-inch cards in English or in Swahili, depending
on which was used, were shown to the respondent in the order below. His

reaction to each card was recorded on a special sheet so that his choices could be circled and additional comments written to the side.]

1. If the President wished to change local leadership, what would he do?

   1. consult the National Assembly

   2. consult the local people, local leaders, or M.P.

   3. consult cabinet or advisors

   4. consult general public opinion, possibly by calling for elections

   5. go ahead and act, exercising constitutional powers

   6. go ahead and act, working through ministry of regional administration

2. If a citizen found officials attempting to help one candidate when he went to the polls to vote in an election, what would he do? What would happen?

   1. the citizen would report the matter to the proper official

   2. the citizen would call for an investigation in the press or before the court

   3. the citizen would do nothing, no action against the election would result

3. If an M.P. openly and strongly criticizes the president and his policies, what would the president do in response?

   1. ignore, realize that a president will be criticized

   2. refute the criticism; justify his actions

   3. accept the criticisms and consider their merit

   4. talk to the M.P. privately, persuade or warn him

   5. publicly criticize the M.P.

   6. get M.P. to stop criticism by offer of position or other reward

   7. force M.P. out of Assembly, detain or dismiss him

4a. The government introduces a measure before the legislature which an M.P. is personally against and which he feels his constituents would not like. What would the M.P. do?

   1. express his opinion in the Assembly; not vote for it

   2. oppose it strongly by speeches and discussions with other M.P.'s

   3. explain to his constituency the reasons for its introduction

   4. resign

4b. If a citizen came to a government administrator complaining of the treatment he had received from one of the administrator's subordinates, what would the administrator do?

   1. call the subordinate in before the citizen and investigate

   2. investigate privately after the citizen leaves

   3. listen to the complaint, but ignore or forget about it later

   4. warn the subordinate, discipline him if necessary

5a. An M.P. believes corruption is occurring within a ministry. What would he do about this?

1. inform the minister or ministry
2. investigate personally
3. raise the matter in the National Assembly
4. inform the president
5. inform the commission of inquiry
6. demand money from the corrupt individuals
7. ignore it and do nothing

5b. An administrator has initiated a policy which has resulted in unforeseen bad consequences and is bringing hardships to a number of people. What would the administrator do?

1. alleviate hardships caused; correct mistakes, compensate for loss
2. change or abandon policy or modify policy slightly
3. seek advice on if and how policy might be changed
4. nothing, policy can't be changed
5. remove or shift blame for the bad policy

6. Opposition to the government breaks out among a rural tribal group. What action would the president order to be taken?

1. use force to suppress and to maintain law and order
2. try to reconcile—use of persuasion, investigation to learn mistakes
3. declare emergency
4. arrest and detain leaders

7. There was a law which a citizen felt to be unjust. What would he do about it?

1. inform or see M.P.
2. appeal through press or mass media to public opinion
3. approach relevant authorities in government
4. refuse to obey
5. consult friends; ask for advice and support
6. nothing

8. A court rules the president has exceeded his authority in a particular matter and declares his action void. What would the president do?

1. president will accept and retract his action
2. president will ask Parliament to change law or constitution so that he can act legally
3. president will do as he pleases—has dictatorial powers
4. president will not accept; sack judge
5. resign

9a. Local TANU *leaders disagree with the M.P. from their area and inform him they have expelled him from the party. What would the M.P. do?*

1. M.P. would make amends, reconcile himself to the party
2. M.P. would appeal to electorate; ask for local support

3. M.P. would appeal to superiors in party (Executive Committee) or government
4. M.P. would resign
5. this is illegal—local leaders do not have the authority

9b. *A TANU official not holding a government post gives an order to a government administrator. What would the administrator do?*

1. do it
2. not do it; ignore the matter
3. report to superior
4. depends on government regulation; accept it if it is within the duty of the administrator
5. depends on his rank in the party; accept if he is a high official
6. discuss with the party official

10. *The president finds a majority of his ministers opposing his views. What would he do?*

1. resign
2. persuade others of his views
3. change his views
4. turn to Parliament for support
5. dismiss his cabinet or those opposing
6. dissolve Parliament and/or resign in order to hold elections

11. *A citizen is told by a policeman to obey a regulation which he believes either doesn't exist or is not legally enacted. What would he do?*

1. obey the policeman
2. refuse the policeman's order
3. explain to the policeman
4. seek the appropriate authority (e.g., police commissioner)
5. take legal (court) action against the policeman

12a. *An M.P. wants to be recognized and liked by ministers and other important people. What will he do?*

1. work hard and be virtuous
2. display new, sensible, and good ideas in the Assembly
3. support the government and ministers fully; never oppose
4. spend time with ministers and VIP's and praise them
5. work in his constituency

12b. *A government administrator wishes to be promoted to a higher position. What would he do?*

1. indicate his desire for advancement; make an application
2. work hard or efficiently
3. act in an outstanding or noticeably distinguished manner
4. please superiors by special attention; favors or gifts

5. undertake further study and pass exams

13. *An M.P. is defeated at the polls in an election. What sort of work should he expect to secure next and what sort of political activity will he engage in after his defeat?*
   1. accept defeat and refrain from politics
   2. keep active in politics locally or regionally; attempt to regain support for the next election
   3. get a government job of some sort
   4. find a job like anyone else, returning to his old job if he had one
   5. start or join an opposition to challenge government

[After the series of cards, 12 in procedure 1, 13 in procedure 2, had been completed, the interviewer said:]

Finally, the students were also asked their opinions on various questions. Would you mind looking at a few of these attitudes and tell me what you think? Some of the students agreed with these statements, while others disagreed. Perhaps if I showed you a list of these attitudes you would tell me what you think about them, whether you would agree or disagree with them.

[Below is a list of the 12 statements that were handed the respondent. The statements were typed on university stationery in English and Swahili versions. In a few cases, both lists were handed to the respondent.]

   a. Most people are fundamentally cooperative and inclined to help others.
   b. It is hard to tell nowadays who a person really can count on.
   c. Obedience and respect for authority are the most important virtues for children to learn.
   d. What this country needs most, more than laws and political programs, is a few courageous, tireless, and devoted leaders in whom people can put their faith.
   e. Leaders should always be obeyed.
   f. People can be divided into two distinct classes: the weak and the strong.
   g. Fundamentally, the world we live in is a pretty lonely place.
   h. Laws are wrong which prevent disagreement with a government from being expressed.
   i. Most people can't be trusted.
   j. Most people who don't get ahead just don't have enough will power.
   k. Nowadays a person has to live pretty much for today and let tomorrow take care of itself.
   l. Competition for leadership in open elections undermines a country's unity and purpose.

Appendix C

Attitude items from the 109 elite interviews were organized into five scales. Each question was scored Agree = 0, Uncertain = 1, Disagree = 2. The scaling technique and items included in each scale are reported below.

Authoritarianism. Five items form a Guttman scale with a coefficient of reproducibility of .926 and a minimal marginal reproducibility of .70.[1] They are:

	% Agree	% Error
1. Obedience and respect for authority are the most important virtues for children to learn.	84.2*	4.6
2. What this country needs, more than laws and political programs, is a few courageous, tireless, and devoted leaders in whom the people can put their faith.	71.2	13.8
3. Most people who don't get ahead just don't have enough will power.	58.3	7.4
4. Leaders should always be obeyed.	27.8	9.2
5. Superiors should say just what is to be done and how to do it if people are going to do a good job.	22.2	1.9

* Includes those who were "uncertain" in contrast to the figure reported in table 3.13.

One item, "People can be divided into two distinct classes: the weak and the strong," was dropped from the scale. Most of these items are from T. W. Adorno, Else Frenkel-Brunswick, Daniel J. Levinson, and R. Nevitt Sanford, *The Authoritarian Personality* (New York: Harper, 1950).

Anomie. Four questions were used to construct this scale. The third item comes from Rokeach's dogmatism scale and the second and fourth are adapted from Leo Srole's anomie scale reported in "Social Integration and Certain Cor-

---

1. For a discussion of Guttman scaling see Samuel Stouffer et al., *Measurement and Prediction* (Princeton: Princeton University Press, 1950), and Warren S. Torgerson, *Theory and Methods of Scaling* (New York: John Wiley and Sons, 1958), pp. 307–36. The program used to compute this scale is BMDO5S, "Guttman Scale #1," Biomedical Computer Programs (BMD) (Los Angeles: UCLA School of Medicine, 1965 rev.), pp. 379–89.

ollaries: An Exploratory Study," *American Sociological Review* 21 (December 1956), 709–16. The four items whose summed scores form this scale are:

	% Agree
1. Things are changing so fast these days no one can tell what will happen or who will cause things to happen.	20.5
2. It is hard to tell nowadays who a person really can count on.	26.9
3. Fundamentally, the world we live in is a pretty lonely place.	18.6
4. Nowadays a person has to live pretty much for today and let tomorrow take care of itself.	12.1

Faith in People (Misanthropy). Two items were combined in this scale. Both are derived from Morris Rosenberg, "Misanthropy and Political Ideology," *American Sociological Review,* 21 (December 1956), 690–95. The items are:

	% Agree
1. Most people are fundamentally cooperative and inclined to help others.	87.0
2. Most people can't really be trusted.	23.1

Democratic Practices. The summed scores on three items form this scale. The first question is adapted from a question used by Wendell Bell and Charles C. Moskos, Jr., reported in "Attitudes Towards Democracy Among Leaders in Four Emergent Nations," *British Journal of Sociology, 15* (December 1964), 320.

	% Agree
1. Giving people the right to vote a political leader out of office can be dangerous, because the average voter is not competent to choose leaders who will serve the long-range interests of Tanzania.	27.8
2. Laws are wrong which prevent disagreement with a government from being expressed. [This shows the scoring of this item was reversed— disagrees and agrees switched—for scaling purposes.]	14.8
3. Competition for leadership undermines a country's unity and purpose.	13.1

Appendix D

Role Expectations

Role Strength

Role expectation questions from the elite interviews were examined to see whether common dimensions underlying several questions could be discovered. One dimension, that of the assertiveness or strength of a role, was found in 10 of the 17 role questions relating to the roles of the president, M.P., and administrator. (These questions are reported in appendix B, interview part II, questions 1–13.) Response categories have been rearranged and collapsed in order to produce a three-point continuum of assertiveness from weak to strong role expectations for each question. The items for each role, the revised categories (the original categories are given in parentheses), and the scaling technique utilized are included in the discussion of the measures of role strength below.

The scale for presidential role strength is based on five items. With responses to 1 and 2 dichotomized as indicated, these items form a Guttman scale with a coefficient of reproducibility of .905 and a minimal marginal reproducibility of .61. The five items with the error each contributes are:

	% in Each Category	*% Error*

1. *If the president wished to change local leadership, what would he do?*

a. President will consult public (1, 2, 4)	20.8	
b. President will consult advisors, discuss privately (3) c. President will act (directly or indirectly)	79.2	4.8

2. *If an M.P. openly and strongly criticizes the president and his policies, what would the president do in response?*

a. President will accept or ignore criticisms (1, 3) b. President will respond to criticism (2)	70.5	
c. President will respond to individual criticizing (4–7)	29.5	2.9

3. Opposition to the government breaks out among a rural tribal group. What action would the president order to be taken?

a. President will use persuasion, investigation (2)   75.0
b. President will use force (1)   20.2
c. President will use extreme or emergency   8.6
   powers (3, 4)   4.8

4. A court rules the president has exceeded his authority in a particular matter and declares his action void. What would the president do?

a. President will accept (1)   44.8
b. President will ask Parliament (2)   44.8   12.4
c. President will override court (3, 4)   10.5

5. The president finds a majority of his ministers opposing his views. What would he do?

a. President will discuss, use persuasion
   (1, 2, 3)   38.0
b. President will turn to Parliament for sup-
   port (4)   32.0   18.1
c. President will act dramatically alone (5, 6)   30.0

The three questions which form the scale for legislative role strength do not meet the requirements of Guttman scaling.[1] The technique of summed scores was used, therefore, to construct this measure.

Consensus among Roles

The nature of the responses to role expectation questions makes measuring role consensus particularly complex. Two measures of consensus were calculated using the original categories (see appendix B interview part II, questions 1–13). These, however, were deemed inadequate and have not been included in our discussion. The reasons why these measures were rejected, the formulas for their calculation, and some of the relationships they indicated are explained below.

In order to overcome difficulties in measuring consensus, items whose categories of responses could be rearranged in a three-point continuum of role strength, as outlined above, were used to calculate consensus. The other items were not used in this analysis. An examination of the excluded items will show that they contain no special pattern of responses. Two items deal with paths

---

1. See Torgerson, *Theory and Methods of Scaling.*

to success of M.P.'s and administrators, the others largely with expectations for the role of citizen.

The consensus on each role is a product of both the nature of the role questions and the distribution of responses. If items on one role delve into more ambiguous terrain, then it is the nature of the question that statistical differences will reflect. However, the ten questions used in our analysis all touch on areas that seemed equally ambiguous and important prior to the interview results. Therefore, we will assume different response patterns reflect differences in the degree of role consensus and not differences in the items. Comparison of consensus among groups on the same item, of course, do not need to rest on this assumption.

Using the ten items discussed in chapter 4–6 (see table D.1)—five items on the president's role, three on the M.P.'s role, and two for the role of admin-

TABLE D.1. Items for Role Consensus

Item	Interview Question No.	Variance	Role Consensus*
1. If the president wished to change local leadership	1	.556	
2. If an M.P. openly criticized the president	3	.627	
3. Opposition to the government breaks out	6	.305	President .519
4. A court rules the president has exceeded his authority	8	.435	
5. President finds a majority of his ministers oppose him	10	.674	
6. M.P. is against government-sponsored measure	4a	.458	
7. M.P. believes corruption exists in ministry	5a	.224	M.P. .394
8. Local TANU leaders expel M.P. from party	9a	.500	
9. Administrator initiates policy resulting in bad consequences	5b	.429	Administrator .521
10. TANU official gives an order to administrator	9b	.613	

* Calculated as the average variance of the relevant role items.

istrator—consensus among the roles was calculated by using the variance (V) statistic. This has been recommended to measure role consensus by Neal Gross and others,[2] although their specific application was for intrasample consensus

2. See Gross, *Exploration in Role Analysis*, p. 107.

while we are extending it to compare consensus among roles as well. The formula for the variance is

$$V = \sum_{i=i}^{N} (\overline{X}_i - X)^2/N$$

where: X_i is the score of the ith respondent
$\overline{X}$ is the mean for all scores
N is the number of respondents with scores on this item.

In this calculation, response categories in each item were accorded a cardinal number as follows:

Category A = 0
Category B = 1
Category C = 2

In figure D.1 are three hypothetical distributions that indicate the relationship between high variance and low consensus.[3] Where responses are equally divided, ambiguity of role expectations is indicated, while the third example

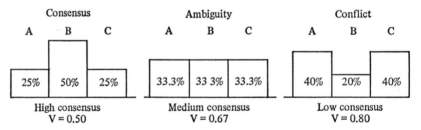

Consensus			Ambiguity			Conflict		
A	B	C	A	B	C	A	B	C
25%	50%	25%	33.3%	33 3%	33.3%	40%	20%	40%
High consensus $V = 0.50$			Medium consensus $V = 0.67$			Low consensus $V = 0.80$		

Figure D.1. Alternative Distributions of Expectations

in figure D.1, which clusters respondents in the most contradictory categories, illustrates role conflict. When responses were treated as strictly nominal categories, the measure of consensus (nominal variability) indicated that the second rather than the third example in figure D.1 was the least consensual. (The calculation of this measure is explained in Hopkins, "Political Roles," pp. 396–98.) This would have been a good measure if all categories were

3. For figure D.1, the variance is calculated for an N of, say, 100 quite simply. The mean $(\overline{X})$ is 1.0, and the differences $(X_i - \overline{X})$ are -1.0 for the 25 respondents in category A, 0.0 for the 50 in category B, and 1.0 for the 25 in category C. Squaring and summing these differences, $\Sigma(X_i - \overline{X})^2$, gives $25 + 0 + 25 = 50$, which divided by N (that is, 100) yields the variance of .50.

equally different. But since this was not the case, the variance calculated for items adjusted to an interval scale seemed the best solution, one that resulted in the least distortion of the data. Table D.1 shows the variances for each item, the results of calculating variability among roles by average variance.

Congruence among Elite

The average of the absolute values of transformed standardized scores for the ten items was used as a measure of the congruence (C) of an individual respondent's expectations with the rest of the elite. The formula for the ith respondent's C score is

$$C_i = \sum_{j=1}^{NI} [2 - |(X_{ij} - \overline{X}_j)/S_j|]/NI$$

where: $S_j = \sqrt{V_j}$
NI = the number of (nonmissing) items
2 = the maximum item score

Scores for congruence were calculated over items for each role and over all items.

The standardized (Z) score, a familiar statistic that allows us to standardize the contribution of each item to a respondent's total score, seems well suited to our needs. The measure used by Gross and others to assess microscopic role consensus (D) is analogous to this procedure.[4] D is calculated as the difference between the role expectations of an individual school superintendent and the mean expectation of the school board, corrected by adding the variance of board expectations. This, however, is equivalent to the dispersion of the school board about the superintendent's expectations. D was calculated on individual items and then summed over items relevant to a particular role or role characteristic. Our procedure was similar, with the individual elite respondent equivalent to the school superintendent and the rest of the elite comparable to the school board against whose normative outlook the individual is assessed. In calculating consensus over a particular item there are several differences between the Gross formula and the one used here. First, since the N is large in all cases and the computation is much simpler but not otherwise greatly affected, the mean is calculated over all elite (equivalent to including the superintendent with the school board). Another dissimilarity is that the standard deviation was used to correct and standardize differences before summing across items, while Gross squared these differences. The effect was similar in both calculation procedures—to accentuate deviant cases.

4. See Gross, pp. 162–74, 369–70.

Appendix E

The Sample

The verbatim debates of the Tanzanian National Assembly are published by the Government Printer in bound volumes, one volume for each meeting. Speeches are not edited, nor is nondebate material included. Assembly meetings have varied in length and regularity; the budget session held each June is the longest and most important regularly scheduled session. I have, therefore, divided the meetings of the Assembly into annual periods ending with the budget session and have analyzed debates for five periods, beginning with the meeting October 10–20, 1961, which immediately followed the last budget session before independence, and ending with the June–July budget session of 1966. All speeches in the first and fifth periods were coded. In the second, third, and fourth periods, days were randomly chosen and all speeches for that day coded. About one half of the days the Assembly met were chosen for coding, thus giving us approximately a 50 percent sample of the middle three periods. The first four periods contain debates from the first National Assembly, the fifth period has the debates of the second Assembly chosen in the election of September 1965. The first Assembly was elected in October 1960 and held four meetings in 1960–61 (36th session, 1–4 of the Tanganyika Legislative Council). The fourth meeting was the 1961 budget session and took place at the time self-government was granted. Because these meetings occurred prior to both self-government and independence, they were not included in the content analysis. Table E.1 presents the periods and sessions covered.

Coding

The coding was done by the author (a portion of period one) and his research assistant, Tom Mkude, a second-year law student at University College, Dar es Salaam. Speeches were coded according to six characteristics: subject, orientation, length, language, position, and period.

Subject. The subject of a speech was determined from 28 possible subject categories created after initial work on the coding procedure. Some correspond to the various ministerial divisions of government activity, but these governmental distinctions themselves are often not clear and over the five-year period several ministries had their portfolios revised. In spite of this, the vast majority

TABLE E.1. National Assembly Speeches Coded

Period	Hansard Session/Meeting	Total Days	Days Coded	Dates of Coded Meetings
1	36/5	8	8	October 10–20, 1961
(1961–62)	36/6	3	3	November 30–December 2, 1961
	1/1	6	6	Dec. 11, 1961–Feb. 17, 1962
	1/2	21	21	June 5–July 3, 1962
	Total	38	38	
2	1/3	3	2	September 26–27, 1962
(1962–63)	1/4	4	2	November 22, 27, 1962
	1/5	6	2	February 13, 16, 1963
	1/6	3	2	April 23, 25, 1963
	1/7	14	7	June 12, 15, 17, 19–20, 24, 1963
	Total	30	15	
3	1/8	3	1	September 12, 1963
(1963–64)	1/9	3	2	December 4–5, 1963
	1/10	4	3	February 18, 20–21, 1964
	1/11	1	1	April 25, 1964
	1/12	1	0	May 14, 1964
	1/13	13	5	June 16, 19, 22, 25, July 1, 1964
	Total	25	12	
4	1/14	2	2	September 8–9, 1964
(1964–65)	1/15	3	1	December 1, 1964
	1/16	3	3	March 16–18, 1965
	1/17	21	9	June 14–18, 21–23, 1965
	Total	29	15	
5	2/1	2	2	October 12–13, 1965
(1965–66)	2/2	9	9	December 14–23, 1965
	2/3	6	6	February 22–28, 1966
	2/4	33	33	June 10–July 25, 1966
	Total	50	50	

of speeches fell clearly into one or another of the devised categories. The substantive issue of a speech determined its subject, hence a legal dispute over revising agricultural statutes was coded as agriculture and not law. If a speech was on more than one distinct subject and had no dominant theme, it was coded for each relevant subject but recorded only once in other categories. Regularly a few long speeches received this special coding. The total number of speeches by subject, therefore, is larger than the actual number as reflected by other coded characteristics. The 28 subject categories are briefly defined below.

SUBJECT DEFINITIONS

1. *Foreign Policy—External.* Policies and behavior of other nations and international organizations either with respect to Tanzania or in general.
2. *Foreign Policy—Tanzanian.* The foreign policy and actions of Tanzania in the international sphere.
3. *Education.* All educational matters—teachers, schools, curriculum, school integration, etc.
4. *Cooperatives, Commerce.* Marketing, price paid for commodities by the government, cooperative organization, cooperative management, regulation of retail trade.
5. *Agriculture.* Agricultural legislation, extension services, control of diseases, reports on crops.
6. *Economic Planning.* Development plans, regional development coordination, economic estimates and projections, National Development Corporation.
7. *Water, Land, Settlement.* Rural development, development and control of land, wildlife, water, expropriation of property.
8. *Police.* Organization, training, duties of police, crimes, criminals, and prisons.
9. *Military.* Questions of national defense, security of borders, army size, recruitment, activities.
10. *Refugees.* Treatment of refugees, laws affecting them, and number crossing into Tanzania.
11. *Health.* Hospitals, health care, control of disease, drug regulations, licensing of medical personnel.
12. *Labor, Unions.* Union regulation and control, protection for workers, wage and salary legislation.
13. *National Culture, Youth.* Cultural activities, art, language (especially Swahili), youth activity, national service, development and spread of Tanzanian culture.
14. *Community Development.* Government extension efforts at local level to promote adult education, new skills, and more advanced health, safety, and work habits, advice for local planning activity.
15. *Administration.* Civil service, salaries, recruitment, treatment of the public, question of expatriates, national government buildings, organization.
16. *News, Radio, Publicity.* Radio Tanzania, coverage of events by local and foreign news services, tourism, promotion of Tanzania at home and abroad.
17. *Housing.* Accommodation of government personnel, public housing projects.
18. *Industries, Utilities.* Matters relating to industrial investment, development, location regulation, development and regulation of electrical, phone, postal services.
19. *Roads, Railroads, Harbors.* Building and maintaining roads, railroads, harbors and all matters relating to communication infrastructure.

20. *Finances, Taxation.* Government budget, estimates of revenue and expenses, tax and tariff legislation, money and banking matters.
21. *Elections.* Matters of elections, qualifications of candidates, and procedures.
22. *TANU, ASP.* Party affairs, the role, organization, and actions of the two legal political parties.
23. *Praise.* Comments lauding an individual or an action.
24. *Laws, Courts.* Judicial concerns, changes in statutes (technical), matters relating to the attorney-general.
25. *National Unity.* Speeches stressing, acknowledging, or criticizing (usually the lack of) Tanzanian solidarity.
26. *African Socialism.* Socialism, African socialism, or the relation of government programs to socialist goals.
27. *Procedures.* Points of order, motions to adjourn, seconds to motions.
28. *Constitution.* Constitutional matters, including revision.

Orientation. If a speech dealt only with local issues or the implications of a general problem in terms of a particular area or district, it was considered to reflect local orientation. On the other hand, if it was on a national plane or examined national issues it was coded as national. Only if a speech equally combined local and national orientations was it coded as mixed.

Length. By reading the Hansard aloud it was possible to find rough equivalences of 1½ and 7 minutes in terms of print. These two cutting points enabled speeches to be classified into three categories; short, medium, and long. Short speeches were largely the questions and answers that normally occupied the first hour of each day's sitting. Points of order, adjournments, and other procedural interjections were also generally short. Lengthy responses to questions and speeches of clarification and support generally fell into the category for medium length. Major speeches often lasted for twenty minutes to an hour. However, since members were forbidden to read speeches, the necessary lack of formal preparation and the eventual boredom of fellow members usually limited the longer speeches to 10 to 20 minutes. If a speech was briefly interrupted it was counted as only one speech, while if a major break occurred in a speaker's comments, such as an intervening speech or period of adjournment, the procedure was to count it as two separate speeches.

Language. Speeches were made in English, Swahili, or a mixture of the two. Swahili did not become an official language of debate until December 1962, when the republican constitution came into effect.

Position. The most difficult trait of a speech to code was its position vis-à-vis the government. If there was no government position on a subject or if the speaker studiously balanced support for the government with criticism, the speech was considered neutral. If the speech's overall effect was clearly in opposition to or at least critical of the government, it was coded as critical. If the speech openly endorsed the government position, praising or defending it, the speech was coded as supportive. A number of speeches did not easily fit any of these three categories, particularly the short questions and answers, so a fourth category was created. Although it is labeled question-answer, not all questions and answers were automatically put in this category. If an M.P. were to inquire about a matter of fact, such as how much food a particular prison produced, the question and answer were considered neutral. If an M.P. asked when the government was going to build the new school planned for his district, this was considered a demand or request for action. A majority of questions were of this type, with the government's answer usually being a promise to move ahead as fast as funds and priorities allowed; these speeches were coded under the special question-answer category. A few questions were considered critical of the government, for example, questions that related to preventive detention and the union—both subjects the government preferred not to debate; the responses generally were coded as supportive.

Period. The final characteristic coded for each speech—the time at which it was given—was comparatively trivial. However, this information was necessary to sort out speeches into the appropriate periods for computer work. As explained above, speeches fell into *five* time periods: 1961–62, 1962–63, 1963–64, 1964–65, and 1965–66.

Excerpts of some speeches from an early session (which was in English) are given below in order to illustrate the coding procedure used.

A. *Mr. Baghdelleh* asked:

> In view of the hardship caused to people of Kilwa through the lack of land or sea communication with Lindi will the Minister state when the Kilwa/Lindi road is likely to be passable for through traffic?

The Minister for Communications, Power and Works replied:

> Whilst the road will be open from time to time, as the hon. Member is aware, its present characteristics are such that it goes out of service after comparatively slight rainfall and it is therefore unlikely that it will be open to traffic continuously before the end of the coming long rains.[1]

Both of these speeches were coded as follows:

> Subject—roads, etc.
> Orientation—local
> Time—short
> Position—question-answer
> Period—first

---

1. *Tanganyika Parliamentary Debates* (Hansard), December 11, 1961, to February 17, 1962 (Dar es Salaam: Government Printer, 1962), Col. 19.

B. *Chief Humbi Ziota:*

> Mr. Deputy Speaker, Sir, I stand to support the Motion. I support the Motion because I am satisfied that the creation of Regional Commissioners is a necessity in the present democratic Tanganyika. These Regional Commissioners are going to be very beneficial in their areas because the Government of today is an elected Government and it is a democratic Government which has been created by the people themselves under the leadership of the ruling party that is T.A.N.U. The reasons that I am satisfied with the work of the Regional Commissioners is . . . Another problem which the Regional Commissioners are going to face is that of drunkenness in the country. I must say that it is on the increase. . . . They [Regional Commissioners] should combine with the work of the Community Development because that could assist a lot in putting across the emphasis on the Three-year Development Plan with which these Regional Commissioners are going to deal in their day to day activities. With these few remarks, I support the Motion.[2]

Chief Humbi Ziota, who soon afterward became a regional commissioner, gave a typical medium-length supportive speech. His speech was coded as follows:

> Subject—government administration
> Orientation—national
> Time—medium
> Position—supportive
> Period—first

C. *Mr. Mtaki:*

> Mr. Speaker, Sir, I first congratulate the Minister for Finance for introducing this bill. It gives me great pleasure to stand here in this House and criticize the introduction of this Bill. I am standing here not to support the introduction of this Bill; I am standing here to criticize very strongly this Bill. My criticism will be based on the African tradition.[3]

This speech went on for about ten minutes—with one interruption—to attack proposed legislation that would impose a personal tax on women. It was coded:

> Subject—finance
> Orientation—national
> Time—long

2. Ibid., Cols. 292–93.
3. Ibid., Cols. 236–38.

Position—critical
Period—first

Mr. Mponji:

Mr. Speaker, Sir, I am very thankful to be given this opportunity to propound my views on this particular bill. The introduction of a Unified Teaching Service, Mr. Speaker, Sir, is whole-heartedly welcomed by the members of the teaching profession. . . . I therefore take this opportunity, Mr. Speaker, to congratulate the Government in the matter.

However, I have some very important remarks to make and I would, therefore, request the Government to consider these remarks very seriously. . . . My main criticism is contained in the Schedules—both in the First and Second Schedule which deal with the constitution of the Central Board and the Area Committees. . . . Teachers who represent the teachers' interests are to be appointed by the Minister. Why? What fear has the Minister got? . . . So it appears, Sir, there is some fear and I assure the Minister he should not fear the teachers and the teachers' organization. . . . One of the rights, Sir, is to be represented by the people who are elected by the teachers themselves on the different Boards. . . . This is one of the very important rights that the teachers demand and they demand it very strongly. Everyone knows that some of the demands which were demanded by the teachers have been denied or if not denied have not been looked after so much as they should be. . . .

I have spoken long enough but as I said earlier I beg the Government, Sir, to consider it very seriously; they will either wreck the whole teaching profession of the country or build it and it is up to them to build it. I want them to build it and the teachers want you to build it. With these necessary amendments, Sir, I beg to support the Motion.[4]

This very long speech by Mponji began and ended by supporting the government's motion, with certain reservations. The entire body of the speech, however, was critical of portions of the legislation. It presented demands of teachers and implied dissatisfaction with present government policy. (Mponji had been a teacher prior to entering politics.) It was coded as follows:

Subject—education
Orientation—national
Time—long
Position—critical
Period—first

4. Ibid., Cols. 306–13.

Reliability

Not all speeches, of course, were as easy to code as the examples above. Sometimes it was difficult to judge whether a speech was, on balance, neutral or critical. At other times a speech might logically be related to two subjects; Africanization of hospitals could relate to either government administration (15) or health (11). A number of particular rules for consistency emerged during the coding. For instance, in the case above, Africanization and not health was the subject chosen because the substance of the debate was on this topic. In order to test the reliability of the coding, intercoder agreement was measured. I gave oral instructions to three coders, along with examples similar to those cited above. Two sections of debate were selected at random, one from period 1 in English (116 speeches) and the other from period 5 in Swahili (198 speeches). Mkude, the principal coder, coded both sets of speeches. Kapinga and Hopkins then coded the period 1 selection and Opanga, a second-year political science student, coded the period 5 selection. Table E.2 gives the percentage of agreement among coders.[5]

TABLE E.2. Intercoder Agreement

| | Agreement Between Coders | | |
	A/B (N = 116)	A/C (N = 116)	A/D (N = 198)
Subject	96.6	94.8	94.9
Orientation	98.3	98.3	97.0
Time	95.7	94.0	94.5
Position	85.3	78.4	96.0
Total	93.9	91.4	95.6

Coders: A = Mkude; B = Hopkins; C = Kapinga; D = Opanga.

Two characteristics, language and period, were sufficiently trivial to be excluded from this measure of reliability. In fact their intercoder agreement in all cases was 100 percent. In spite of the lower agreement on "position" for

5. This measure of agreement among two coders is commonly suggested to compute reliability. See Robert C. North, Ole R. Holsti, M. George Zaninovich, and Dina A. Zinnes, *Content Analysis* (Evanston: Northwestern University Press, 1963), pp. 49–50, and W. S. Robinson, "The Statistical Measurement of Agreement." The formula for computing agreement between coders i and j is

$$\text{Percentage Agreement } i/j = (NA_{i,j}/N) \times 100$$

when $N =$ the number of items coded and $NA_{i,j} =$ the number of items in agreement. Each coder must choose one and only one category for the same material.

the period 1 speeches, these results indicate reasonably high levels of agreement.

Computation and Analysis

A computer program was written to count and classify the 15,421 speeches that were coded. The number and percentage of speeches by period for subject, orientation, language, position, and time were calculated. For each period on each subject the percentage by position and orientation was also calculated. Since long and medium speeches were more important contributions to the debate, a special and arbitrary weighting procedure was devised for all the above relationships whereby long speeches were multiplied by two, medium speeches by one, and short speeches by zero (thus removing short speeches from the analysis). Next, each M.P.'s contribution to the debate (by subject, orientation, and position) was measured as a percentage of both total and weighted speeches in the period(s) in which he spoke and also as a percentage of his own total and weighted speeches by period.

The resulting figures provided both a picture of the total pattern of talk in the National Assembly over time and a series of individual measures for each M.P. indicating the extent and nature of his contributions to the Assembly debates. Tables E.3 to E.5 present the results of the analysis. Periods 2, 3, and 4 represent approximately a 50 percent sample of speeches, while periods 1 and 5 contain all speeches.

Factor Analysis

The percentages of each M.P.'s contribution to speeches by subject ($N = 28$) in period 1 (80 observations) and period 5 (165 observations—20 members never spoke) were submitted to factor analyses to ascertain what underlying dimensions or patterns of talk existed among M.P.'s in these two periods. The individual scores used as raw data for the factor analysis were:

$$\text{Score of } MP_i \text{ on Subject}_j \text{ in period}_k = \frac{\text{No. of speeches by } MP_i \text{ on Sub}_j \text{ in } P_k}{\text{Total number of speeches on Sub}_j \text{ in } P_k}$$

The Yale Computer Center Factor Analysis Program was used to calculate these two factor analyses. The principal component method with varimax rotation was employed.[6] All factors with eigenvalues of 1.0 or greater were rotated. Ten factors for each period met this criteria. These rotated factors with their factor loadings for period 5 are presented in table E.6. Naming of the

6. For a discussion of factor analysis see Harry Harman, *Modern Factor Analysis* (Chicago: University of Chicago Press, 1960).

TABLE E.3. National Assembly Debates: Number of Speeches

	1961–62	1962–63	1963–64	1964–65	1965–66	Total
Total	4303	1613	1347	1964	6194	15421
For. Pol.—Ext.	44	9	17	12	46	128
For. Pol.—Tnz.	99	30	44	17	96	286
Education	538	95	90	96	452	1271
Coops, Comm.	149	130	49	263	637	1228
Agriculture	283	172	103	82	270	910
Dev. Plan	17	5	17	3	123	165
Water, Land	168	81	113	215	435	1012
Police	196	79	106	86	295	762
Military	40	14	24	24	45	147
Refugees	24	0	0	0	3	27
Health	181	73	48	138	298	738
Labor, Unions	131	35	72	21	180	439
Youth, Cultr.	55	26	25	35	48	189
Comm. Dev.	54	19	15	7	110	205
Civil Servs.	447	75	20	58	538	1138
News, Radio	100	16	31	41	128	316
Housing	69	7	25	9	157	267
Industry, Utl.	152	82	63	144	365	806
Roads, RR, Harbors	275	100	56	142	570	1143
Finance, Tax	429	150	61	177	524	1341
Elections	36	13	13	1	26	89
TANU, ASP	21	2	2	7	32	64
Praise	41	7	3	4	11	66
Law Courts	269	88	17	22	90	486
Nat. Unity	38	1	0	12	25	76
Af. Socialism	15	9	16	9	6	55
Procedures	511	307	321	333	702	2174
Constitution	87	0	0	11	11	109
Local	817	386	253	459	1747	3662
National	3648	1237	1098	1508	4475	11966
Mixed	4	2	0	2	1	9
Swahili	4	874	879	1670	6056	9483
English	4297	726	461	287	118	5889
Mixed	2	13	7	7	20	49
Supportive	1361	312	284	377	760	3094
Critical	793	147	47	91	329	1412
Neutral	1274	491	480	522	1193	3960
Quest. Answer	1036	675	540	979	3941	7171
Short	3298	1265	1053	1553	5035	12204
Medium	592	123	111	163	403	1392
Long	413	225	183	248	756	1825

TABLE E.4. National Assembly Debates: Percentage of All Speeches by Category

	1961–62	1962–63	1963–64	1964–65	1965–66	Total
For. Pol.—Ext.	0.98	0.55	1.26	0.61	0.74	0.82
For. Pol.—Tnz.	2.22	1.85	3.26	0.86	1.54	1.83
Education	12.04	5.85	6.66	4.88	7.26	8.13
Coops, Comm.	3.33	8.00	3.63	13.36	10.24	7.85
Agriculture	6.33	10.58	7.62	4.16	4.34	5.82
Dev. Plan	0.38	0.31	1.26	0.15	1.98	1.06
Water, Land	3.76	4.98	8.36	10.92	6.99	6.47
Police	4.39	4.86	7.85	4.37	4.74	4.87
Military	0.90	0.86	1.78	1.22	0.72	0.94
Refugees	0.54	0.00	0.00	0.00	0.05	0.17
Health	4.05	4.49	3.55	7.01	4.79	4.72
Labor, Unions	2.93	2.15	5.33	1.07	2.89	2.81
Youth, Cultr.	1.23	1.60	1.85	1.78	0.77	1.21
Comm. Dev.	1.21	1.17	1.11	0.36	1.77	1.31
Civil Servs.	10.00	4.62	1.48	2.95	8.65	7.28
News, Radio	2.24	0.98	2.29	2.08	2.06	2.02
Housing	1.54	0.43	1.85	0.46	2.52	1.71
Industry, Utl.	3.40	5.05	4.66	7.31	5.87	5.15
Roads, RR, Harbors	6.15	6.15	4.15	7.21	9.16	7.31
Finance, Tax	9.60	9.23	4.52	8.99	8.42	8.58
Elections	0.81	0.80	0.96	0.05	0.42	0.57
TANU, ASP	0.47	0.12	0.15	0.36	0.51	0.41
Praise	0.92	0.43	0.22	0.20	0.18	0.42
Law Courts	6.02	5.42	1.26	1.12	1.45	3.11
Nat. Unity	0.85	0.06	0.00	0.61	0.40	0.49
Af. Socialism	0.34	0.55	1.18	0.46	0.10	0.35
Procedures	11.43	18.89	23.76	16.91	11.28	13.90
Constitution	1.95	0.00	0.00	0.56	0.18	0.70
Local	18.28	23.75	18.73	23.31	28.07	23.42
National	81.63	76.12	81.27	76.59	71.91	76.52
Mixed	0.09	0.12	0.00	0.10	0.02	0.06
Swahili	0.09	54.18	65.26	85.03	97.77	61.49
English	99.86	45.01	34.22	14.61	1.91	38.19
Mixed	0.05	0.81	0.52	0.36	0.32	0.32
Supportive	30.45	19.20	21.02	19.15	12.21	19.79
Critical	17.86	9.05	3.48	4.62	5.29	9.03
Neutral	28.51	30.22	35.53	26.51	19.17	25.32
Quest.-Answer	23.18	41.54	39.97	49.72	63.33	45.86
Short	76.64	78.43	78.17	79.07	81.29	79.14
Medium	13.76	7.63	8.24	8.30	6.51	9.03
Long	9.60	13.95	13.59	12.63	12.21	11.83

TABLE E.5. National Assembly Debates: Percent of Weighted
Speeches by Category

	1961–62	1962–63	1963–64	1964–65	1965–66	Total
For. Pol.—Ext.	1.45	2.86	2.89	1.35	1.47	1.73
For. Pol.—Tnz.	3.36	4.87	9.48	2.69	3.24	3.95
Education	8.34	1.85	3.09	1.20	5.88	5.40
Coops, Comm.	5.04	16.30	4.54	15.99	11.05	9.75
Agriculture	8.63	15.13	6.60	4.78	2.74	6.55
Dev. Plan	1.33	0.84	5.98	0.30	8.06	4.00
Water, Land	2.49	10.25	7.84	21.97	6.84	7.78
Police	3.19	3.36	11.55	3.74	3.14	4.00
Military	2.26	0.00	4.12	4.33	2.94	2.68
Refugees	0.52	0.00	0.00	0.00	0.00	0.17
Health	1.51	1.85	0.21	3.29	3.19	2.26
Labor, Unions	5.50	3.36	9.90	1.20	3.50	4.41
Youth, Cultr.	1.16	3.19	3.30	3.89	0.51	1.67
Comm. Dev.	1.97	1.01	0.62	0.00	1.93	1.49
Civil Servs.	11.41	6.22	1.44	4.04	11.81	9.20
News, Radio	0.98	0.17	2.68	3.14	1.93	1.65
Housing	2.03	0.50	3.71	0.00	2.69	2.00
Industry, Utl.	2.95	4.37	1.86	4.19	3.09	3.21
Roads, RR, Harbors	6.03	1.01	0.00	1.20	6.08	4.37
Finance, Tax	10.08	14.12	8.25	15.70	10.34	11.14
Elections	1.68	0.00	3.71	0.30	1.82	1.56
TANU, ASP	0.81	0.17	0.41	0.00	1.93	1.01
Praise	2.32	0.00	0.41	0.00	0.20	0.84
Law Courts	6.26	6.55	2.06	1.35	1.57	3.62
Nat. Unity	1.39	0.34	0.00	1.94	1.47	1.25
Af. Socialism	0.87	0.50	4.95	2.09	0.35	1.16
Procedures	1.62	1.18	0.41	0.15	2.13	1.47
Constitution	4.81	0.00	0.00	1.20	0.10	1.71
Local	11.76	9.58	5.57	4.93	15.81	11.60
National	87.83	90.42	94.43	95.07	84.09	88.23
Mixed	0.41	0.00	0.00	0.00	0.10	0.17
Swahili	0.42	60.91	70.23	87.56	97.23	62.06
English	99.51	37.00	28.51	11.84	1.72	37.09
Mixed	0.07	2.09	1.26	0.61	1.04	0.85
Supportive	44.03	54.12	68.87	69.96	52.05	53.43
Critical	30.59	18.82	6.39	9.42	22.55	21.64
Neutral	23.12	25.38	22.68	17.49	18.45	20.94
Quest.-Answer	2.26	1.68	2.06	3.14	6.94	3.98
Short						
Medium	41.75	21.47	23.27	24.73	21.04	27.61
Long	58.25	78.53	76.73	75.27	78.96	72.39

TABLE E.6. Rotated Factor Matrix of National Assembly Debates, 1965–1966

	Sovereignty-Security I	Cultural-Image II	Rural Development III	Administrative Performance IV	Economic Management V	Infrastructure Development VI	Socialist Progress VII	VIII	IX	X	Communalities
For. Pol.—Ext.	.92	.06	.01	−.08	−.04	−.01	−.11	−.01	−.11	−.02	.88
For. Pol.—Tnz.	.86	−.00	.01	−.07	−.06	−.00	−.12	−.01	−.03	−.01	.76
Education	−.01	−.01	−.01	.00	.01	.01	.02	.02	.00	−.96	.92
Coops, Comm.	.02	−.02	.04	.01	.07	.05	.03	.03	−.00	.03	.69
Agriculture	−.03	−.03	.82	.03	.00	−.01	−.08	−.02	.04	.02	.69
Dev. Plan	−.05	−.00	.02	.02	−.89	−.04	−.04	−.03	−.05	.00	.79
Water, Land	.03	.02	.85	−.02	−.02	.02	.01	.01	−.04	−.01	.73
Police	−.01	−.02	−.01	.00	.02	−.01	.04	.03	−.92	.11	.86
Military	.85	−.01	−.02	−.03	−.01	−.06	.01	.04	.03	.00	.72
Refugees	.89	−.00	.00	−.06	−.01	−.01	−.02	−.01	−.04	−.01	.80
Health	.01	−.02	−.01	−.02	.01	.00	−.00	.91	.04	.00	.83
Labor, Unions	.76	−.01	−.03	−.00	−.05	.36	.01	.14	−.01	.02	.74
Youth, Cultr.	.43	.82	.06	−.08	.01	.03	.02	.03	−.07	−.03	.87
Comm. Dev.	−.01	.92	.01	−.01	.03	.04	.10	.06	−.04	−.02	.86
Civil Servs.	.42	.02	−.02	−.78	−.06	−.03	−.05	−.01	.01	.01	.80
News, Radio	.11	.02	.00	.02	−.04	−.02	−.11	−.08	−.36	−.25	.23
Housing	.01	−.00	−.02	.84	.02	−.01	−.02	.10	.00	.01	.73
Industry, Utl.	.03	−.02	−.04	.09	−.01	.81	−.12	.23	.02	.01	.73
Roads, RR, Harbors	−.02	−.01	.05	−.12	.01	.71	.05	−.22	.01	−.01	.57
Finance, Tax	.25	.03	.00	−.09	.82	.04	−.00	.02	−.08	−.00	.75
Elections	.44	−.00	.04	−.10	−.09	.14	−.00	−.20	.02	−.01	.55
TANU, ASP	.78	.16	−.03	.05	.03	−.05	.00	−.06	.01	.00	.65
Praise	−.03	.56	−.07	.05	−.07	−.10	−.23	−.12	.12	.05	.42
Law Courts	.93	.04	.01	−.09	−.03	−.01	−.06	.01	−.03	−.02	.89
Nat. Unity	.71	−.01	−.02	−.08	−.05	−.05	−.16	−.06	−.03	−.01	.55
Af. Socialism	.32	.12	.04	−.09	−.15	.02	−.72	−.03	−.07	−.07	.68
Procedures	.82	.17	.12	−.28	−.21	.11	−.00	.16	−.11	−.11	.90
Constitution	.84	.07	−.00	−.10	−.03	−.02	−.03	−.04	.02	.02	.73
% Variance Explained	27.8	6.8	5.1	6.4	5.6	4.8	4.8	3.8	3.7	3.6	Total = 72.6

Note: High loading variables, those above .50, are enclosed in a box on each factor for the reader's convenience. Since factors VIII–X seem to be single issue dimensions, they have not been labeled or discussed.

factors was based on examination of the high-loading subject variables, which by their clustering on the respective factors indicated underlying covariances among these subjects with the factor. These factors represent common themes among groups of members in the Assembly.

Index

YALE STUDIES IN POLITICAL SCIENCE